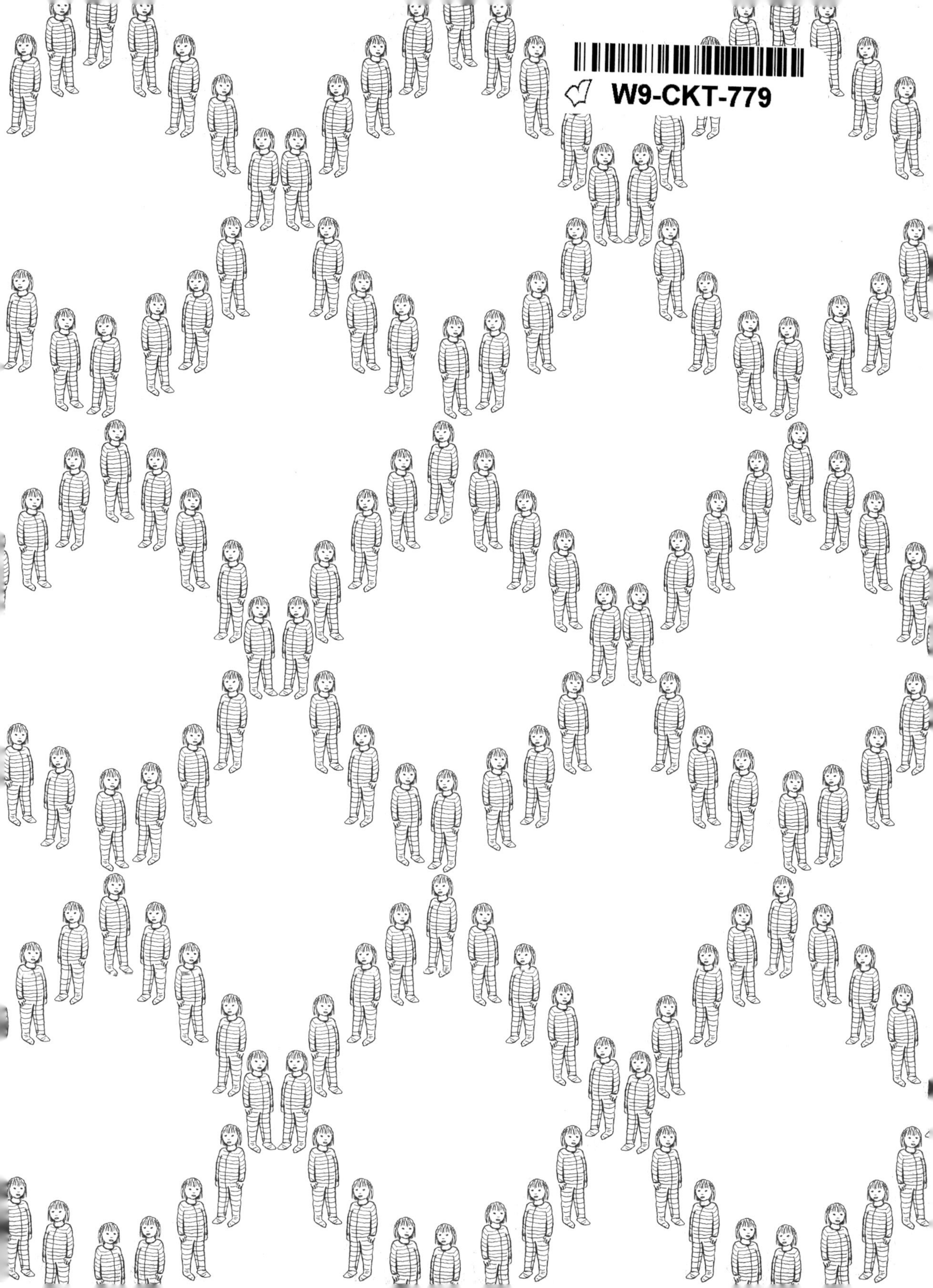

Published by Koyama Press
koyamapress.com

First edition: May 2017
ISBN: 978-1-927668-44-3
Printed in China

SUNBURNING

Keiler Roberts

dedicated to my most endearing characters,
Mom and Dad

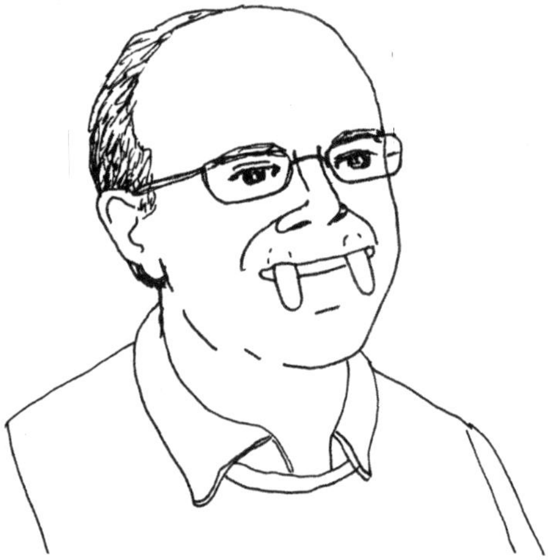

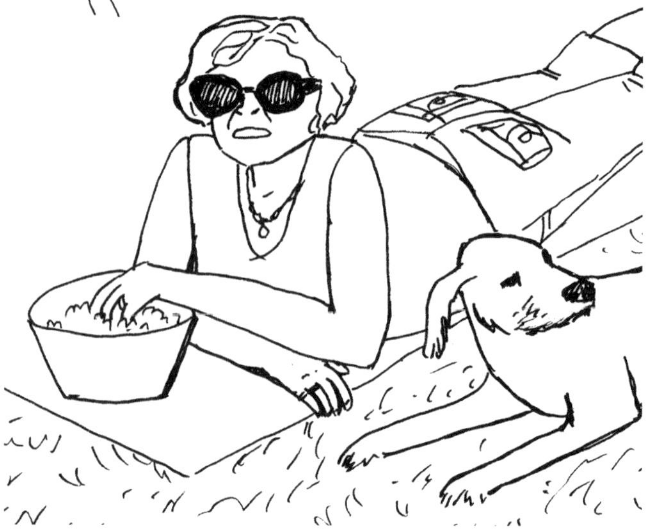

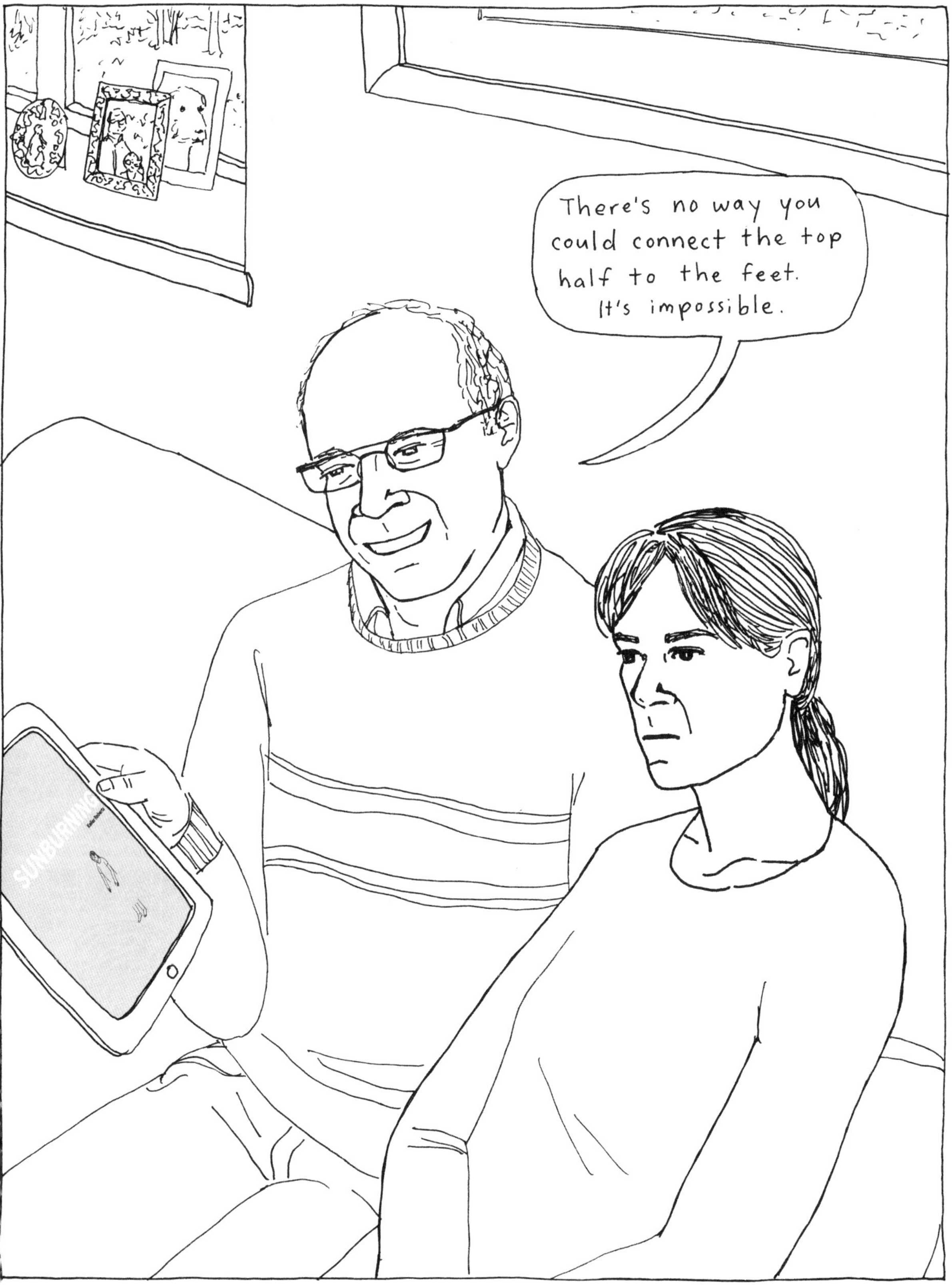
SUNBURNING
Keiler Roberts
There's no way you could connect the top half to the feet. It's impossible.

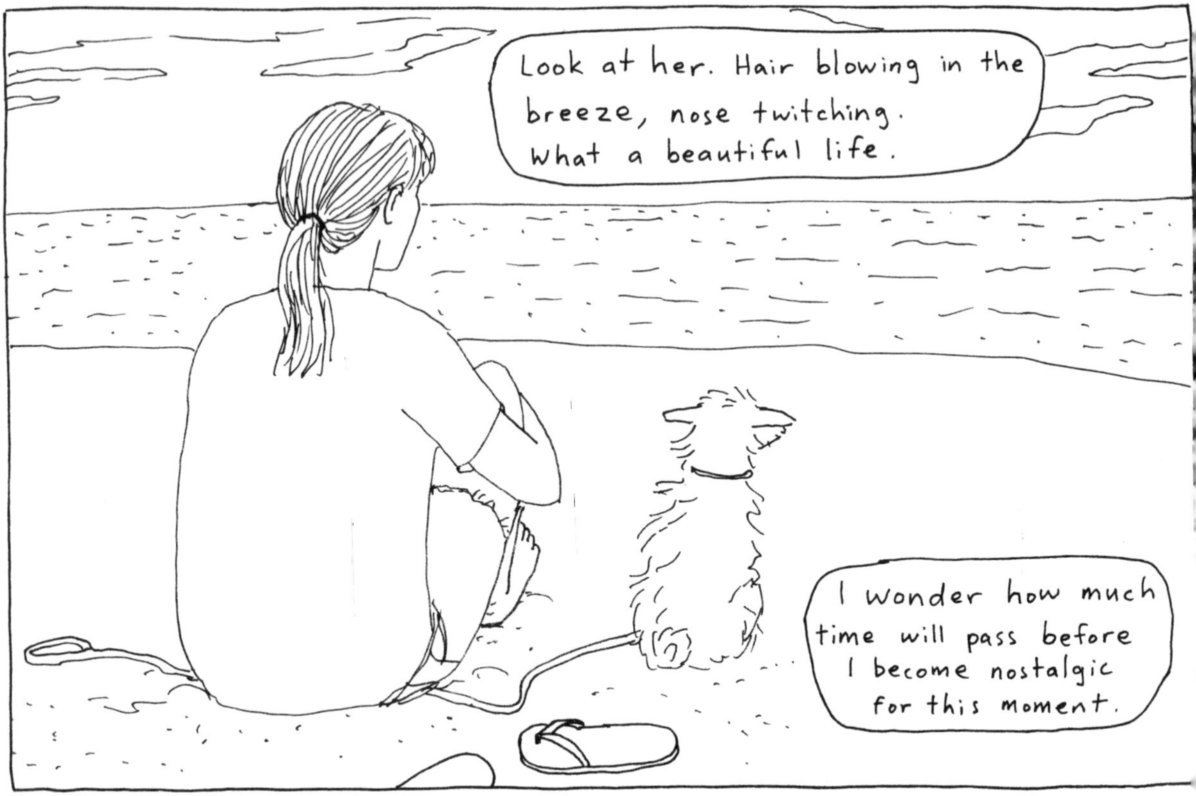
Look at her. Hair blowing in the breeze, nose twitching. What a beautiful life.
I wonder how much time will pass before I become nostalgic for this moment.

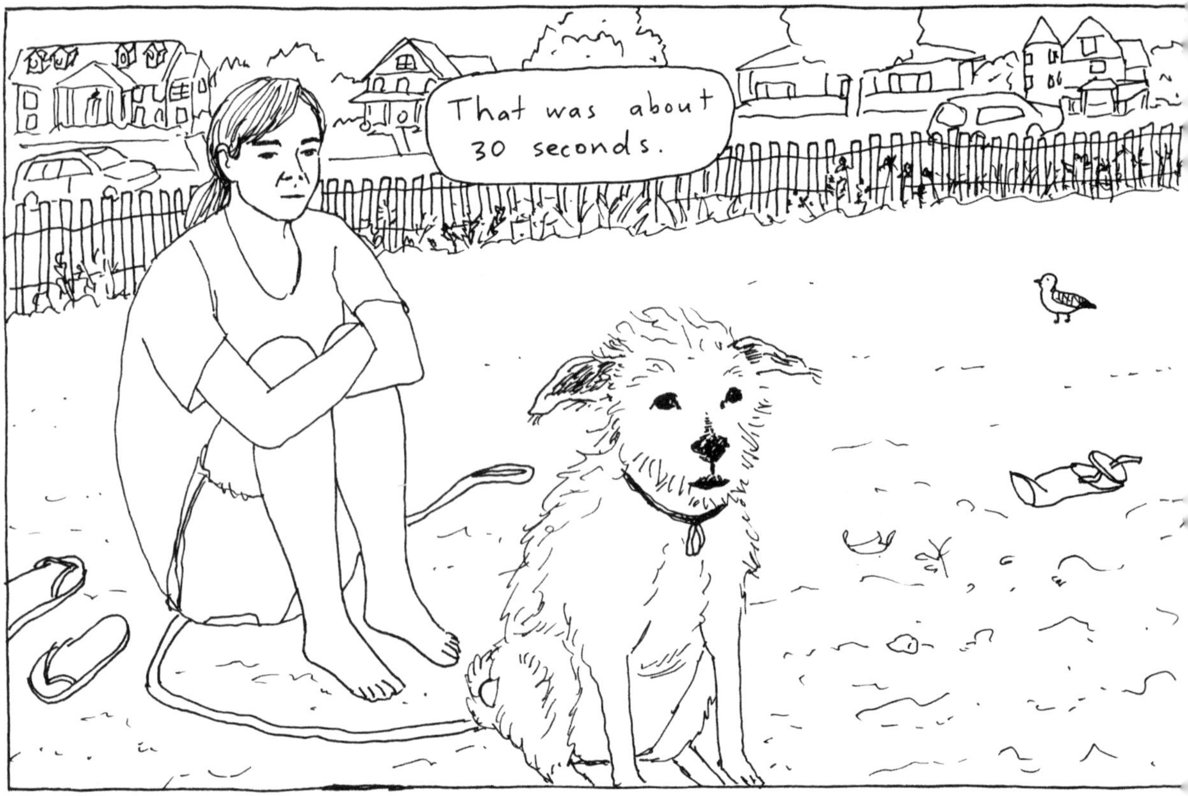
That was about 30 seconds.

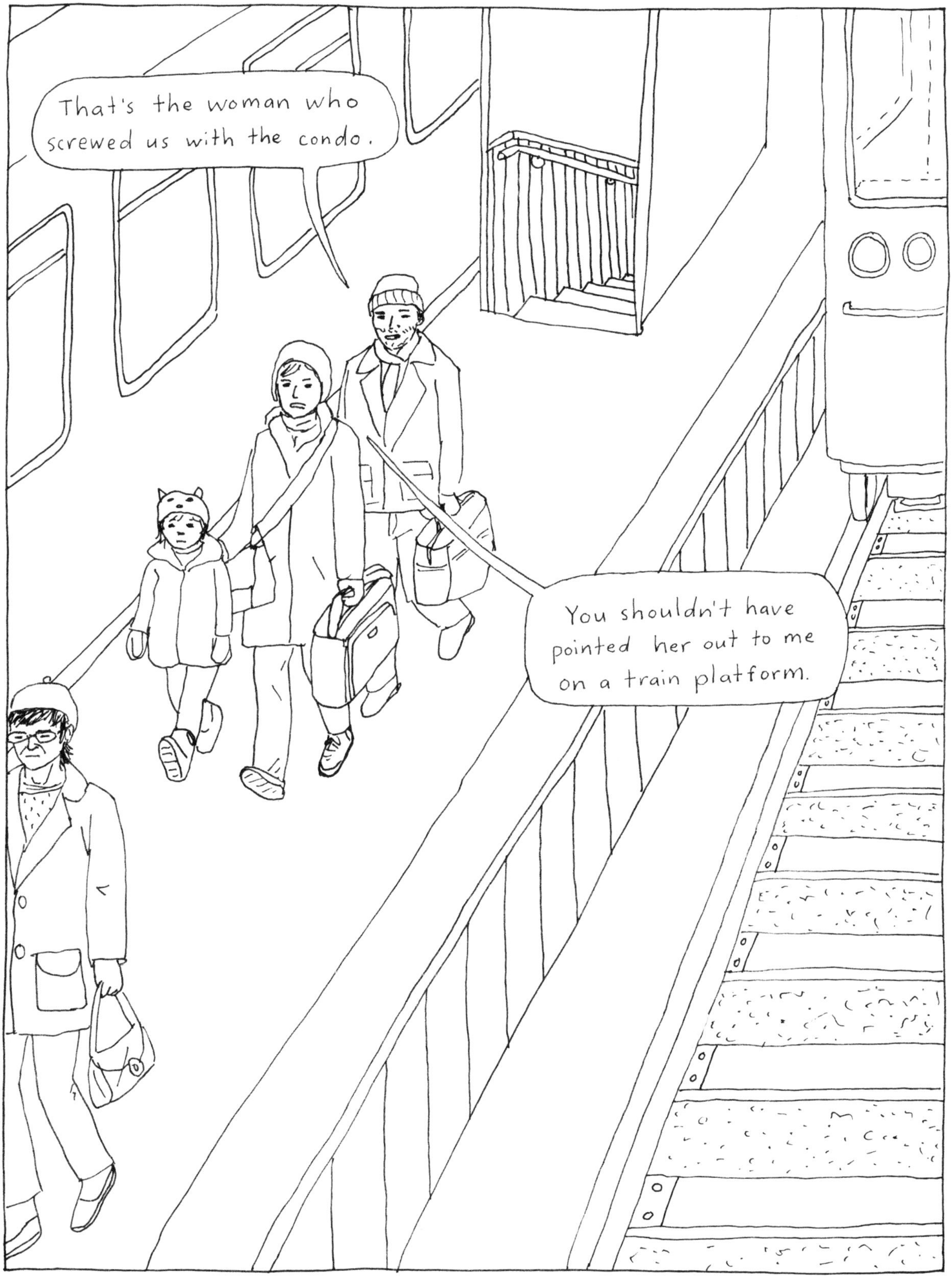
That's the woman who screwed us with the condo.
You shouldn't have pointed her out to me on a train platform.

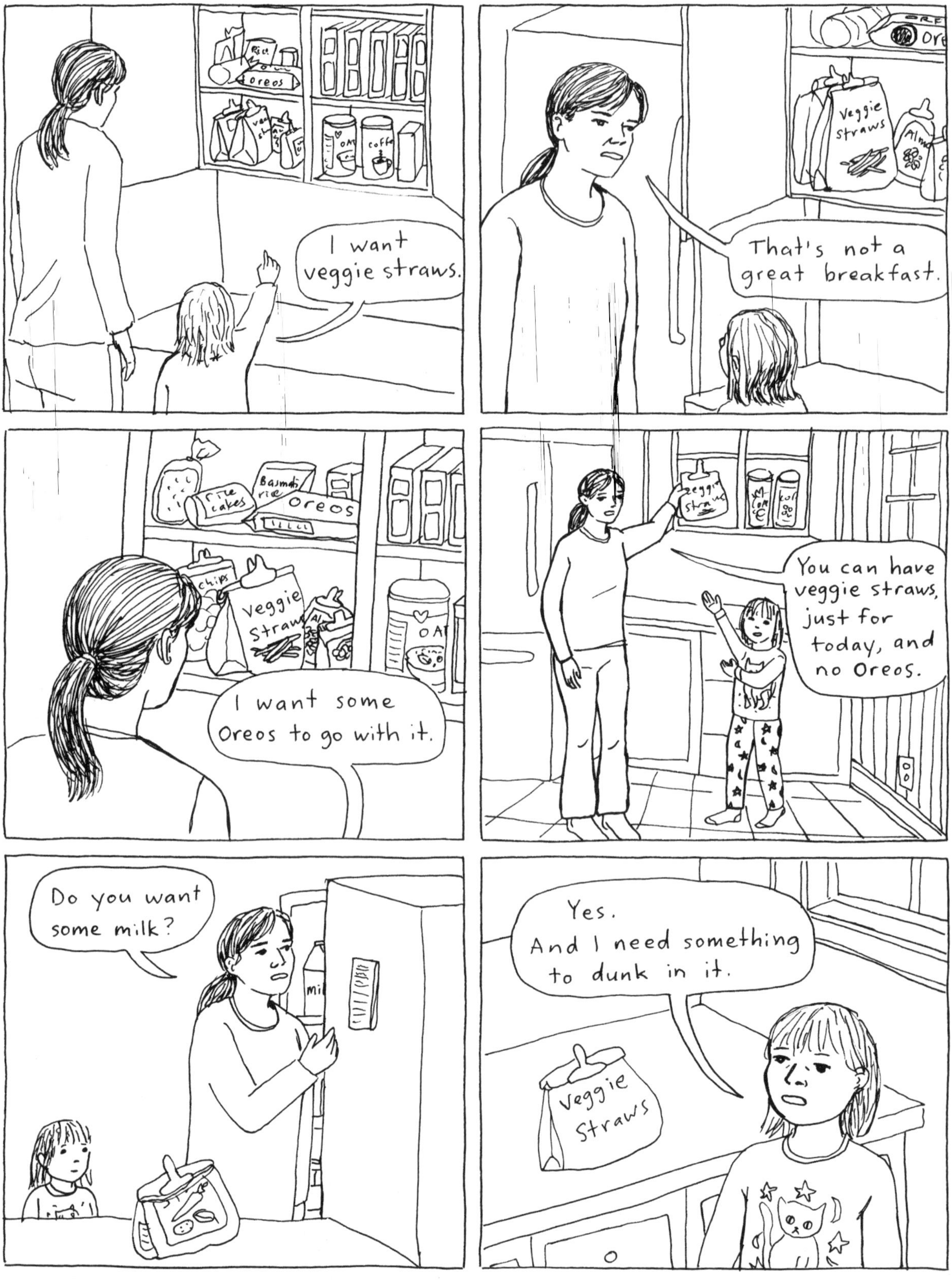
Rice
Oreos
veggie straws
OAT
coffee
I want veggie straws.
OREO
Veggie Straws
That's not a great breakfast.
Basmati rice
rice cakes
Oreos
chips
Veggie Straws
OAT
I want some Oreos to go with it.
You can have veggie straws, just for today, and no Oreos.
Do you want some milk?
Yes. And I need something to dunk in it.
Veggie Straws

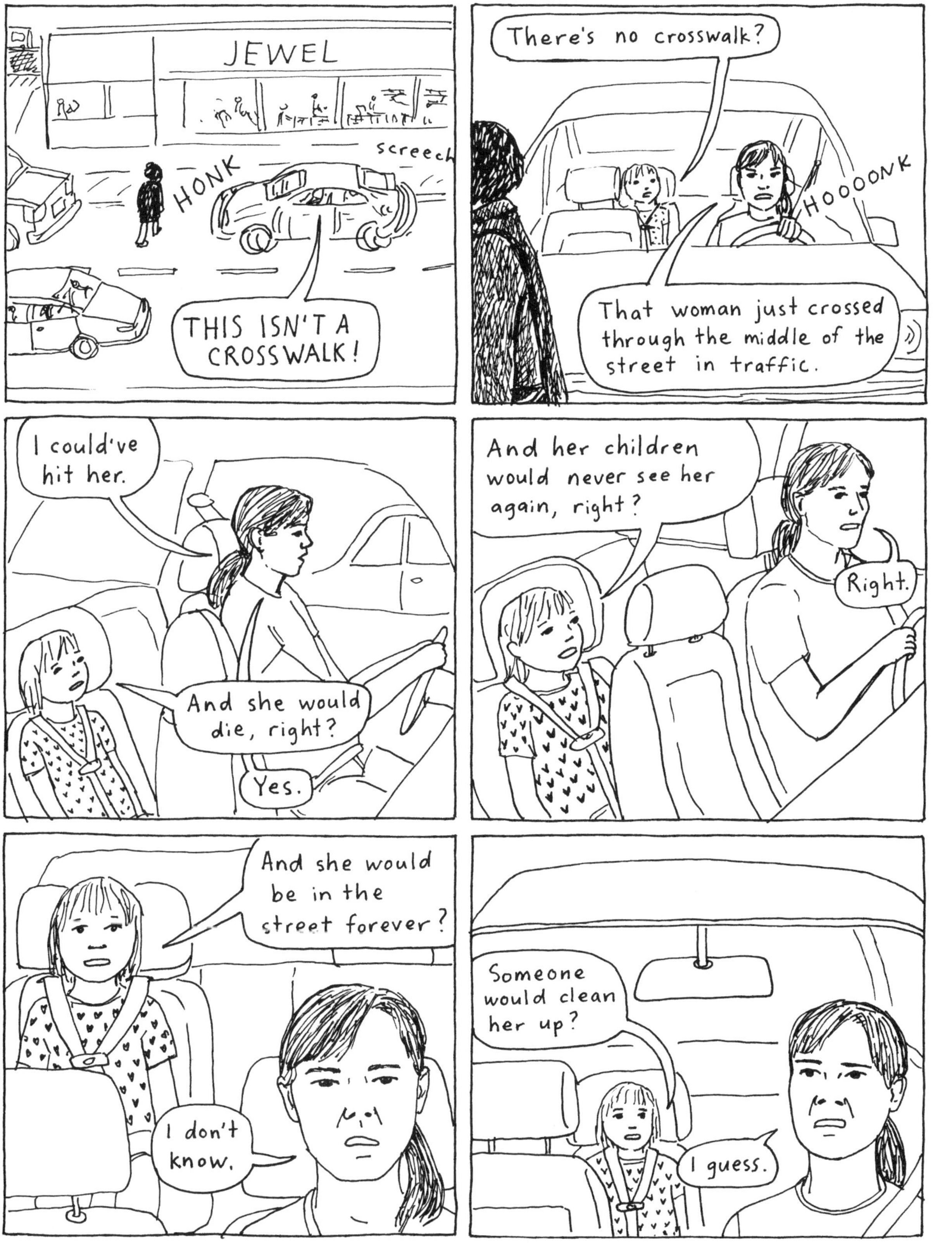
JEWEL
screech
HONK
THIS ISN'T A CROSSWALK!
There's no crosswalk?
HOOOONK
That woman just crossed through the middle of the street in traffic.
I could've hit her.
And she would die, right?
Yes.
And her children would never see her again, right?
Right.
And she would be in the street forever?
I don't know.
Someone would clean her up?
I guess.

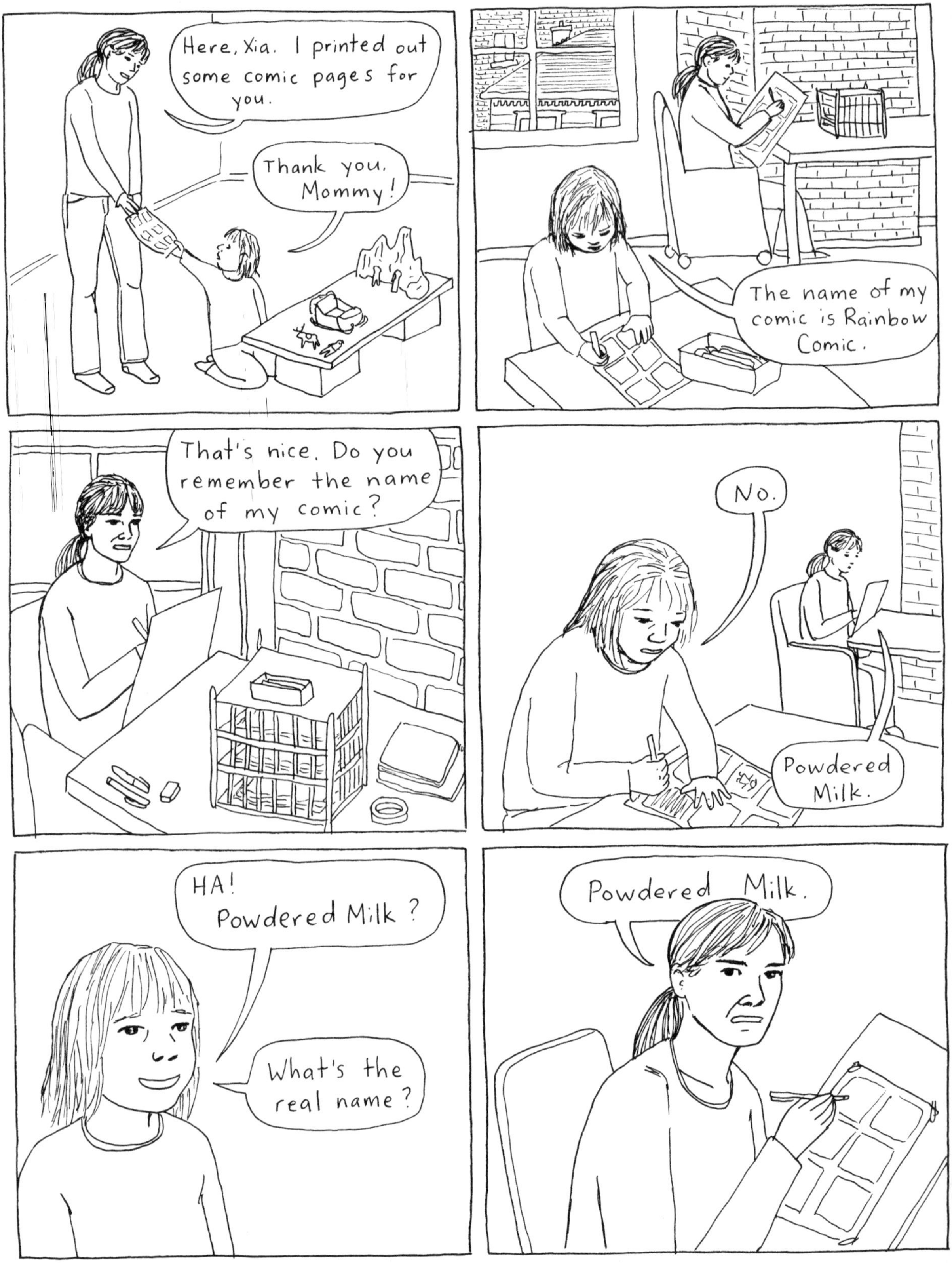
Here, Xia. I printed out some comic pages for you.
Thank you, Mommy!
The name of my comic is Rainbow Comic.
That's nice. Do you remember the name of my comic?
No.
Powdered Milk.
HA! Powdered Milk?
What's the real name?
Powdered Milk.

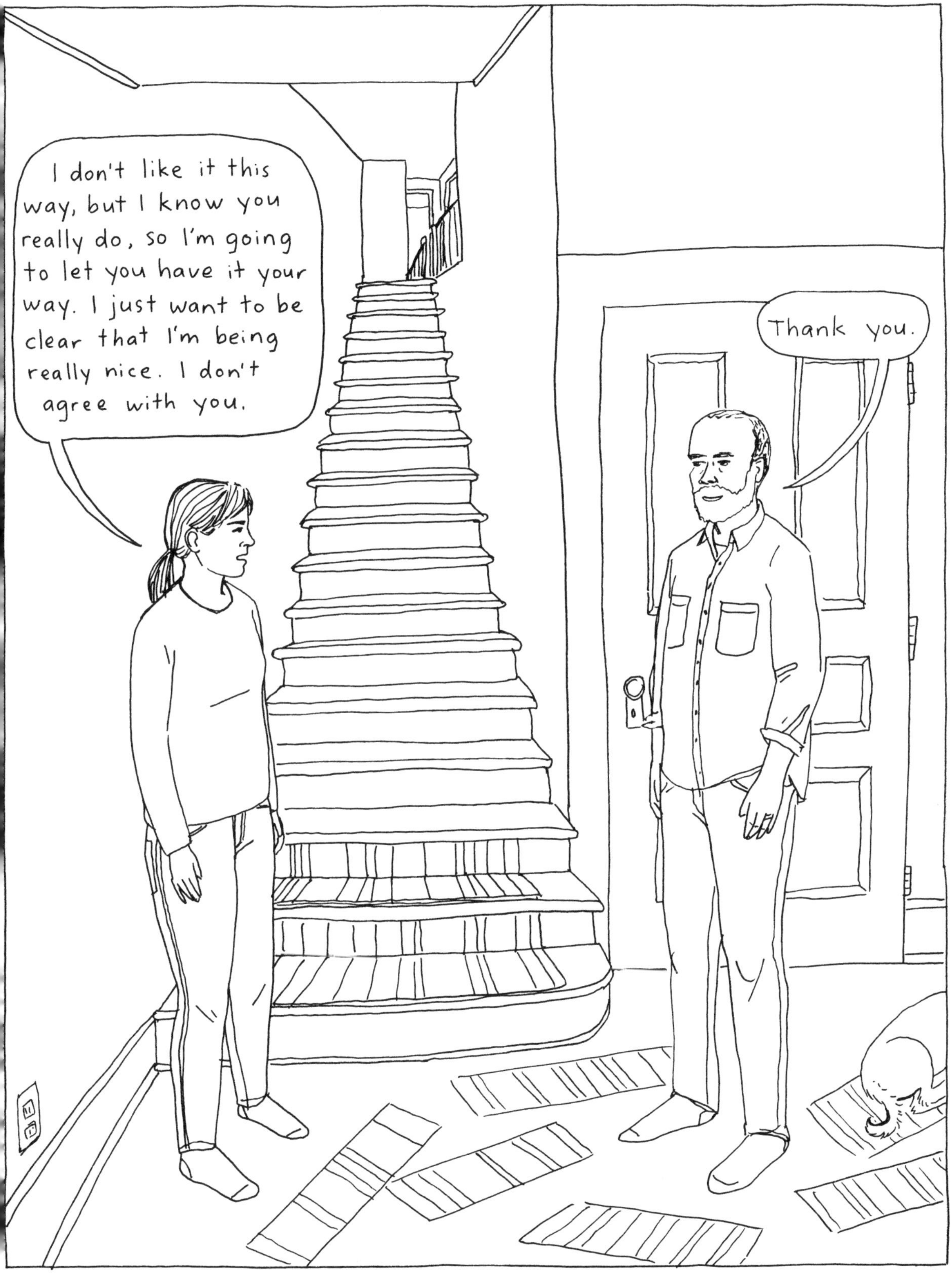
I don't like it this way, but I know you really do, so I'm going to let you have it your way. I just want to be clear that I'm being really nice. I don't agree with you.
Thank you.

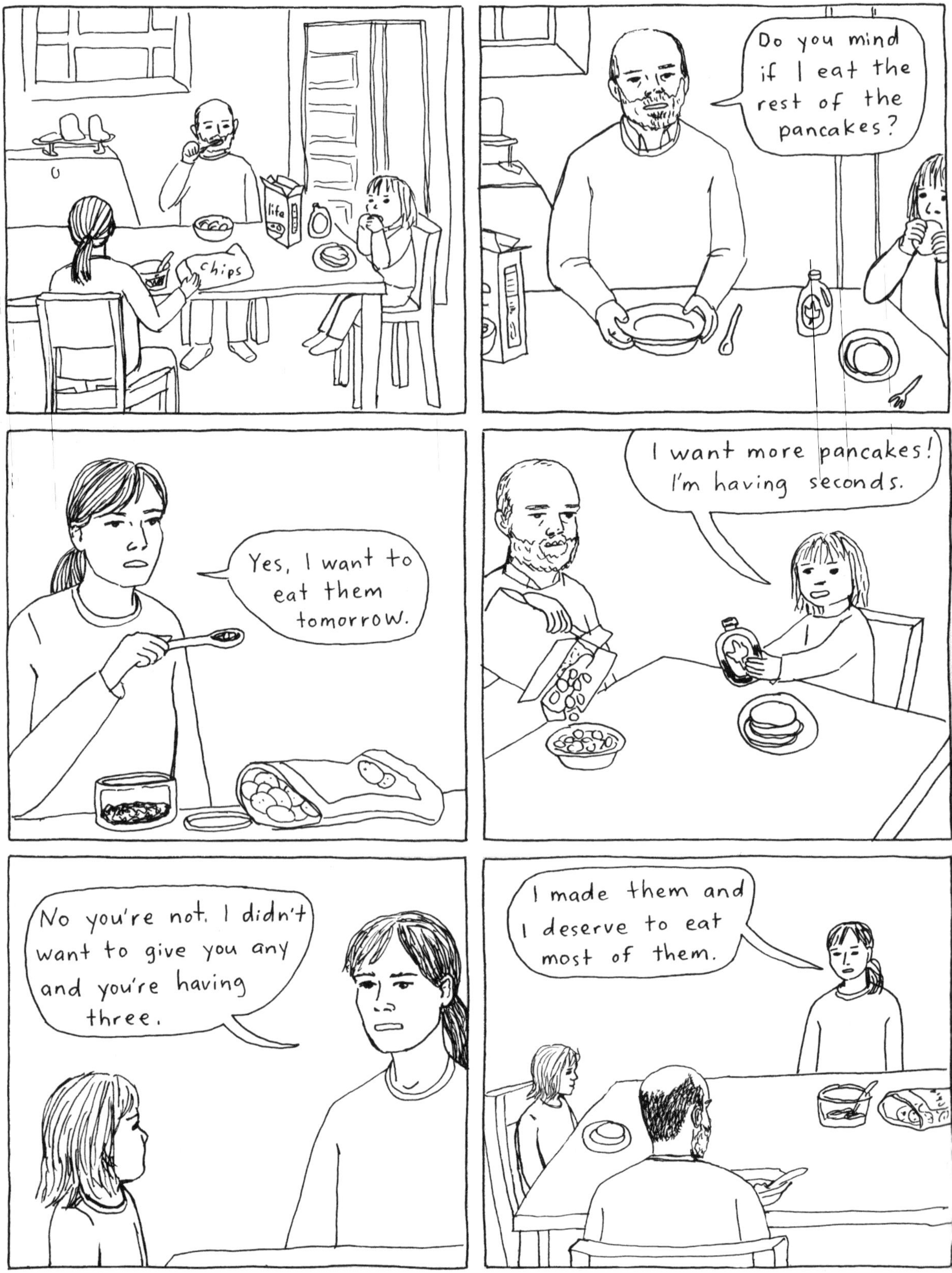
chips
lifa
Do you mind if I eat the rest of the pancakes?
Yes, I want to eat them tomorrow.
I want more pancakes! I'm having seconds.
No you're not. I didn't want to give you any and you're having three.
I made them and I deserve to eat most of them.

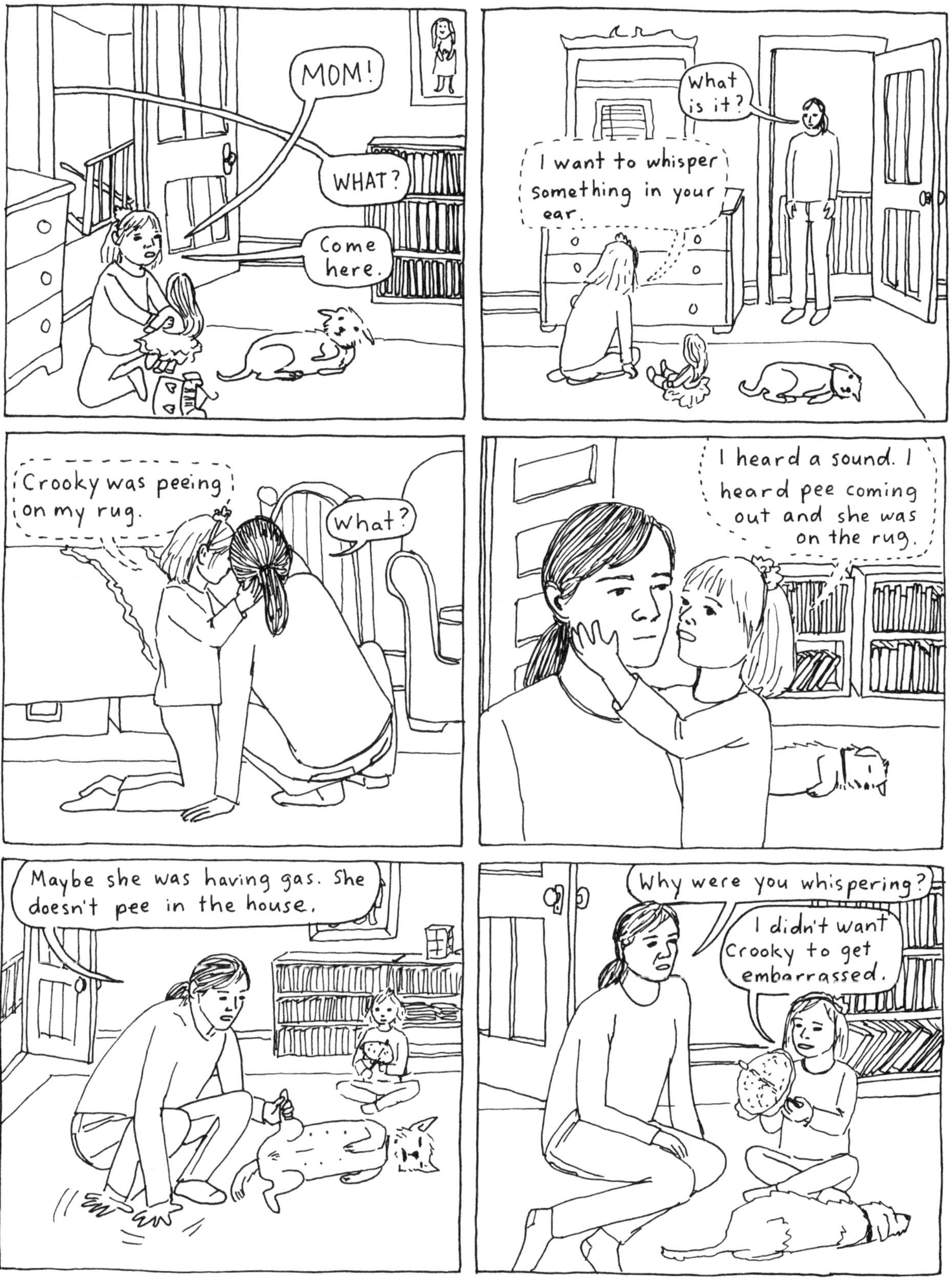
MOM!
WHAT?
Come here.
What is it?
I want to whisper something in your ear.
Crooky was peeing on my rug.
What?
I heard a sound. I heard pee coming out and she was on the rug.
Maybe she was having gas. She doesn't pee in the house.
Why were you whispering?
I didn't want Crooky to get embarrassed.

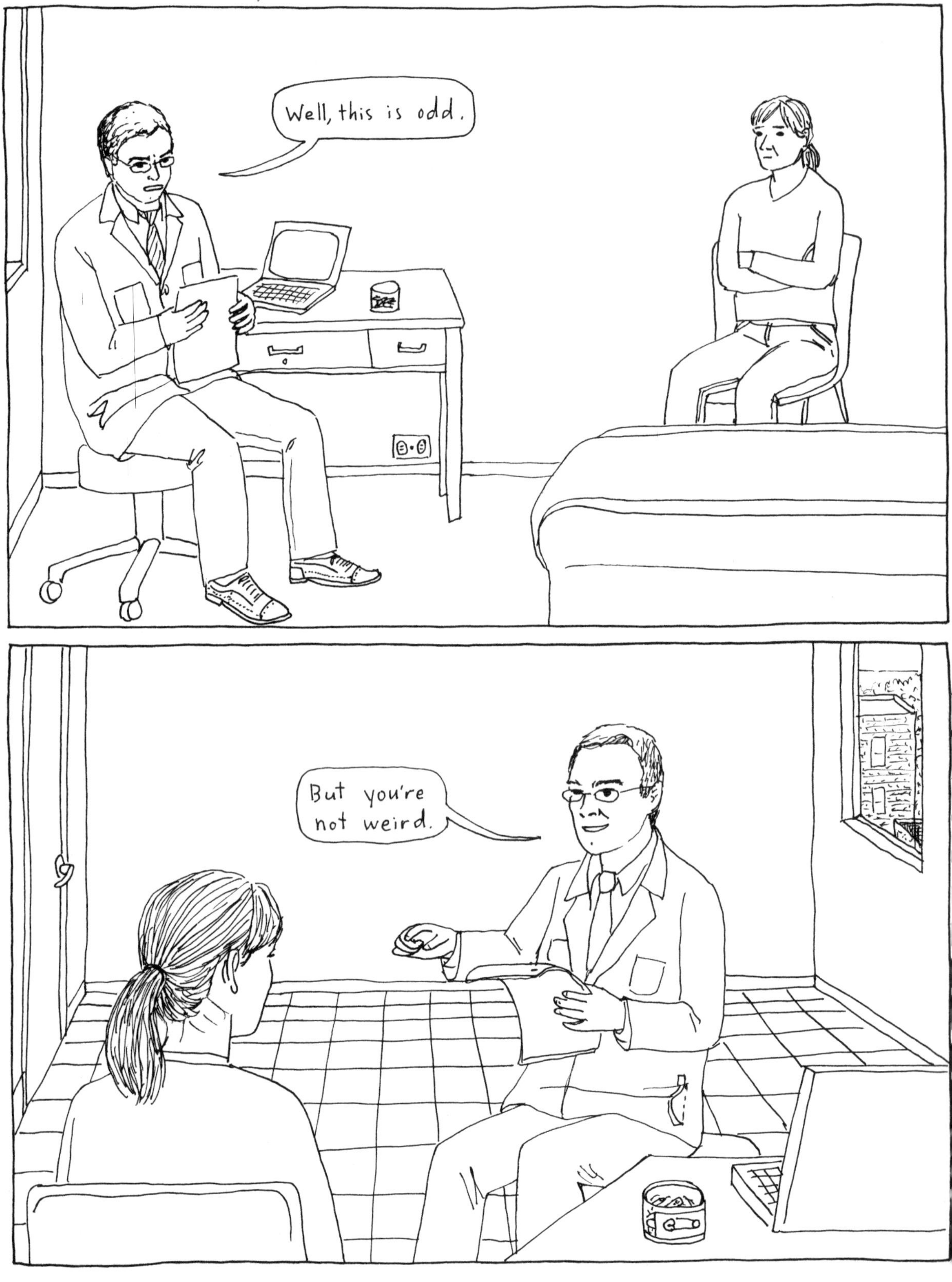
Well, this is odd.
But you're not weird.

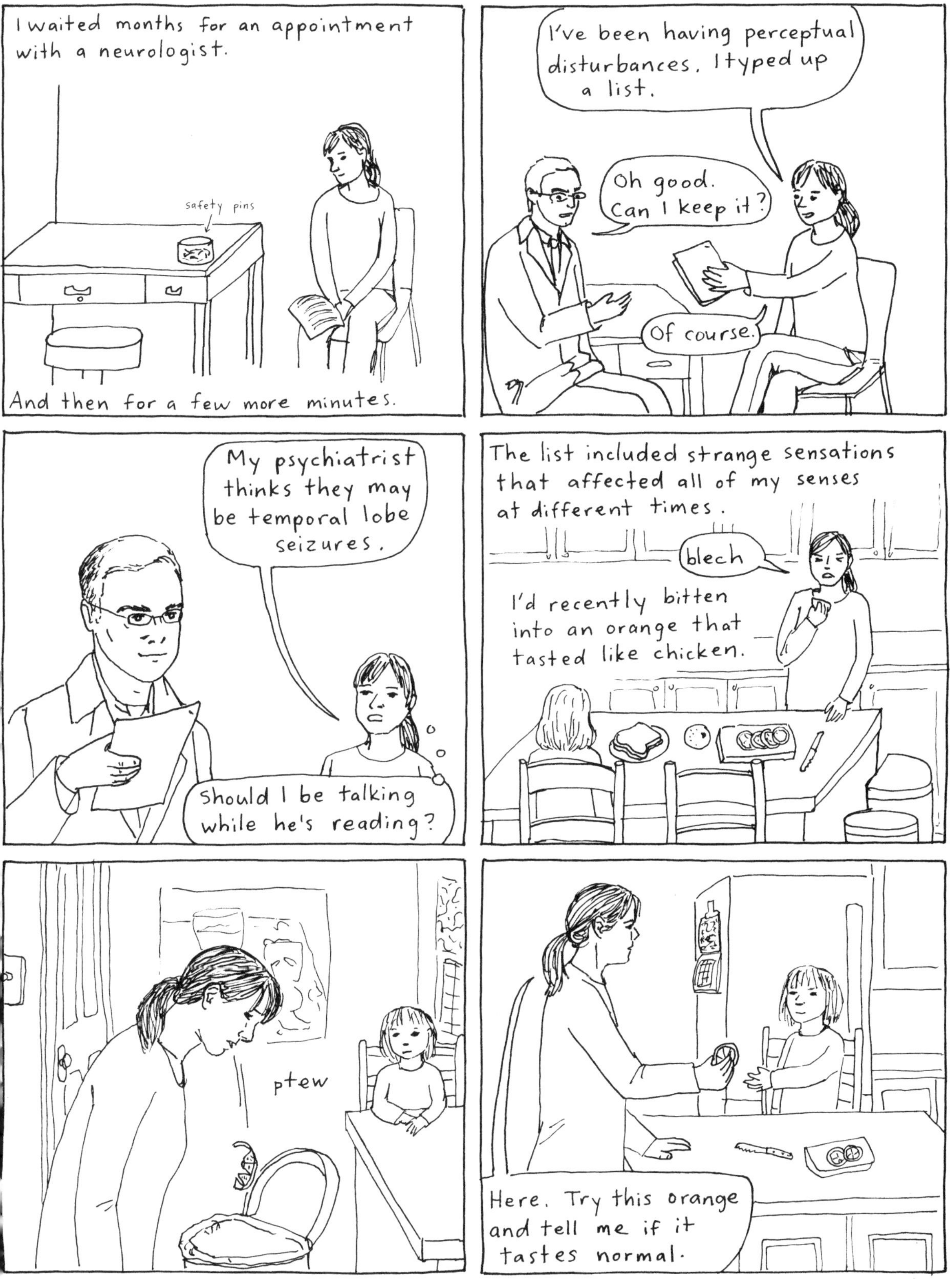
I waited months for an appointment with a neurologist.
safety pins
And then for a few more minutes.
I've been having perceptual disturbances. I typed up a list.
Oh good. Can I keep it?
Of course.
My psychiatrist thinks they may be temporal lobe seizures.
Should I be talking while he's reading?
The list included strange sensations that affected all of my senses at different times.
blech
I'd recently bitten into an orange that tasted like chicken.
ptew
Here. Try this orange and tell me if it tastes normal.

I hear sounds through other noise. Xia seems to be shouting for me, but every time I turn the hairdryer off, it's quiet.

zhzhzh zhmam zhzh zhzh Mom zhMom zhh zhcome he zhh zhMam zhh zhh zhzh

On our first date seventeen years ago, Scott and I were talking while looking at the lake. I heard him say

I love you.

One of us is crazy!

When I looked at him I realized he definitely hadn't said that.

My vision is the most affected. I'm startled by people and animals that appear in my peripheral vision.

I've got to move that stupid coat.

It's most distracting when I'm teaching.

I have no idea what I was saying.

← not real

When I drive on a sunny day it often looks like a strobe light. I feel like I'm missing short amounts of time and cars, bikes, and people appear out of nowhere.

give

I hate these people. It is not safe to collect money in traffic.

If you get hit it's your own fault!

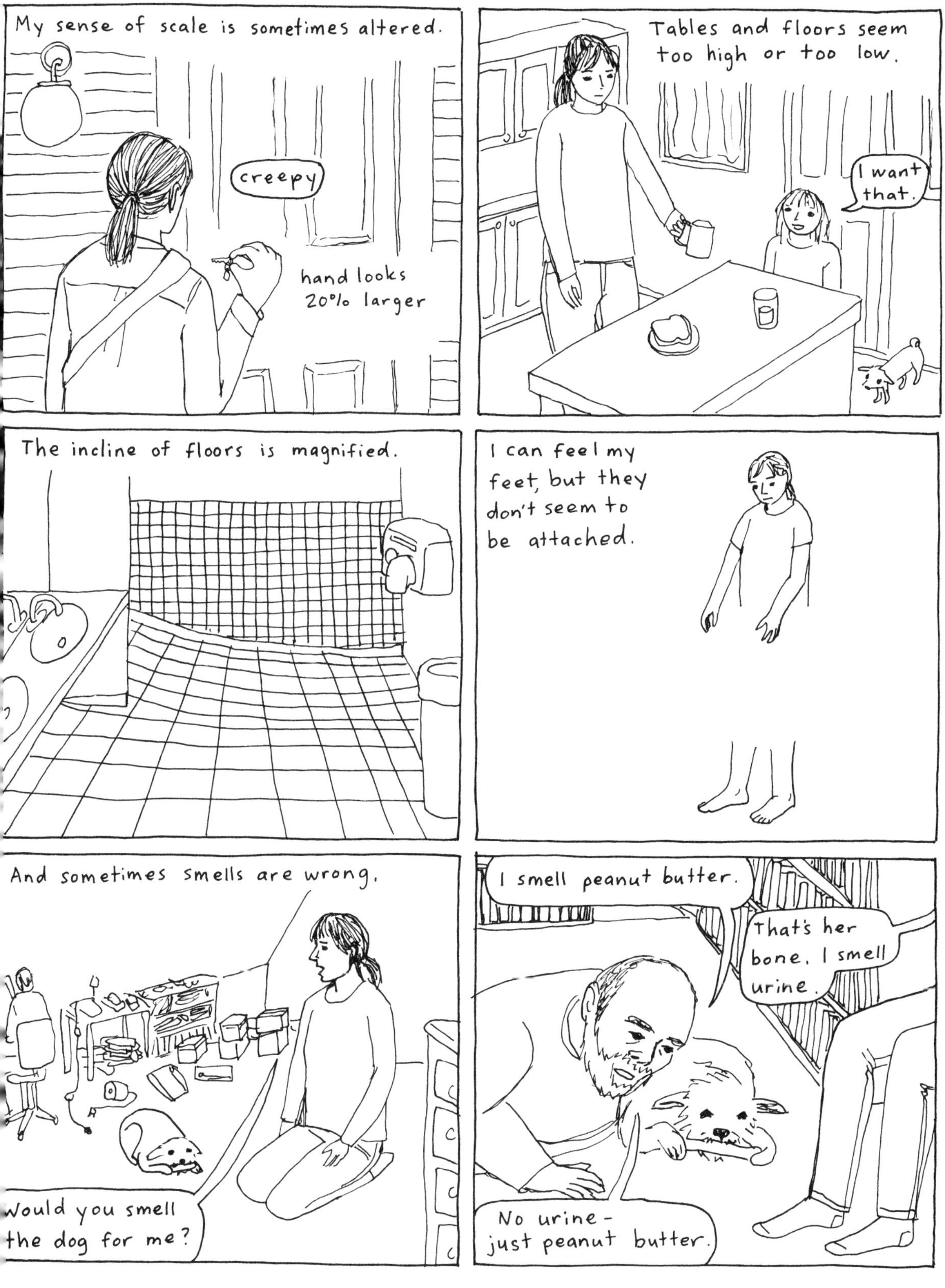
My sense of scale is sometimes altered.
creepy
hand looks 20% larger
Tables and floors seem too high or too low.
I want that.
The incline of floors is magnified.
I can feel my feet, but they don't seem to be attached.
And sometimes smells are wrong.
Would you smell the dog for me?
I smell peanut butter.
That's her bone. I smell urine.
No urine - just peanut butter.

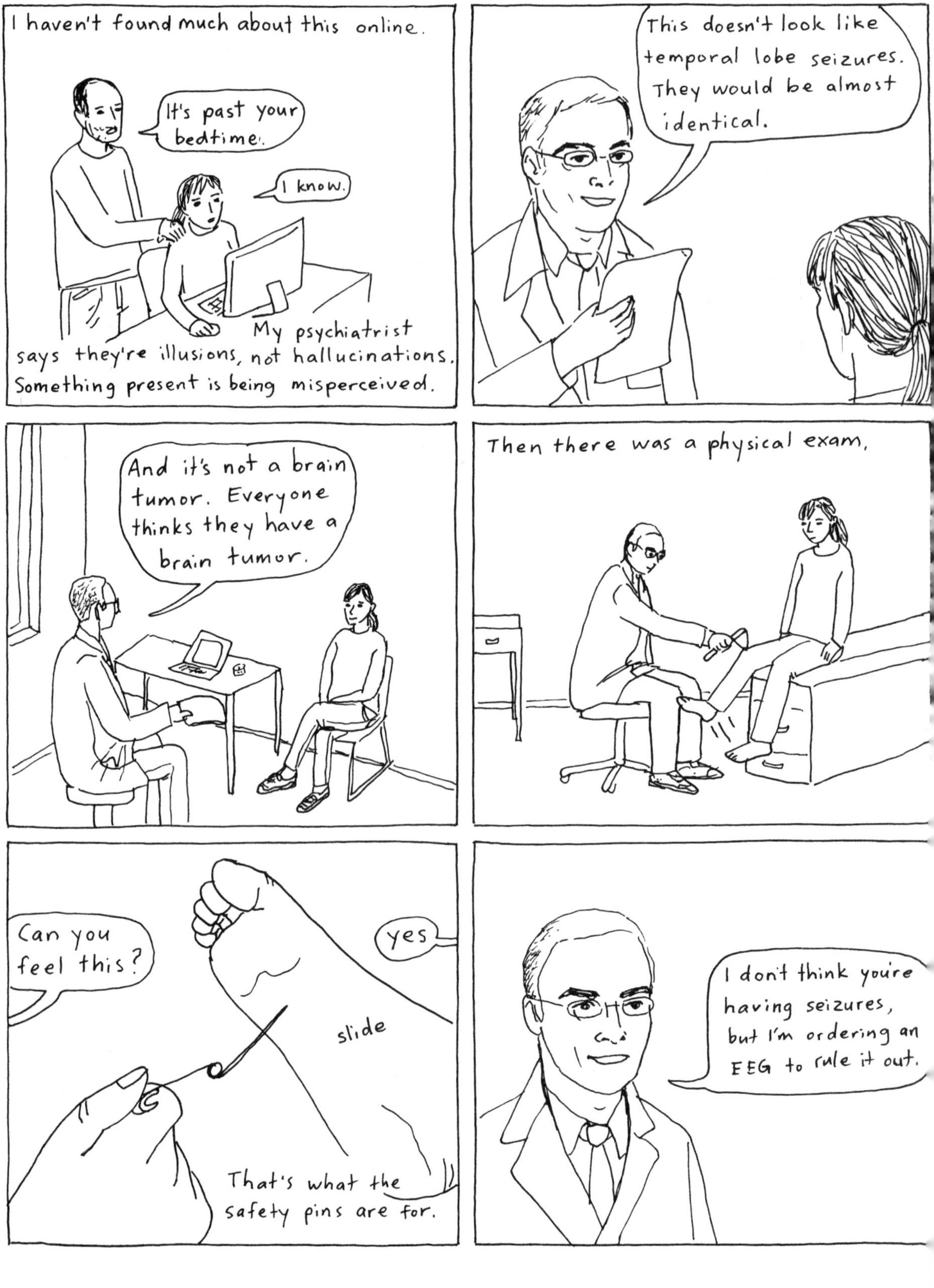
I haven't found much about this online.
It's past your bedtime.
I know.
My psychiatrist says they're illusions, not hallucinations. Something present is being misperceived.
This doesn't look like temporal lobe seizures. They would be almost identical.
And it's not a brain tumor. Everyone thinks they have a brain tumor.
Then there was a physical exam.
Can you feel this?
yes
slide
That's what the safety pins are for.
I don't think you're having seizures, but I'm ordering an EEG to rule it out.

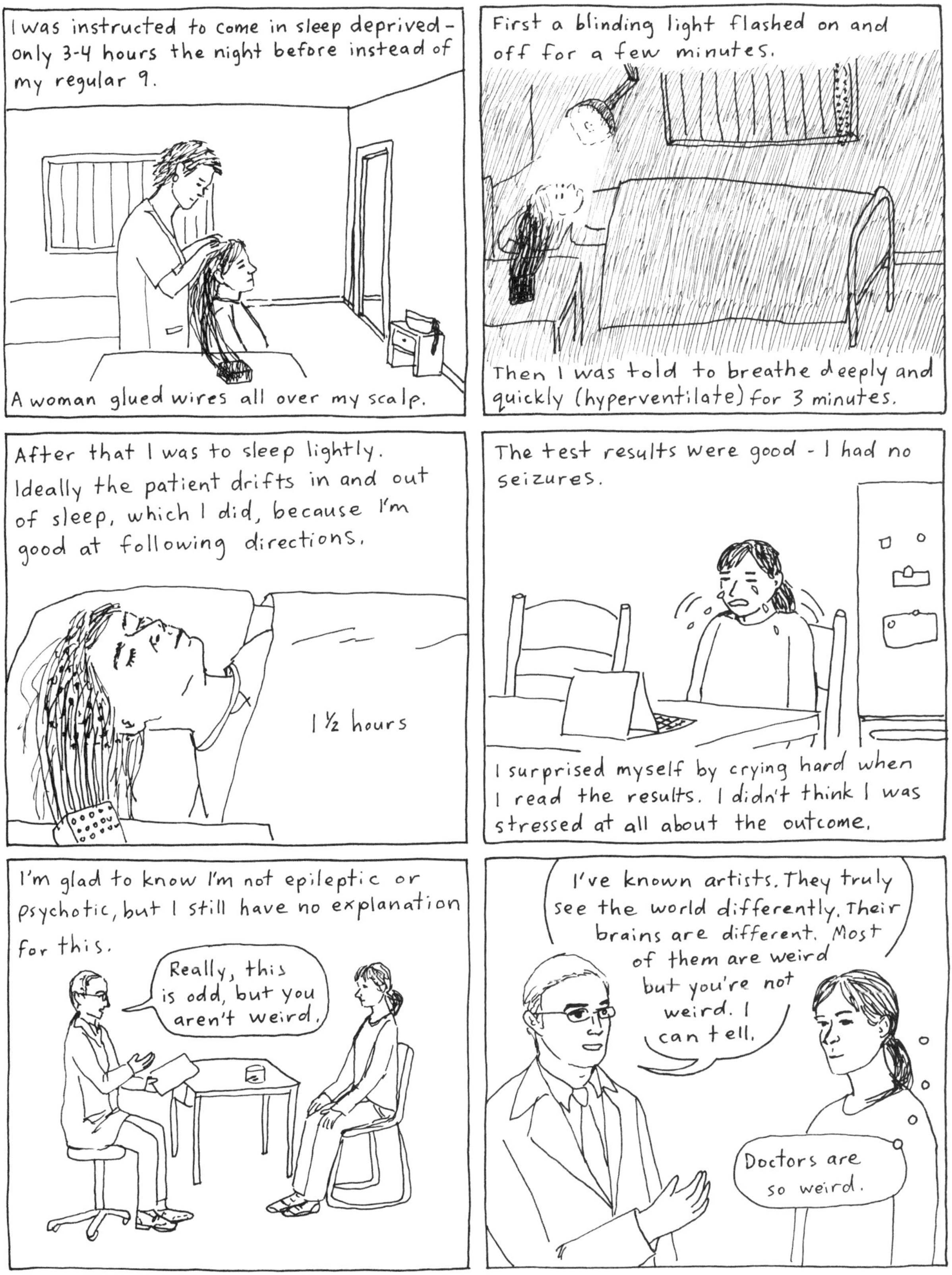
I was instructed to come in sleep deprived - only 3-4 hours the night before instead of my regular 9.
A woman glued wires all over my scalp.
First a blinding light flashed on and off for a few minutes.
Then I was told to breathe deeply and quickly (hyperventilate) for 3 minutes.
After that I was to sleep lightly. Ideally the patient drifts in and out of sleep, which I did, because I'm good at following directions.
1½ hours
The test results were good - I had no seizures.
I surprised myself by crying hard when I read the results. I didn't think I was stressed at all about the outcome.
I'm glad to know I'm not epileptic or psychotic, but I still have no explanation for this.
Really, this is odd, but you aren't weird.
I've known artists. They truly see the world differently. Their brains are different. Most of them are weird but you're not weird. I can tell.
Doctors are so weird.

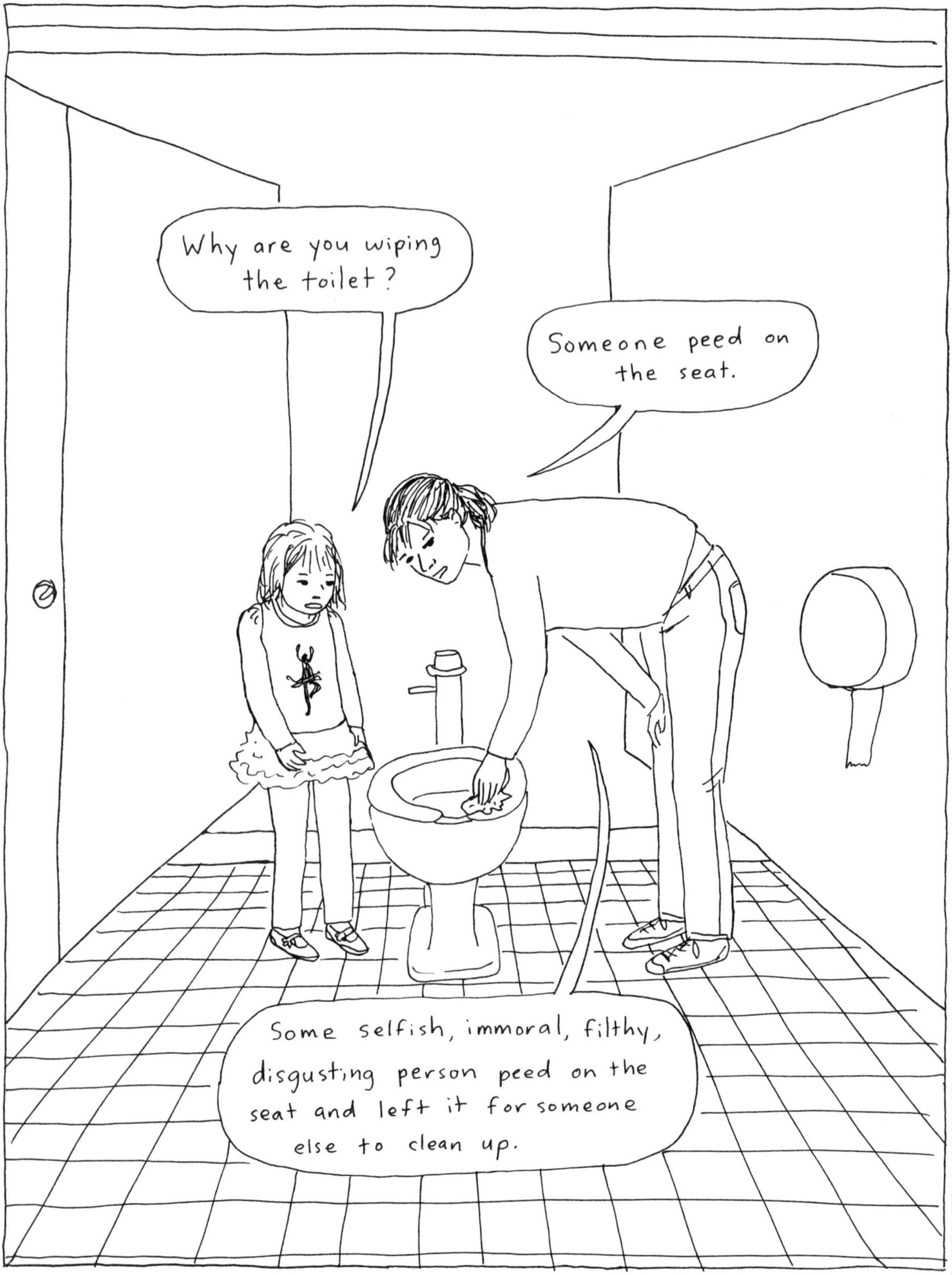
Why are you wiping the toilet?
Someone peed on the seat.
Some selfish, immoral, filthy, disgusting person peed on the the seat and left it for someone else to clean up.

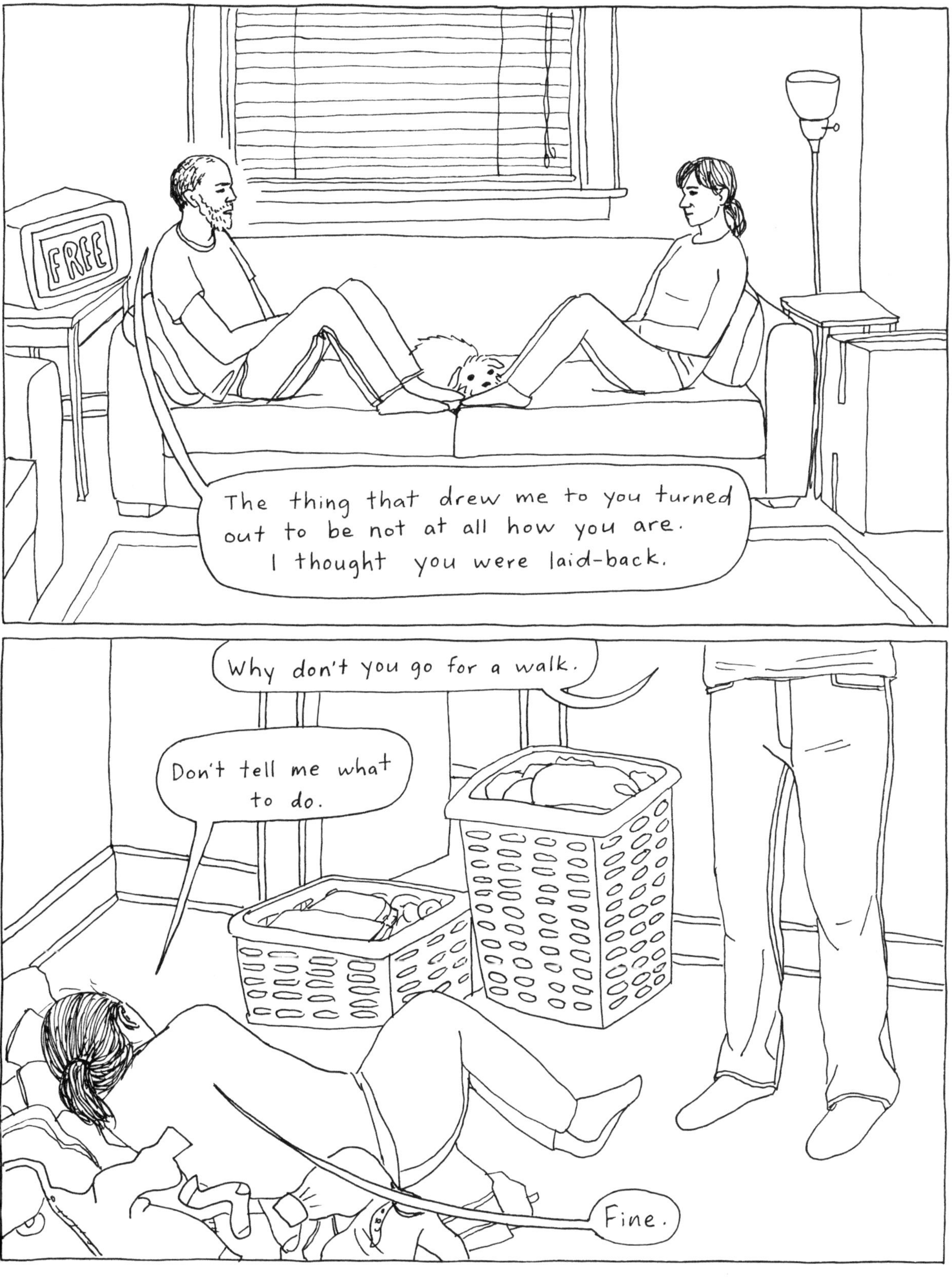
FREE
The thing that drew me to you turned out to be not at all how you are. I thought you were laid-back.
Why don't you go for a walk.
Don't tell me what to do.
Fine.

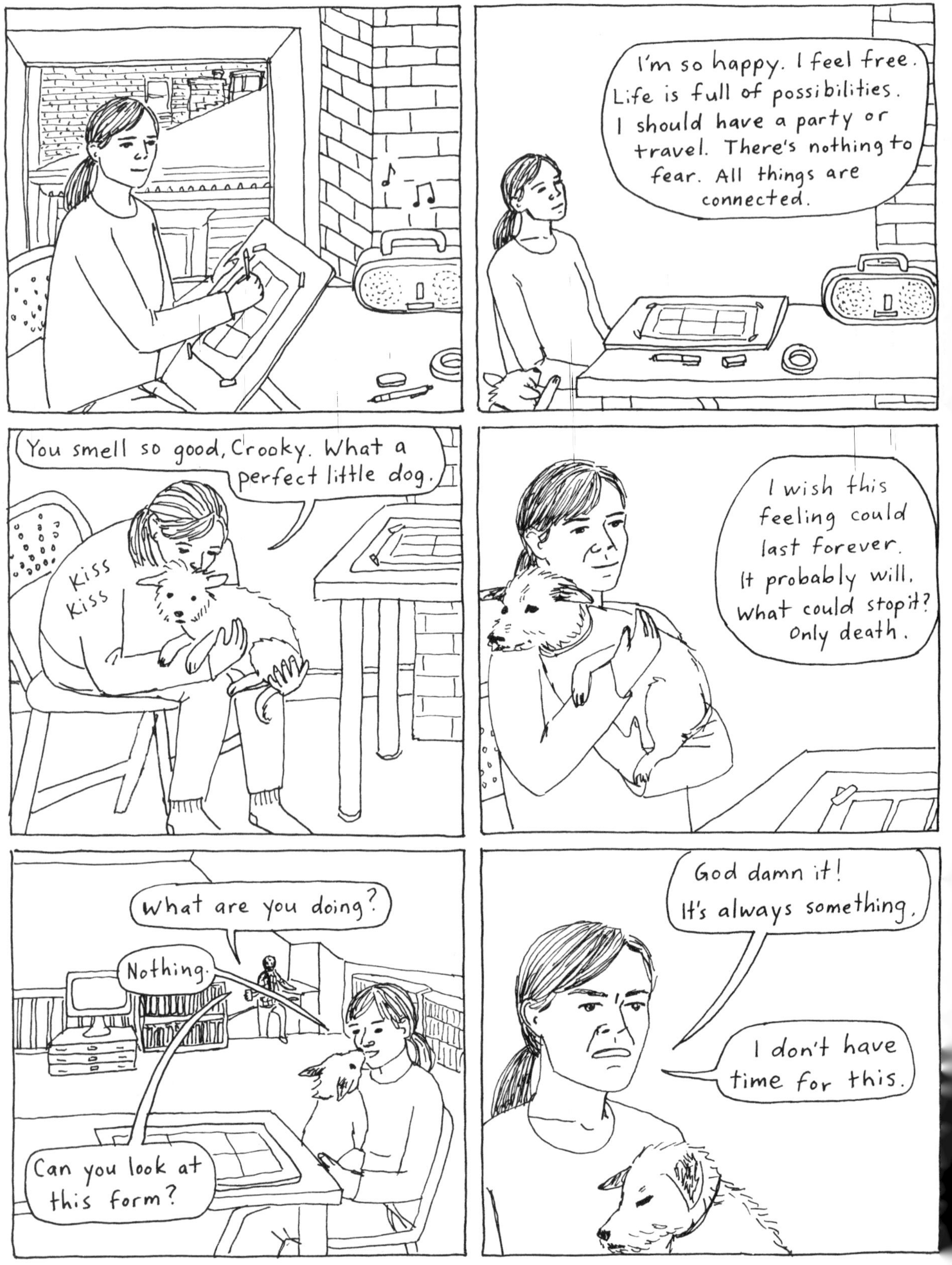
I'm so happy. I feel free. Life is full of possibilities. I should have a party or travel. There's nothing to fear. All things are connected.
You smell so good, Crooky. What a perfect little dog.
Kiss Kiss
I wish this feeling could last forever. It probably will. What could stop it? Only death.
What are you doing?
Nothing.
Can you look at this form?
God damn it! It's always something.
I don't have time for this.

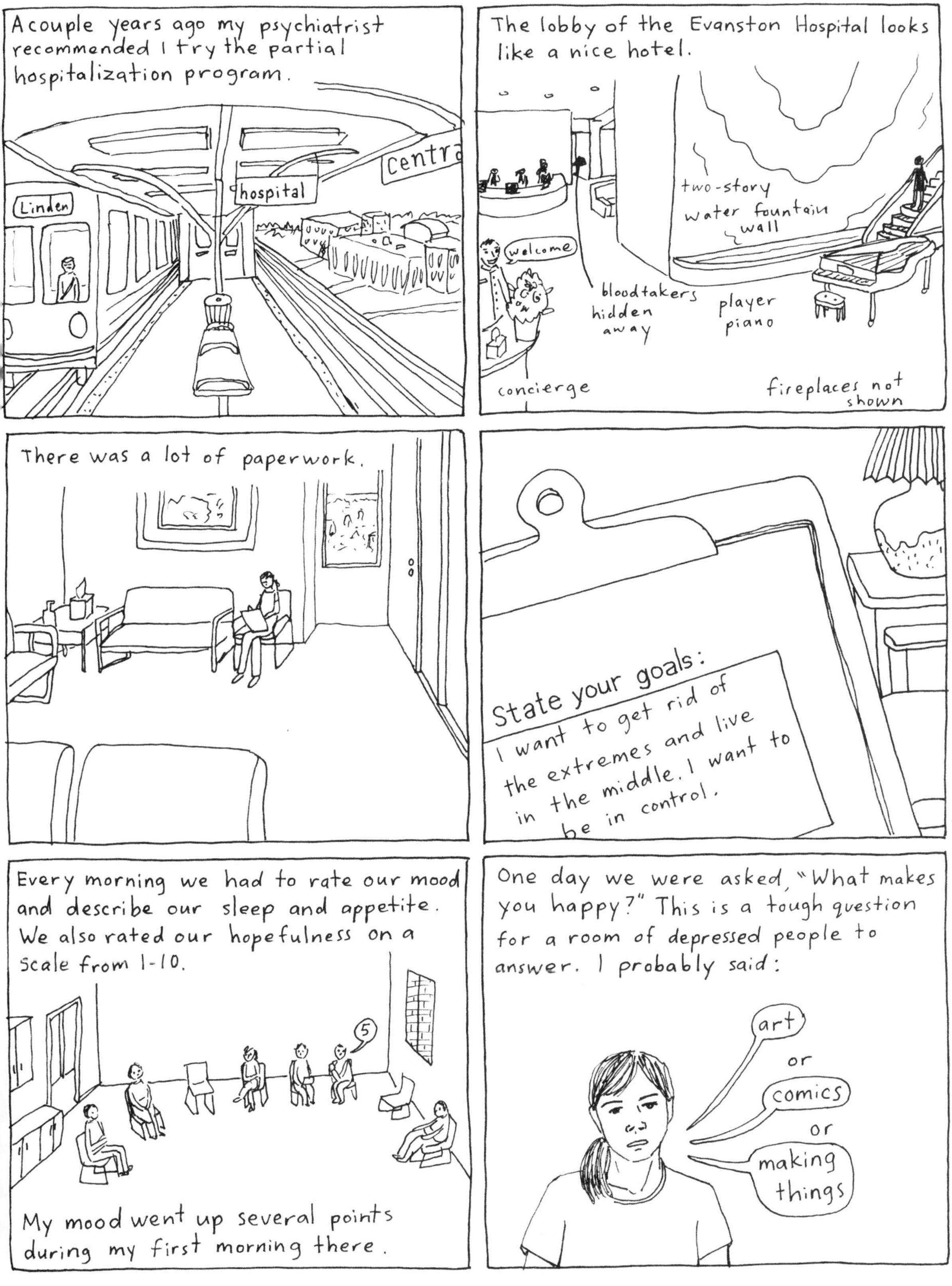
A couple years ago my psychiatrist recommended I try the partial hospitalization program.
Linden
hospital
Centra
The lobby of the Evanston Hospital looks like a nice hotel.
welcome
two-story water fountain wall
bloodtakers hidden away
player piano
concierge
fireplaces not shown
There was a lot of paperwork.
State your goals:
I want to get rid of the extremes and live in the middle. I want to be in control.
Every morning we had to rate our mood and describe our sleep and appetite. We also rated our hopefulness on a scale from 1-10.
5
My mood went up several points during my first morning there.
One day we were asked, "What makes you happy?" This is a tough question for a room of depressed people to answer. I probably said:
art
or
comics
or
making things

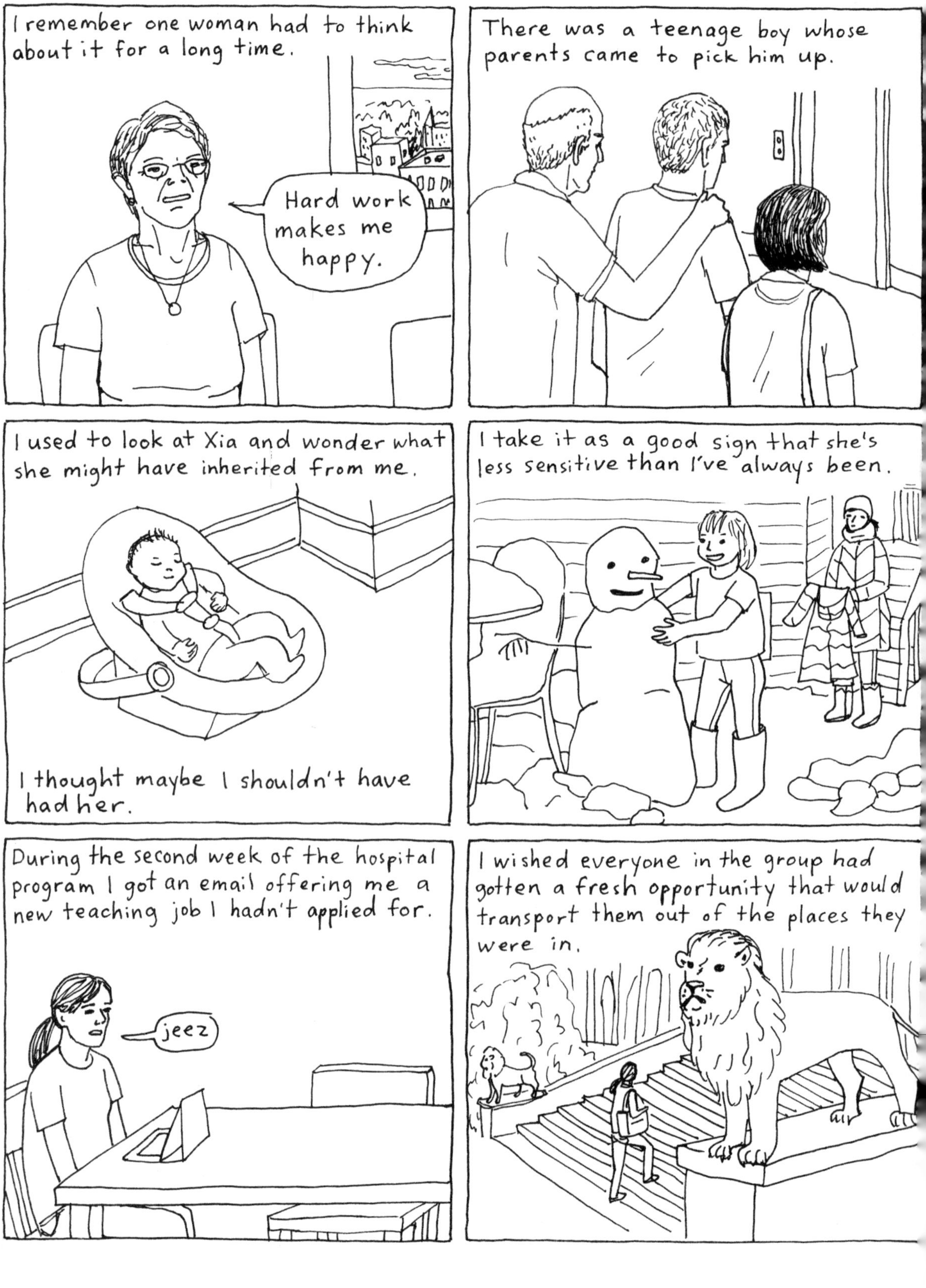
I remember one woman had to think about it for a long time.
Hard work makes me happy.
There was a teenage boy whose parents came to pick him up.
I used to look at Xia and wonder what she might have inherited from me.
I thought maybe I shouldn't have had her.
I take it as a good sign that she's less sensitive than I've always been.
During the second week of the hospital program I got an email offering me a new teaching job I hadn't applied for.
jeez
I wished everyone in the group had gotten a fresh opportunity that would transport them out of the places they were in.

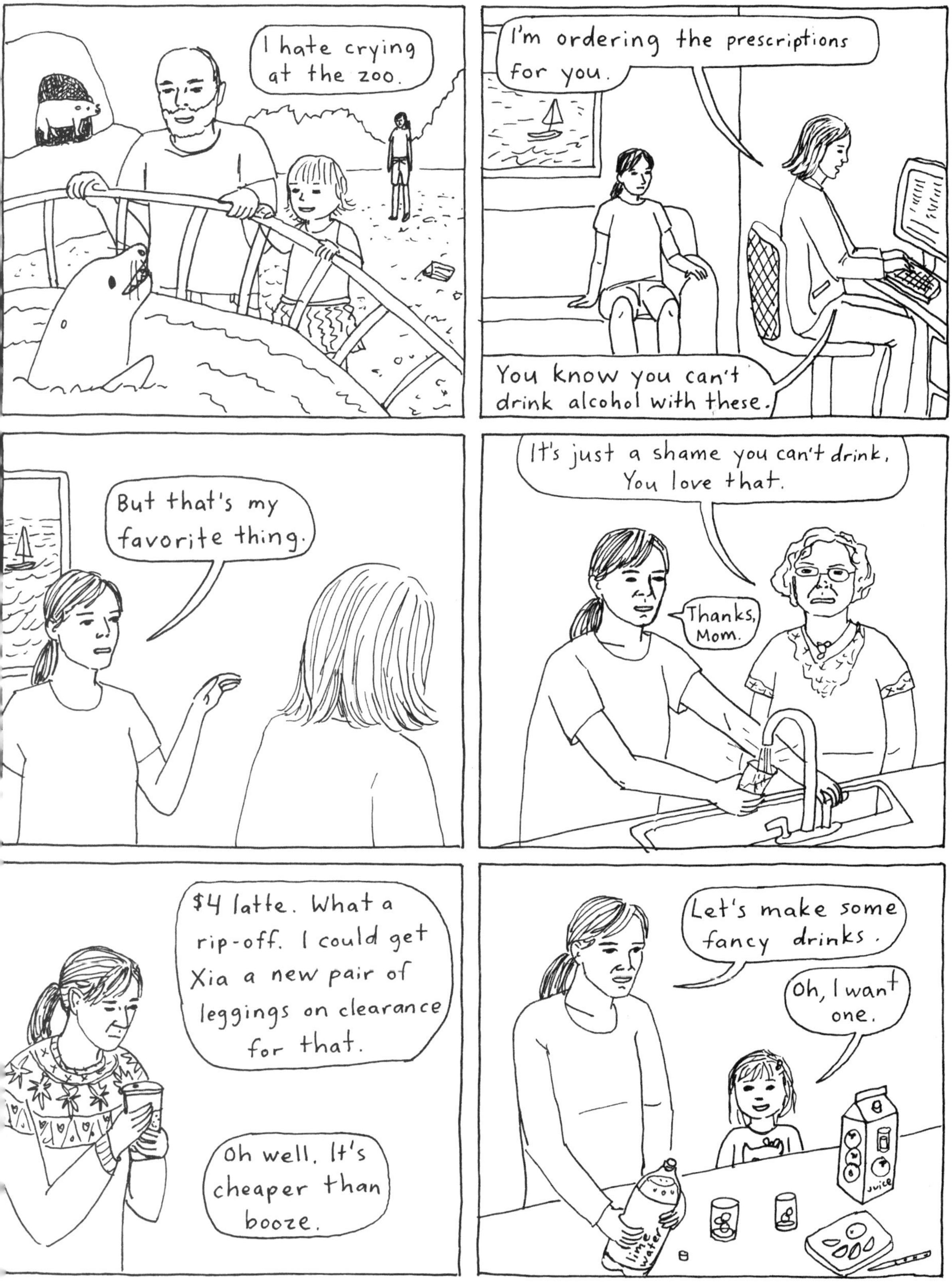
I hate crying at the zoo.
I'm ordering the prescriptions for you.
You know you can't drink alcohol with these.
But that's my favorite thing.
It's just a shame you can't drink. You love that.
Thanks, Mom.
$4 latte. What a rip-off. I could get Xia a new pair of leggings on clearance for that.
Oh well. It's cheaper than booze.
Let's make some fancy drinks.
Oh, I want one.
juice
lime water

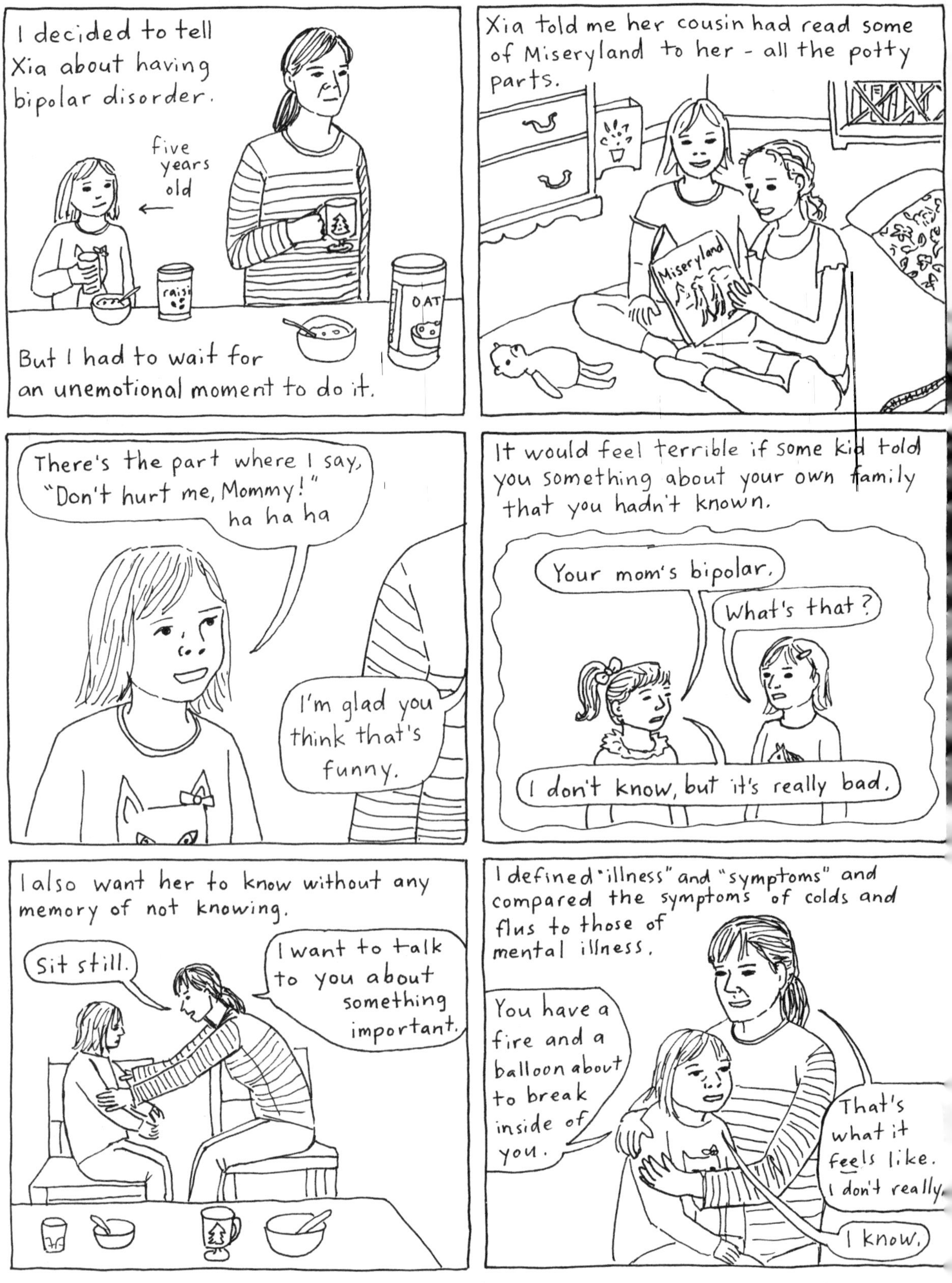

I decided to tell Xia about having bipolar disorder.
five years old
raisi
OAT
But I had to wait for an unemotional moment to do it.
Xia told me her cousin had read some of Miseryland to her - all the potty parts.
Miseryland
There's the part where I say, "Don't hurt me, Mommy!" ha ha ha
I'm glad you think that's funny.
It would feel terrible if some kid told you something about your own family that you hadn't known.
Your mom's bipolar.
What's that?
I don't know, but it's really bad.
I also want her to know without any memory of not knowing.
Sit still.
I want to talk to you about something important.
I defined "illness" and "symptoms" and compared the symptoms of colds and flus to those of mental illness.
You have a fire and a balloon about to break inside of you.
That's what it feels like. I don't really.
I know.

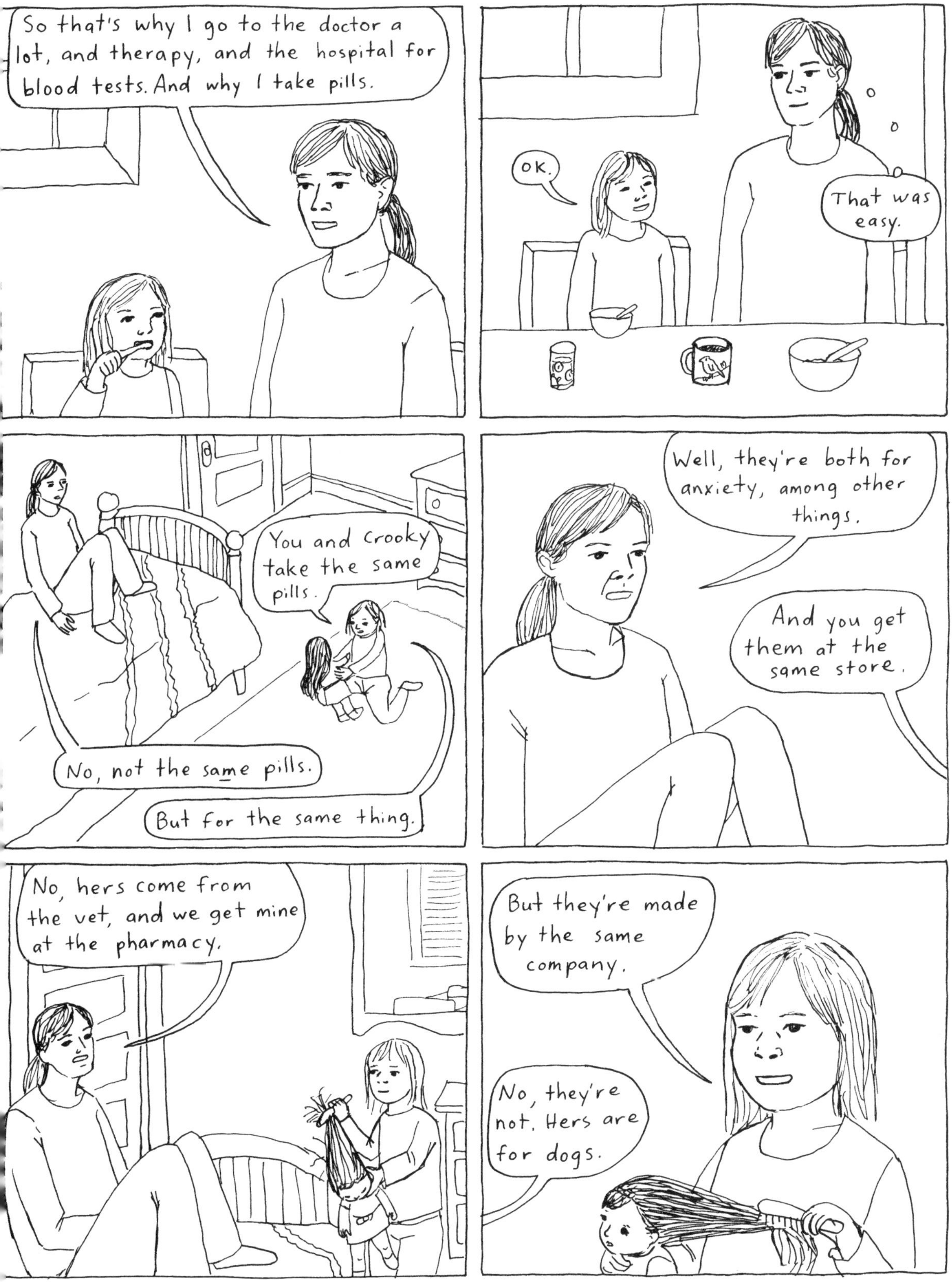
So that's why I go to the doctor a lot, and therapy, and the hospital for blood tests. And why I take pills.
OK.
That was easy.
You and Crooky take the same pills.
No, not the same pills.
But for the same thing.
Well, they're both for anxiety, among other things.
And you get them at the same store.
No, hers come from the vet, and we get mine at the pharmacy.
But they're made by the same company.
No, they're not. Hers are for dogs.

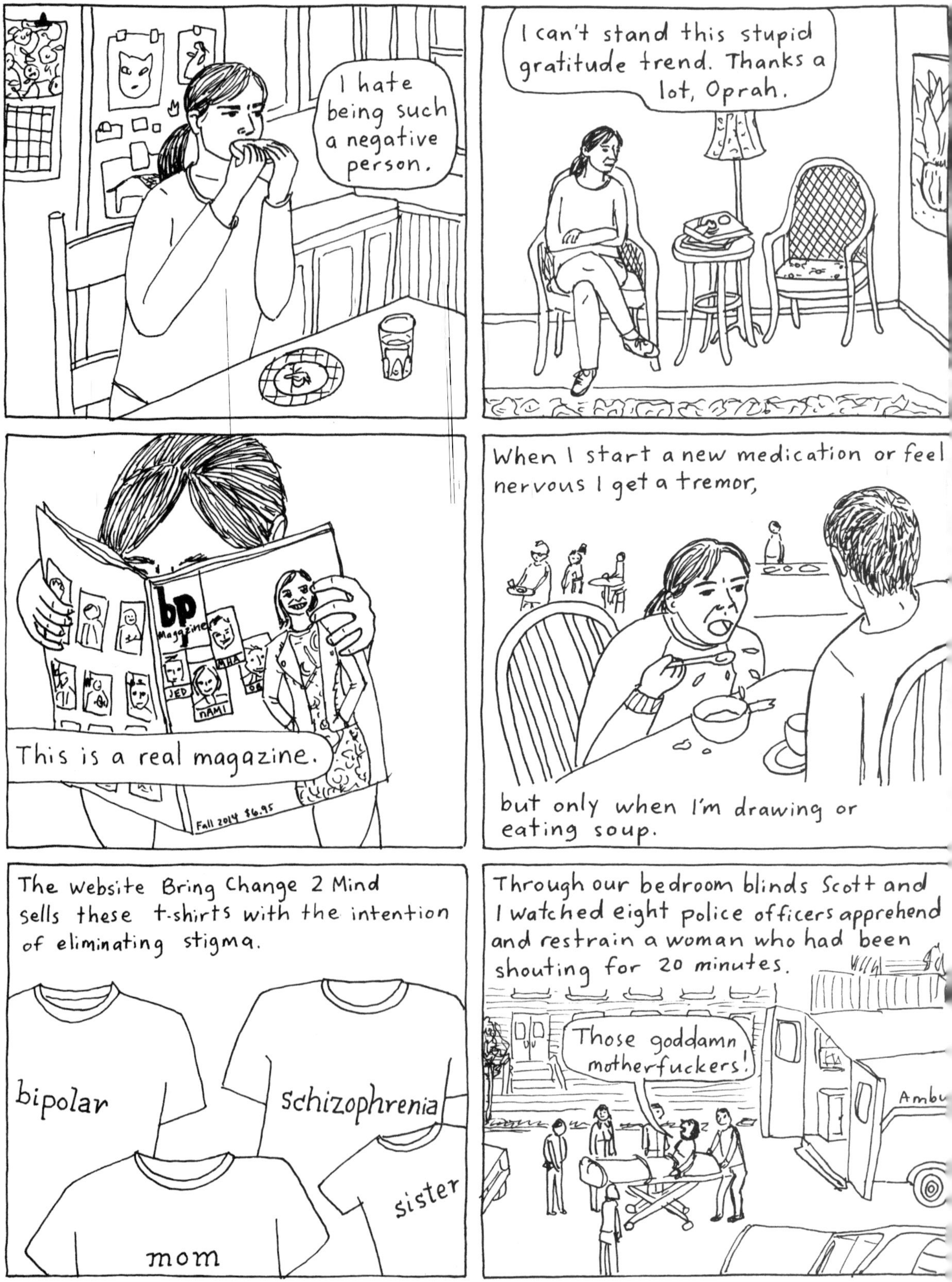
I hate being such a negative person.
I can't stand this stupid gratitude trend. Thanks a lot, Oprah.
bp Magazine
JED
NAMI
MHA
Fall 2014 $6.95
This is a real magazine.
When I start a new medication or feel nervous I get a tremor,
but only when I'm drawing or eating soup.
The website Bring Change 2 Mind sells these t-shirts with the intention of eliminating stigma.
bipolar
schizophrenia
mom
sister
Through our bedroom blinds Scott and I watched eight police officers apprehend and restrain a woman who had been shouting for 20 minutes.
Those goddamn motherfuckers!
Ambu

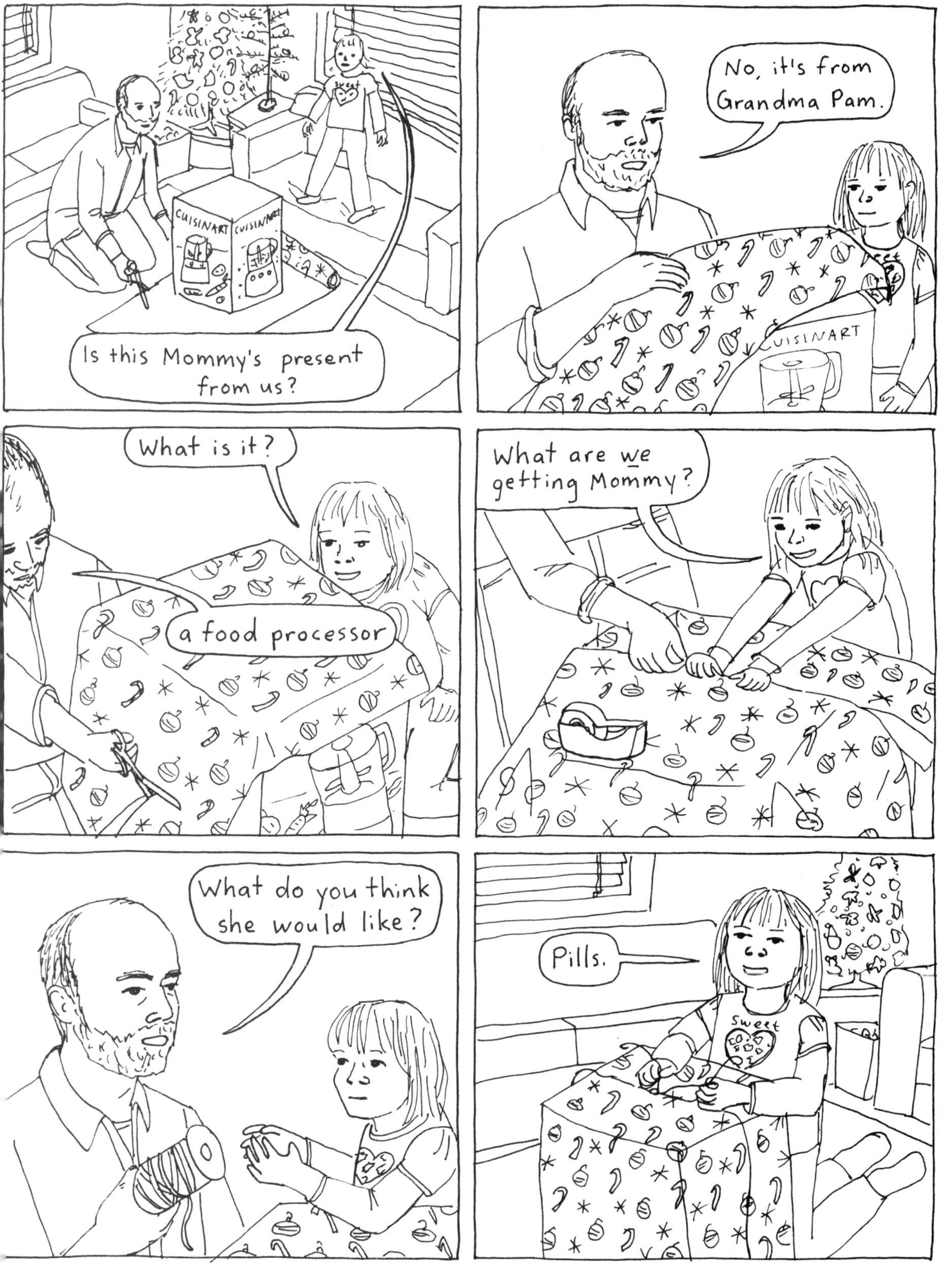
Is this Mommy's present from us?
No, it's from Grandma Pam.
What is it?
a food processor
What are we getting Mommy?
What do you think she would like?
Pills.

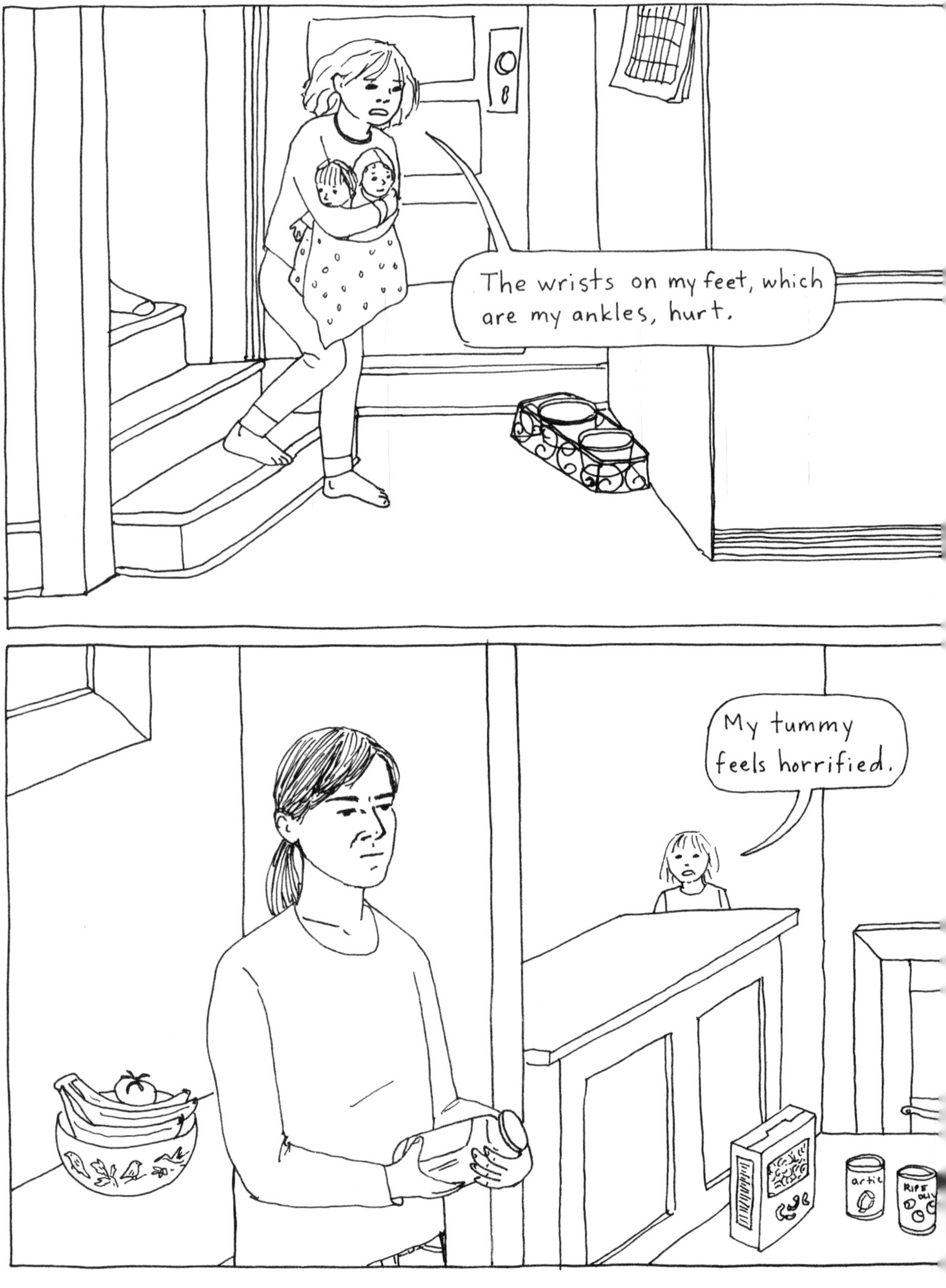
The wrists on my feet, which are my ankles, hurt.
My tummy feels horrified.

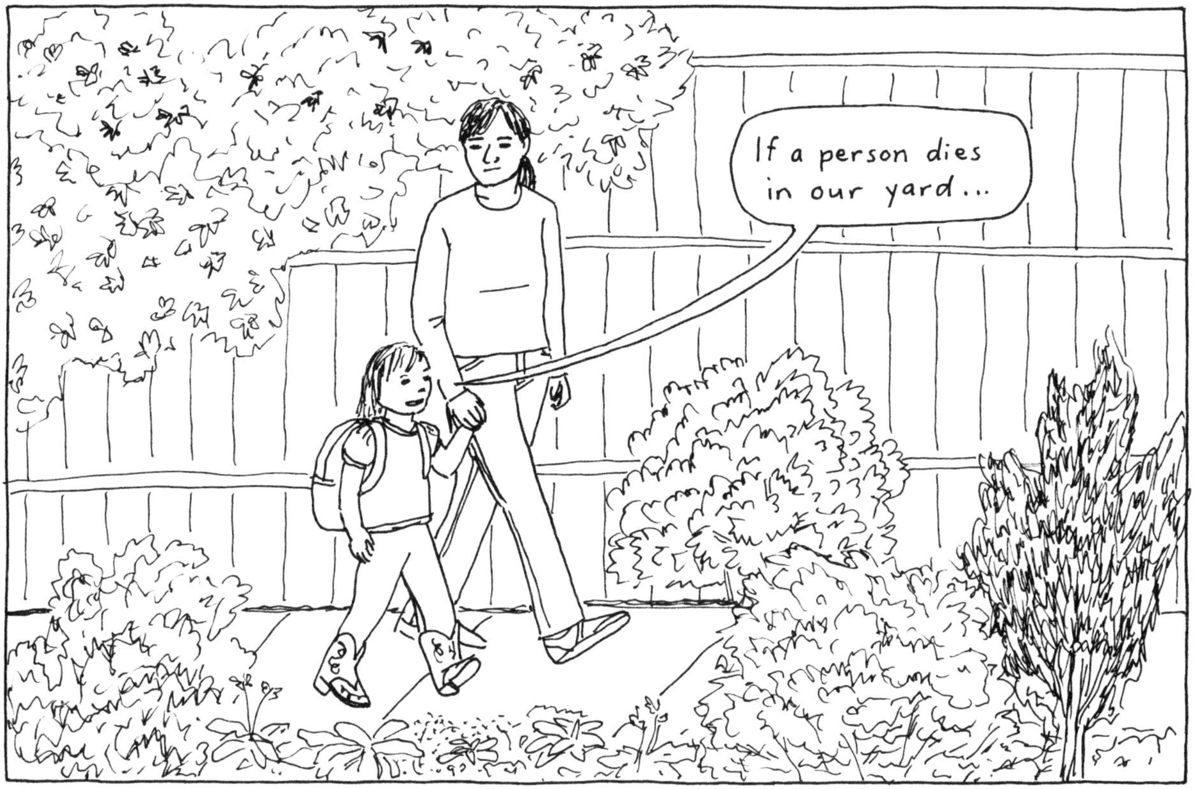
If a person dies in our yard...

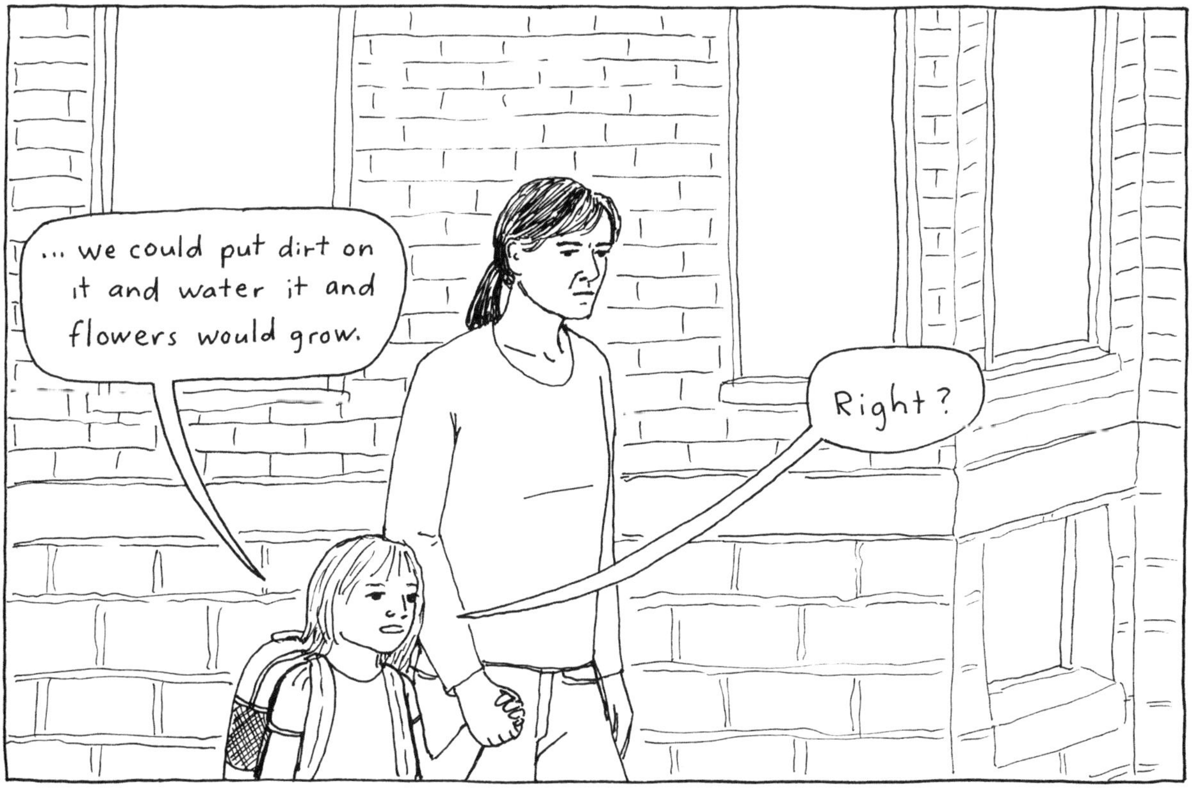
... we could put dirt on it and water it and flowers would grow.
Right?

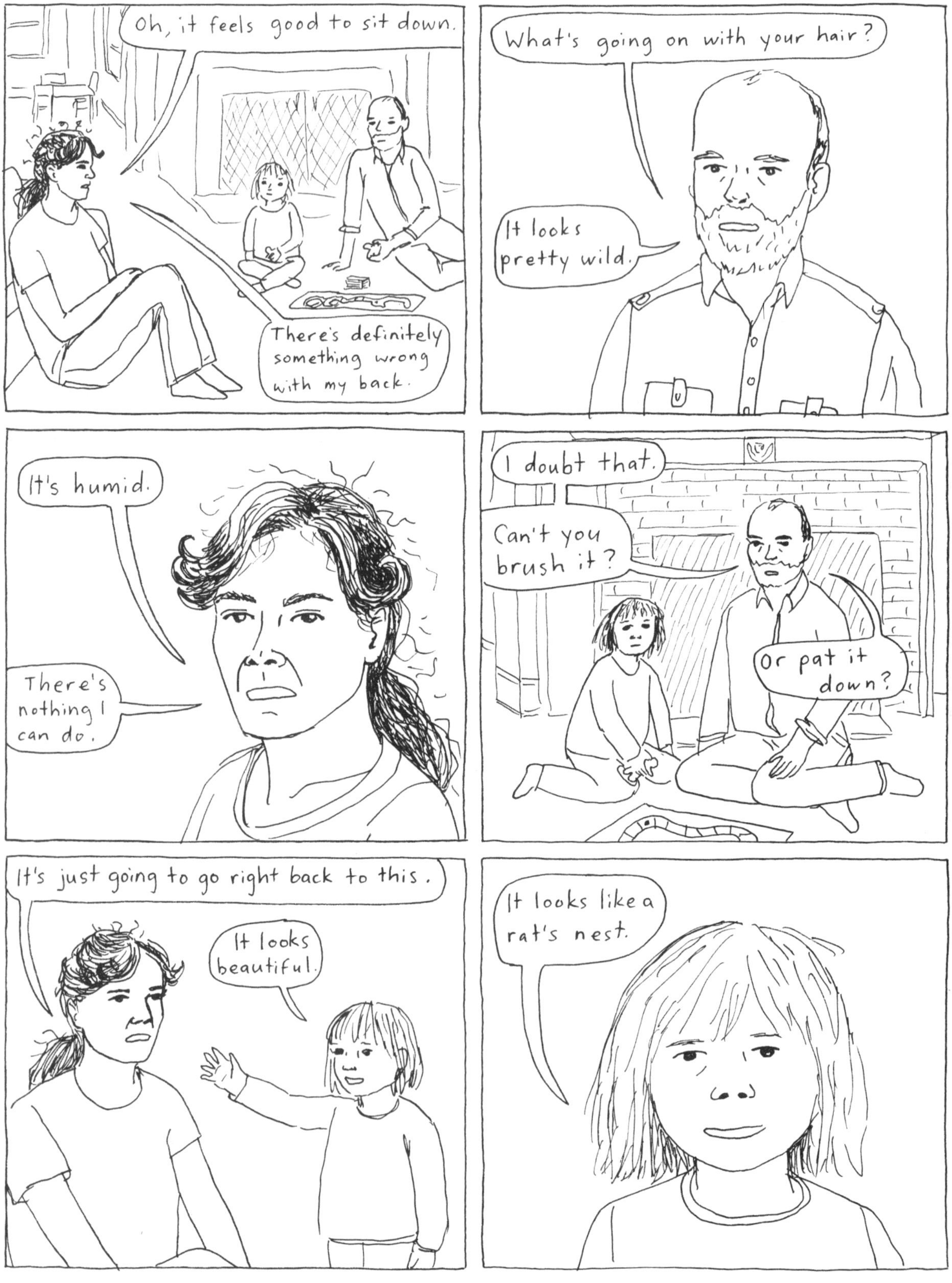
Oh, it feels good to sit down.
There's definitely something wrong with my back.
What's going on with your hair?
It looks pretty wild.
It's humid.
There's nothing I can do.
I doubt that.
Can't you brush it?
Or pat it down?
It's just going to go right back to this.
It looks beautiful.
It looks like a rat's nest.

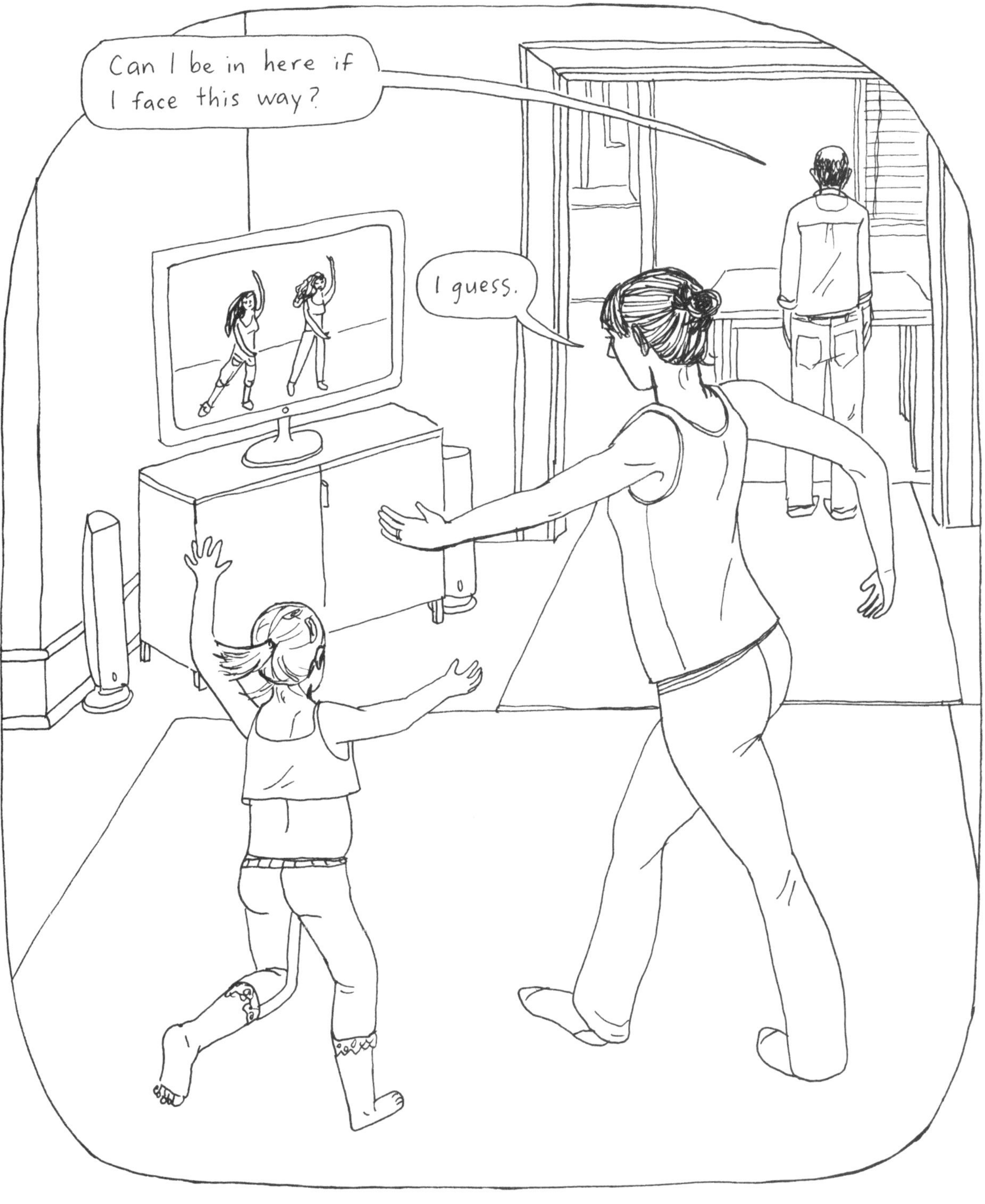
Can I be in here if I face this way?
I guess.

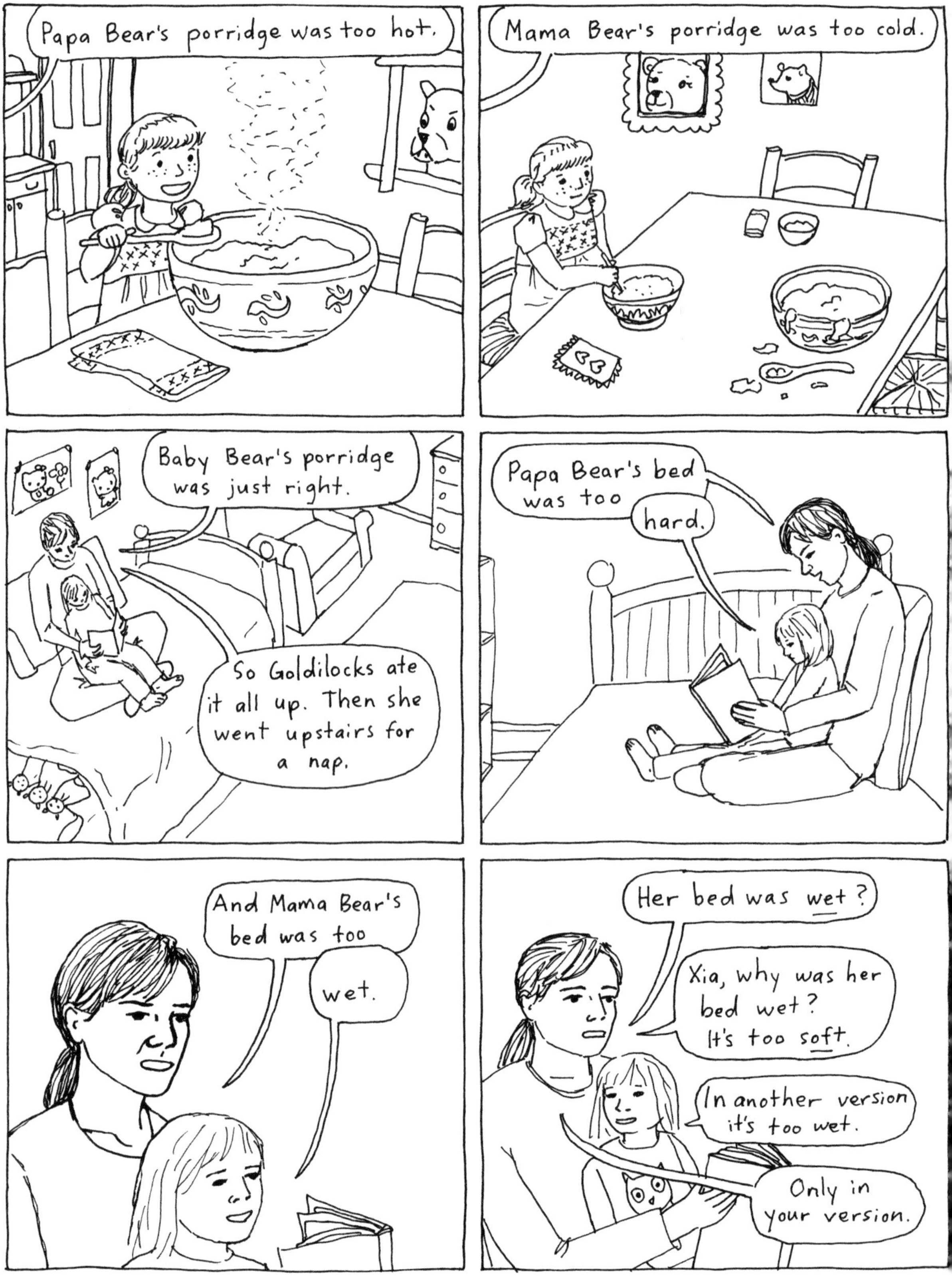
Papa Bear's porridge was too hot.
Mama Bear's porridge was too cold.
Baby Bear's porridge was just right.
So Goldilocks ate it all up. Then she went upstairs for a nap.
Papa Bear's bed was too
hard.
And Mama Bear's bed was too
wet.
Her bed was wet?
Xia, why was her bed wet? It's too soft.
In another version it's too wet.
Only in your version.

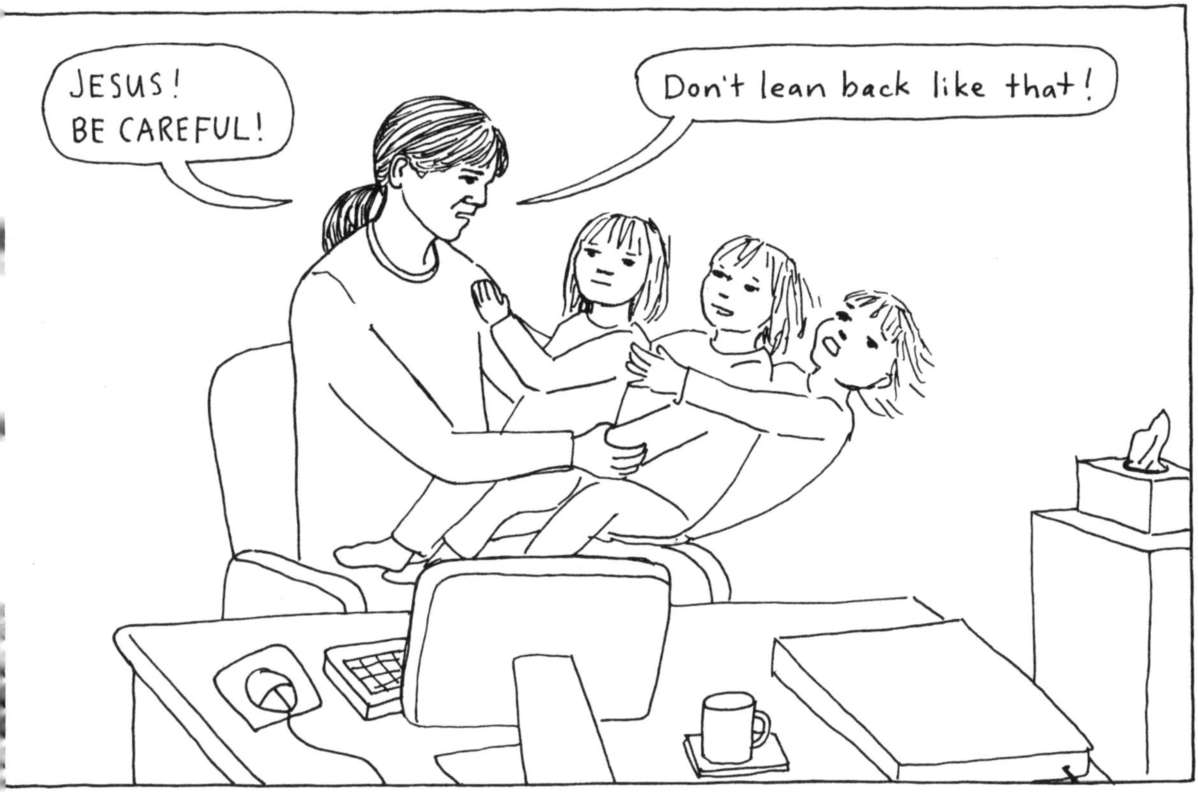
JESUS! BE CAREFUL!
Don't lean back like that!

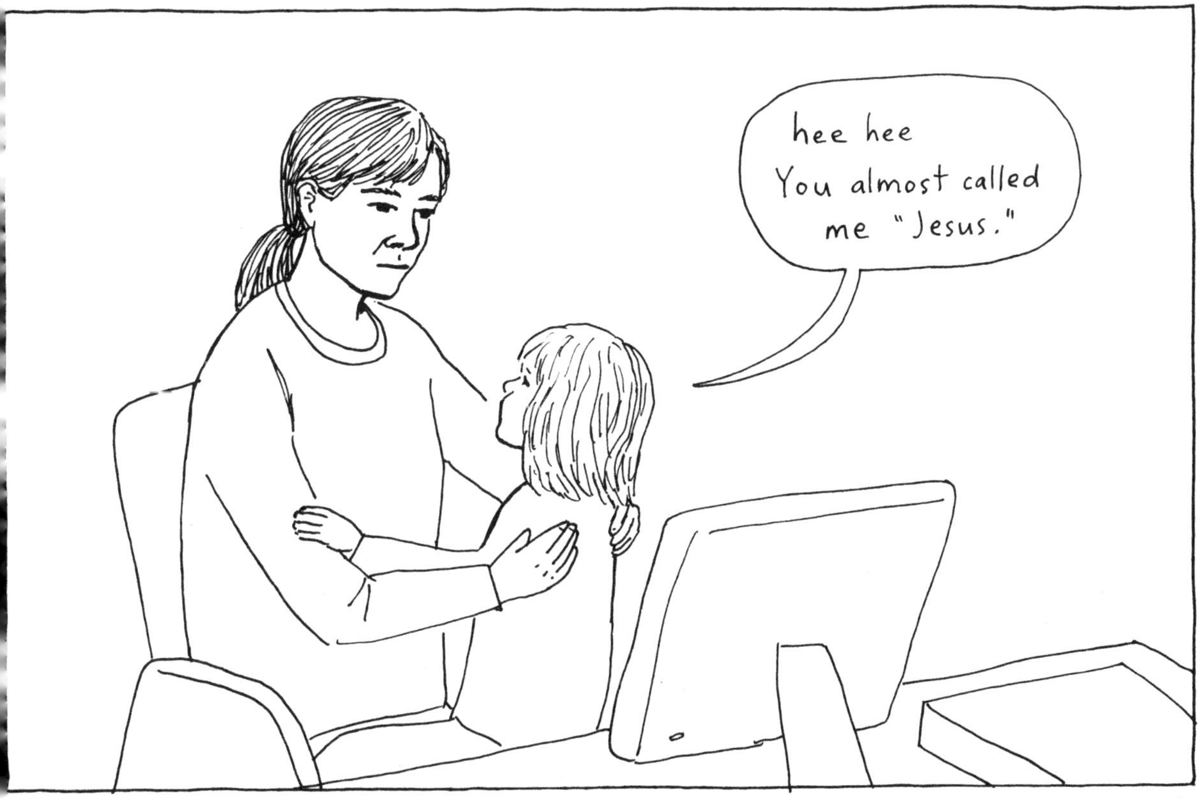
hee hee You almost called me "Jesus."

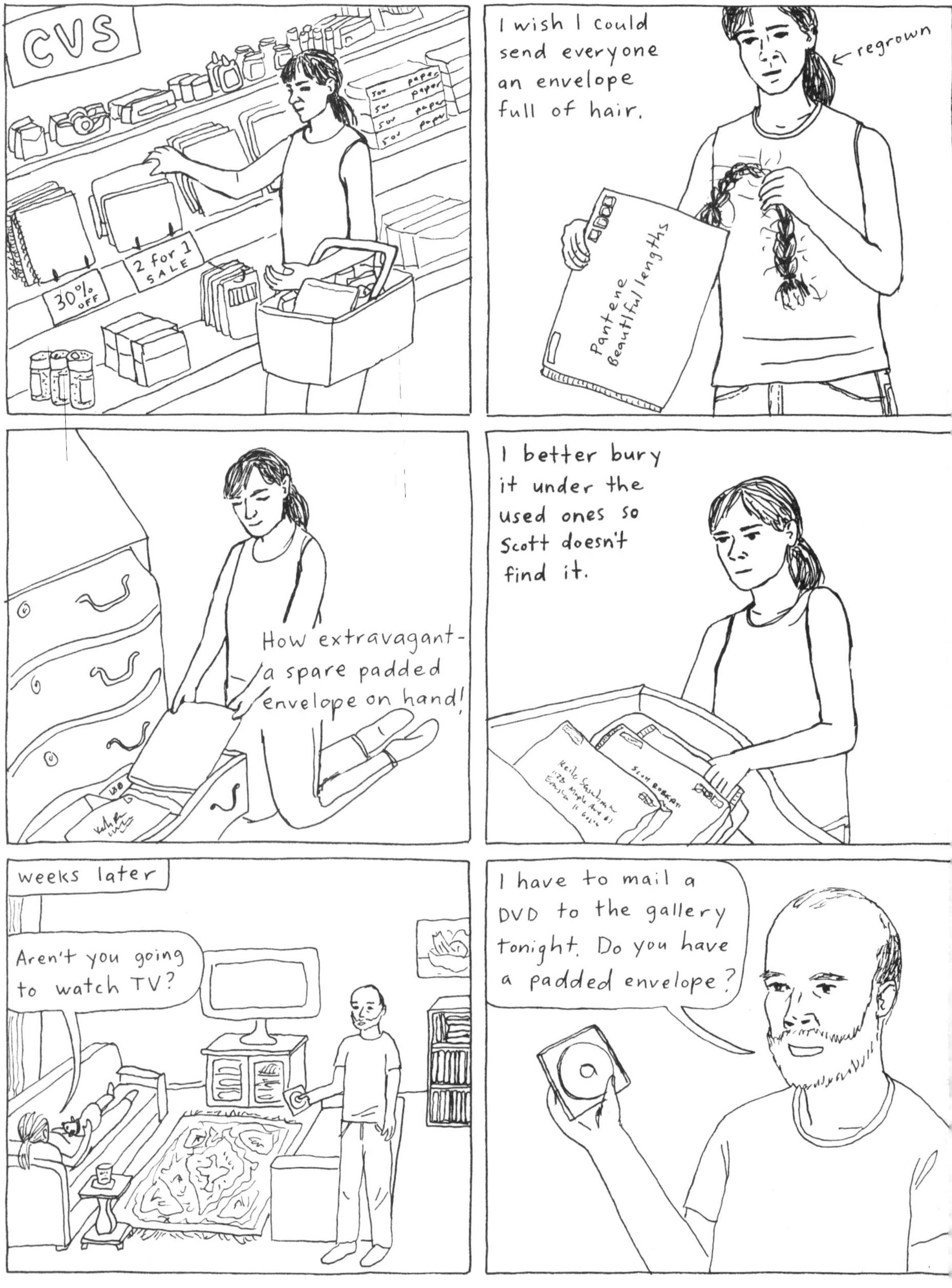
CVS
500 paper
500 paper
500 paper
500 paper
2 for 1 SALE
30% OFF
I wish I could send everyone an envelope full of hair.
← regrown
Pantene Beautiful lengths
How extravagant- a spare padded envelope on hand!
I better bury it under the used ones so Scott doesn't find it.
weeks later
Aren't you going to watch TV?
I have to mail a DVD to the gallery tonight. Do you have a padded envelope?

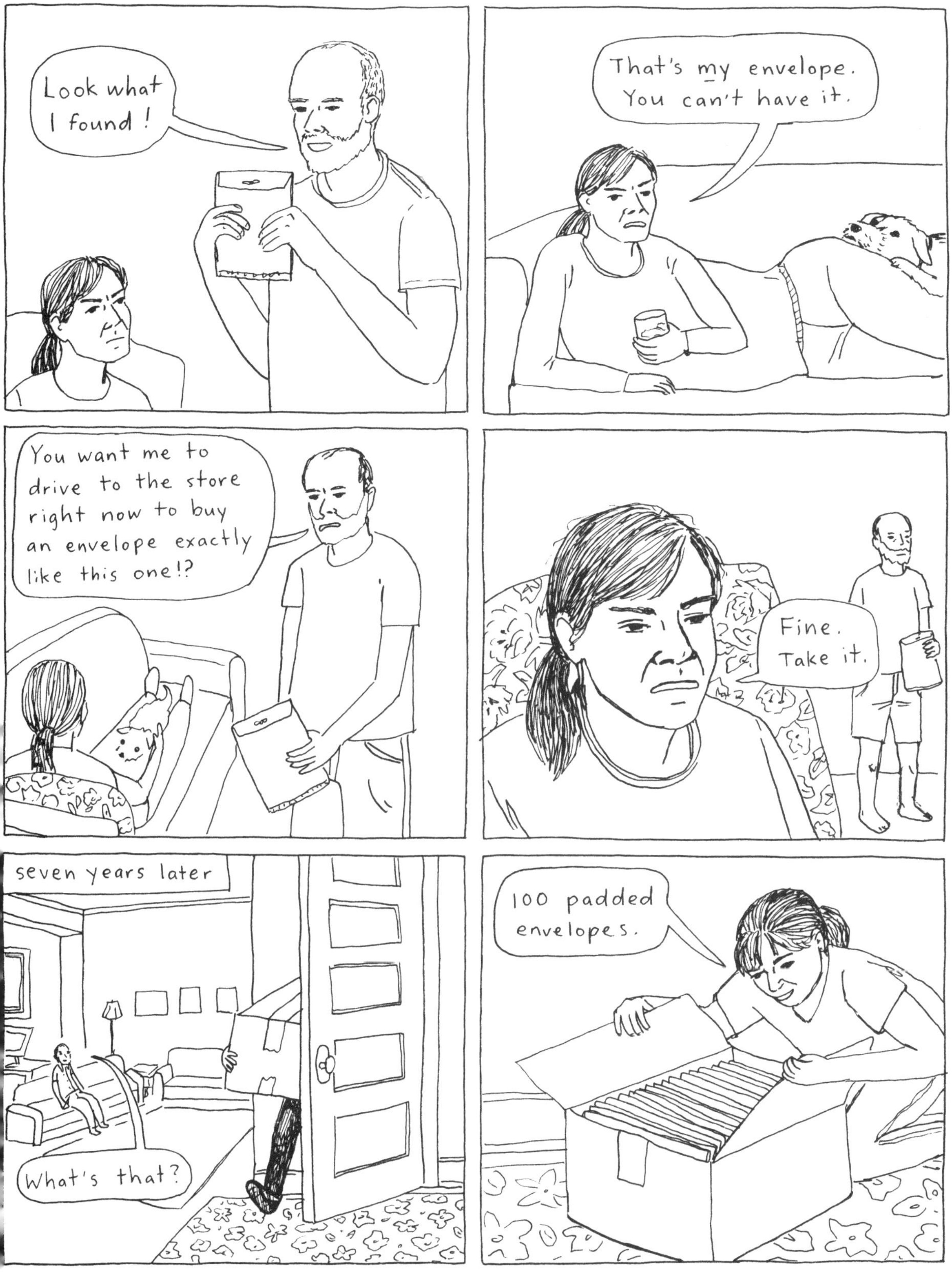
Look what I found!
That's my envelope. You can't have it.
You want me to drive to the store right now to buy an envelope exactly like this one!?
Fine. Take it.
seven years later
What's that?
100 padded envelopes.

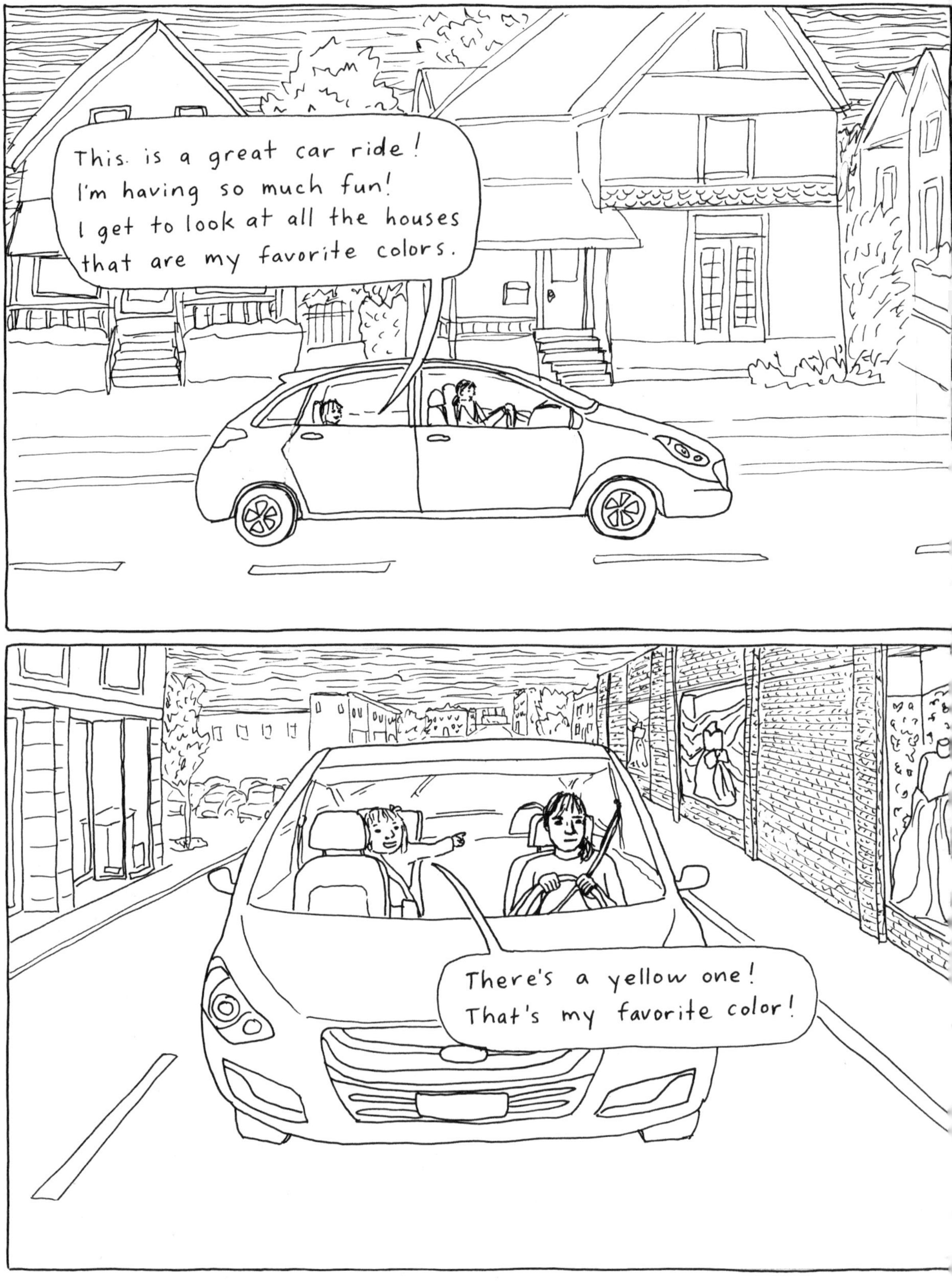
This is a great car ride! I'm having so much fun! I get to look at all the houses that are my favorite colors.
There's a yellow one! That's my favorite color!

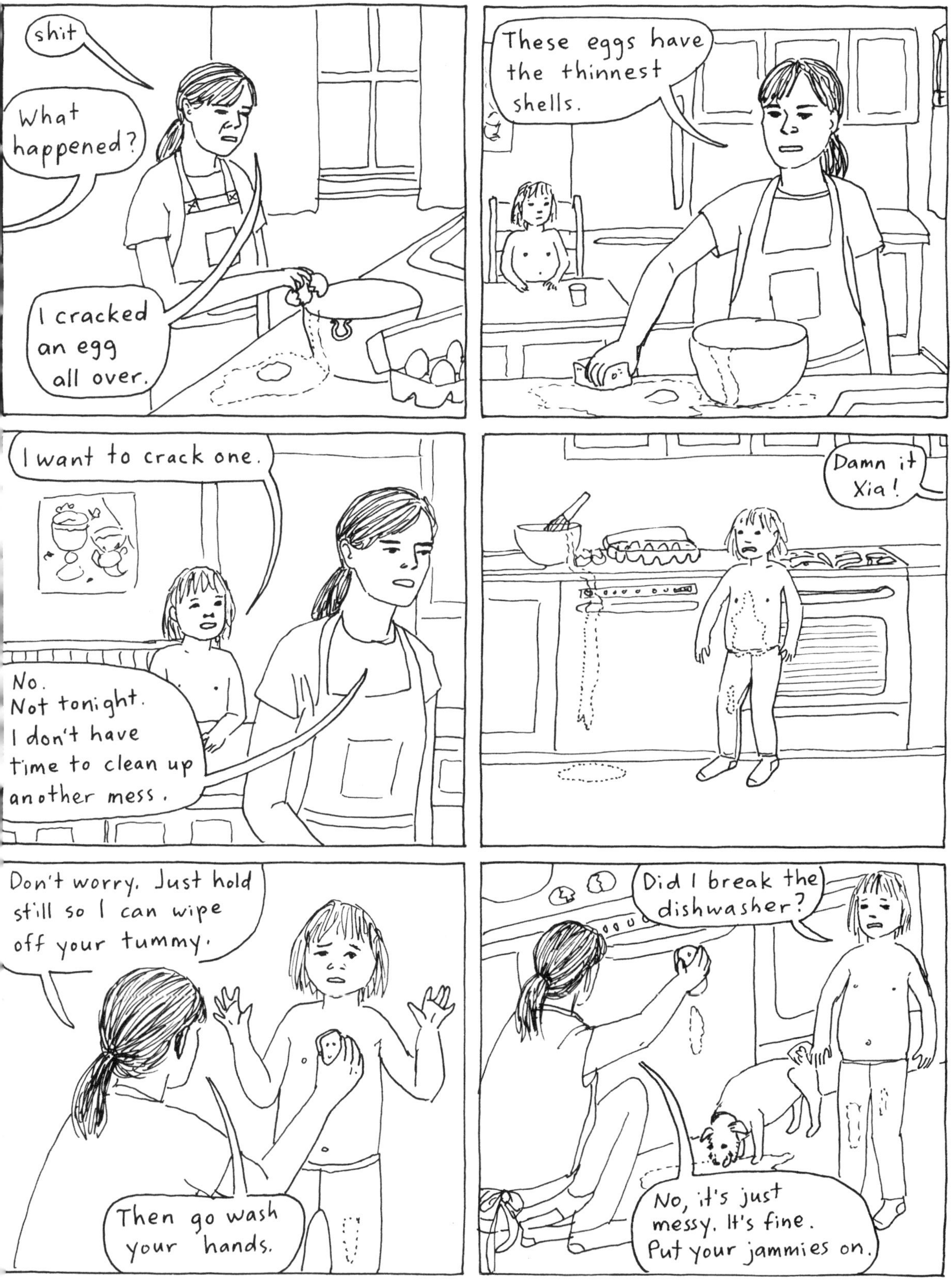
shit
What happened?
I cracked an egg all over.
These eggs have the thinnest shells.
I want to crack one.
No. Not tonight. I don't have time to clean up another mess.
Damn it Xia!
Don't worry. Just hold still so I can wipe off your tummy.
Then go wash your hands.
Did I break the dishwasher?
No, it's just messy. It's fine. Put your jammies on.

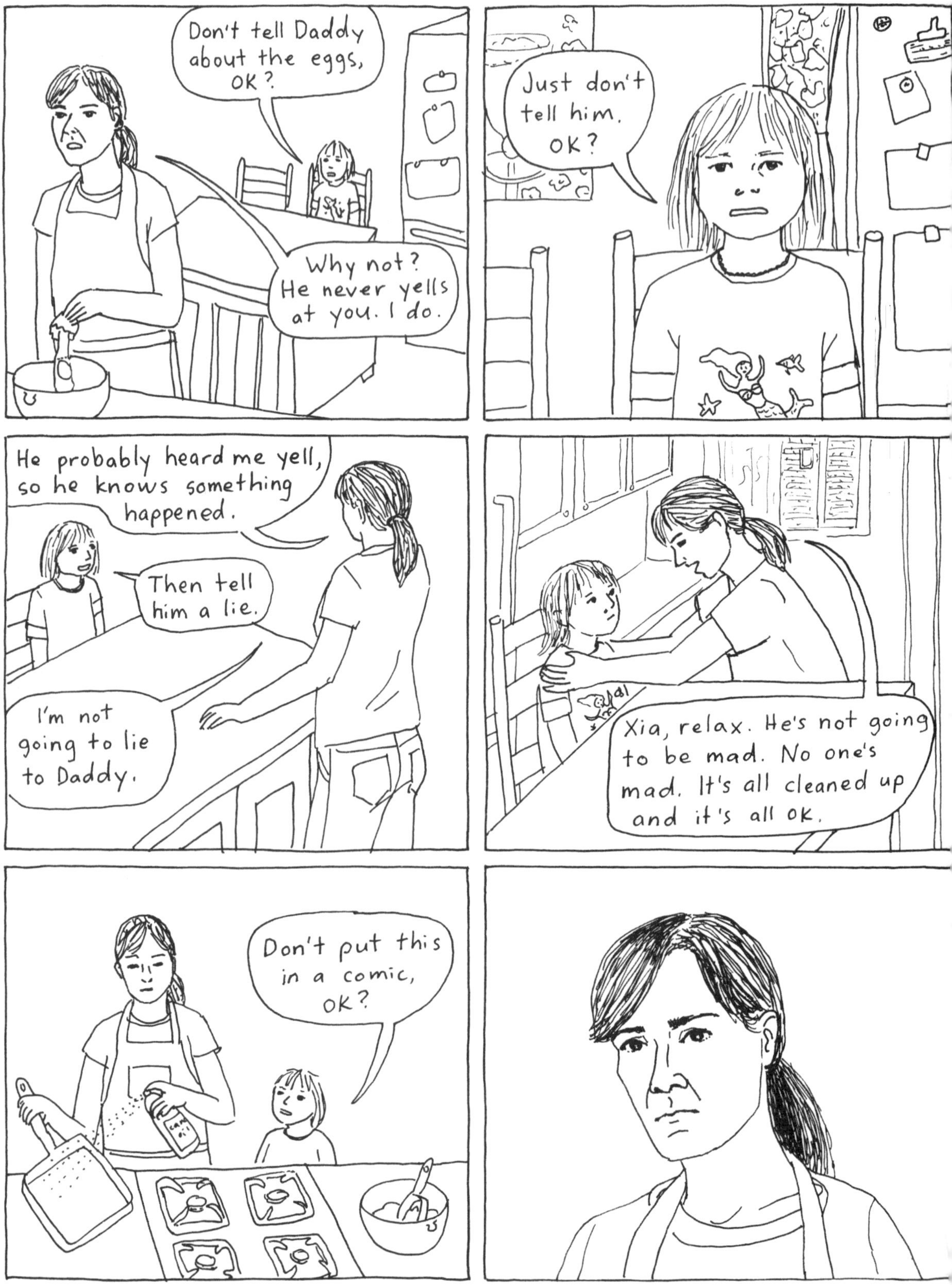
Don't tell Daddy about the eggs, OK?
Why not? He never yells at you. I do.
Just don't tell him. OK?
He probably heard me yell, so he knows something happened.
Then tell him a lie.
I'm not going to lie to Daddy.
Xia, relax. He's not going to be mad. No one's mad. It's all cleaned up and it's all OK.
Don't put this in a comic, OK?

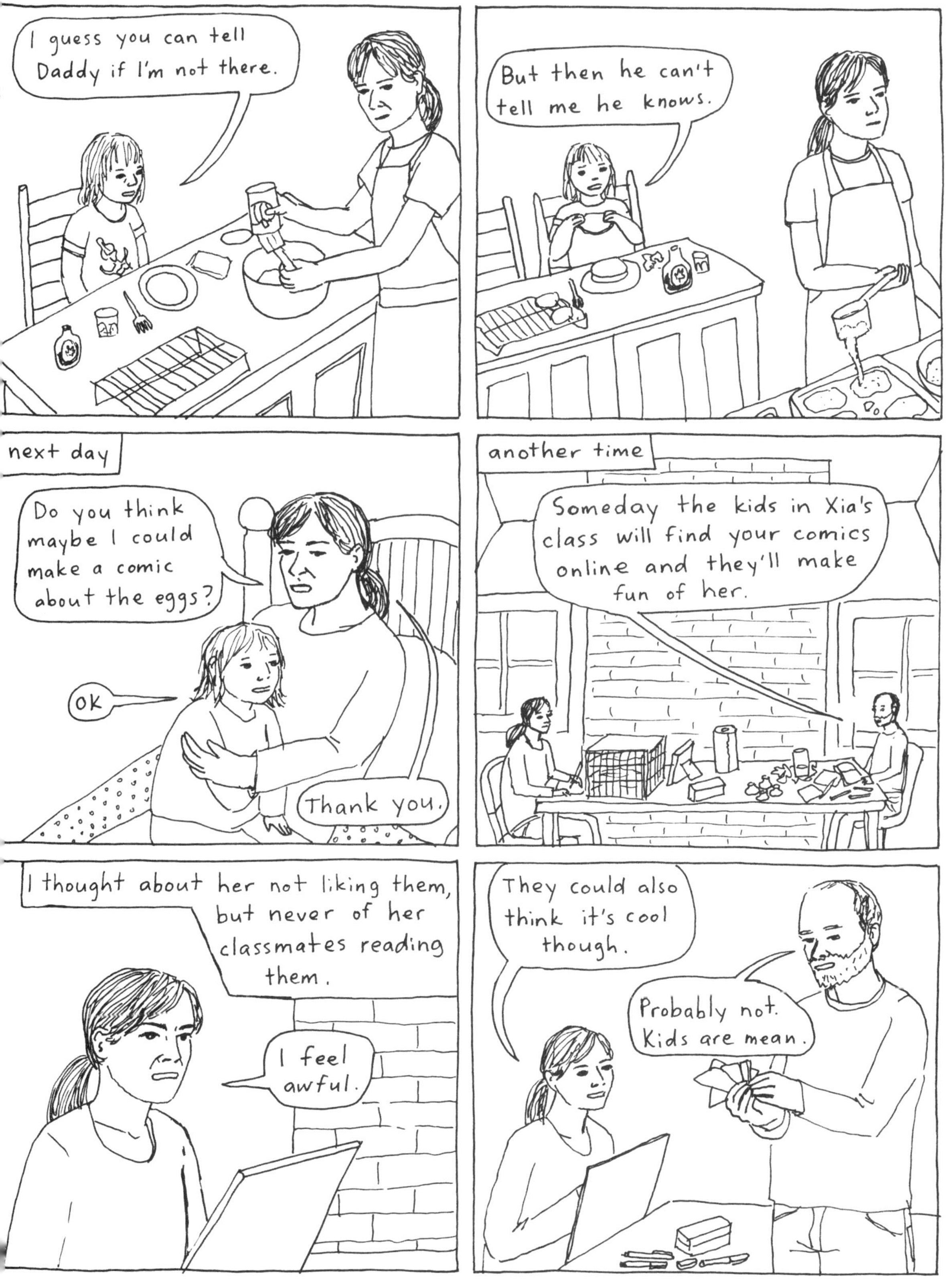
I guess you can tell Daddy if I'm not there.
But then he can't tell me he knows.
next day
Do you think maybe I could make a comic about the eggs?
OK
Thank you.
another time
Someday the kids in Xia's class will find your comics online and they'll make fun of her.
I thought about her not liking them, but never of her classmates reading them.
I feel awful.
They could also think it's cool though.
Probably not. Kids are mean.

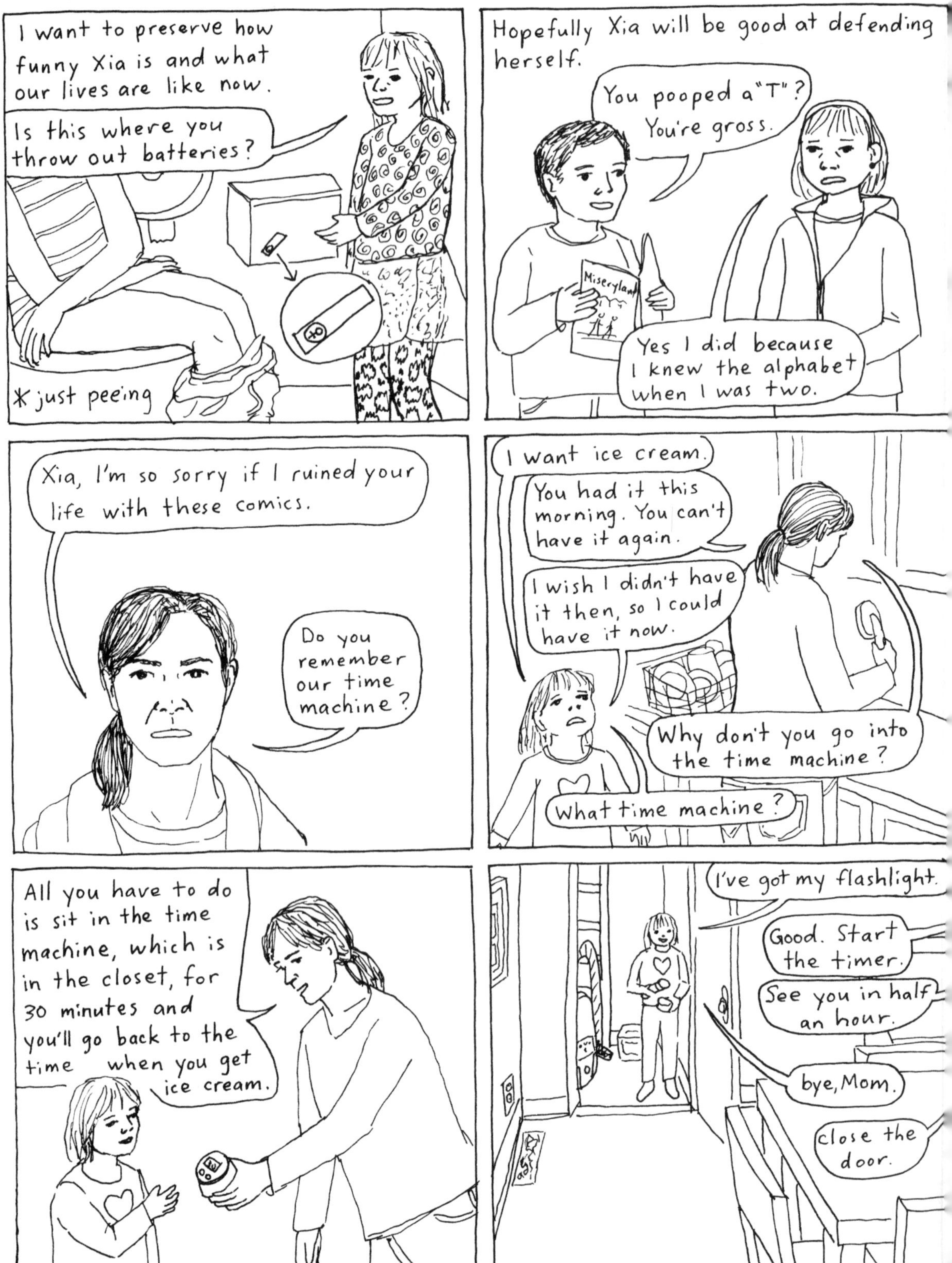
I want to preserve how funny Xia is and what our lives are like now.
Is this where you throw out batteries?
* just peeing
Hopefully Xia will be good at defending herself.
You pooped a "T"? You're gross.
Miseryland
Yes I did because I knew the alphabet when I was two.
Xia, I'm so sorry if I ruined your life with these comics.
Do you remember our time machine?
I want ice cream.
You had it this morning. You can't have it again.
I wish I didn't have it then, so I could have it now.
Why don't you go into the time machine?
What time machine?
All you have to do is sit in the time machine, which is in the closet, for 30 minutes and you'll go back to the time when you get ice cream.
I've got my flashlight.
Good. Start the timer.
See you in half an hour.
bye, Mom.
close the door.

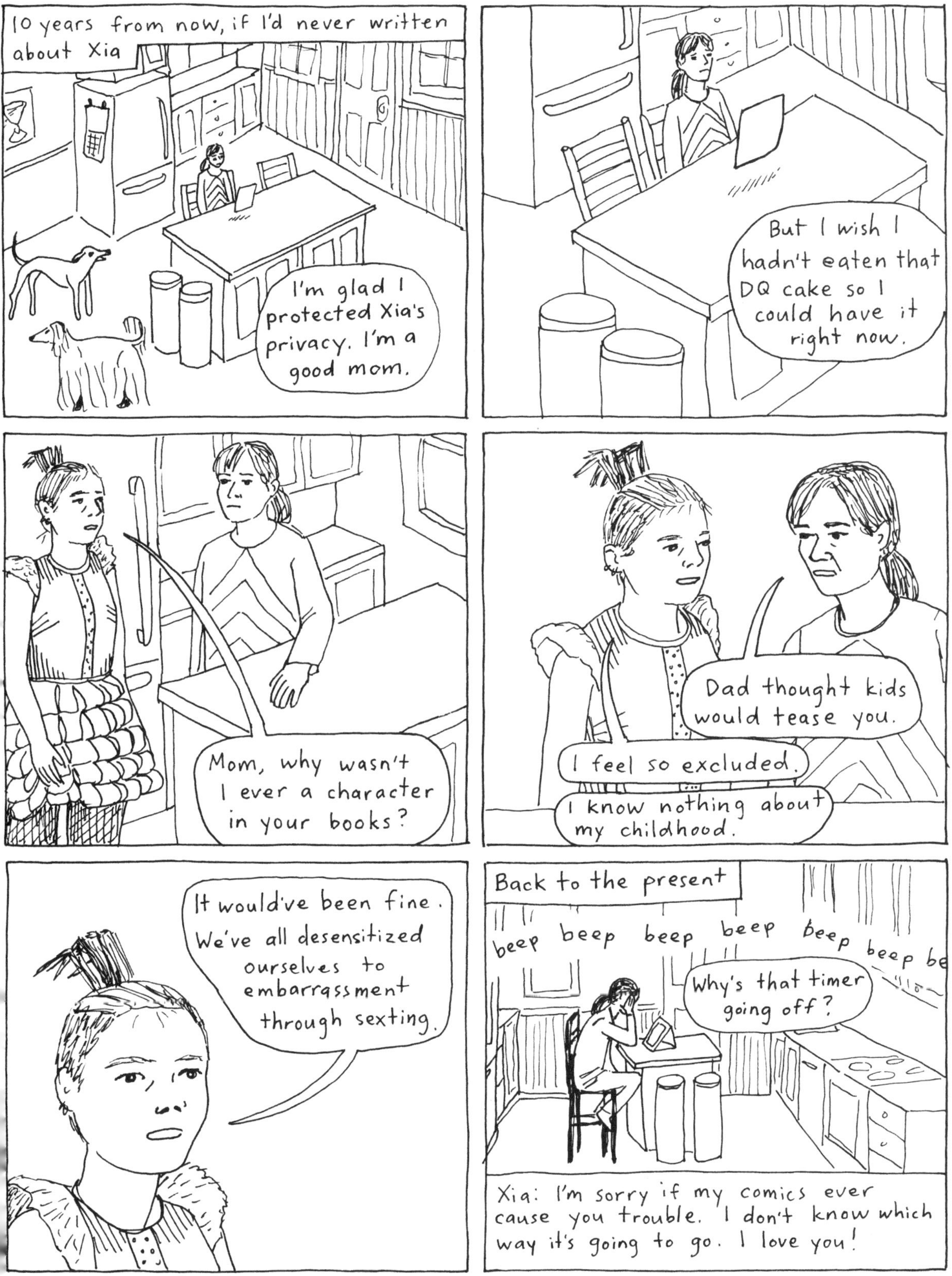
10 years from now, if I'd never written about Xia
I'm glad I protected Xia's privacy. I'm a good mom.
But I wish I hadn't eaten that DQ cake so I could have it right now.
Mom, why wasn't I ever a character in your books?
Dad thought kids would tease you.
I feel so excluded.
I know nothing about my childhood.
It would've been fine. We've all desensitized ourselves to embarrassment through sexting.
Back to the present
beep beep beep beep beep beep be
Why's that timer going off?
Xia: I'm sorry if my comics ever cause you trouble. I don't know which way it's going to go. I love you!

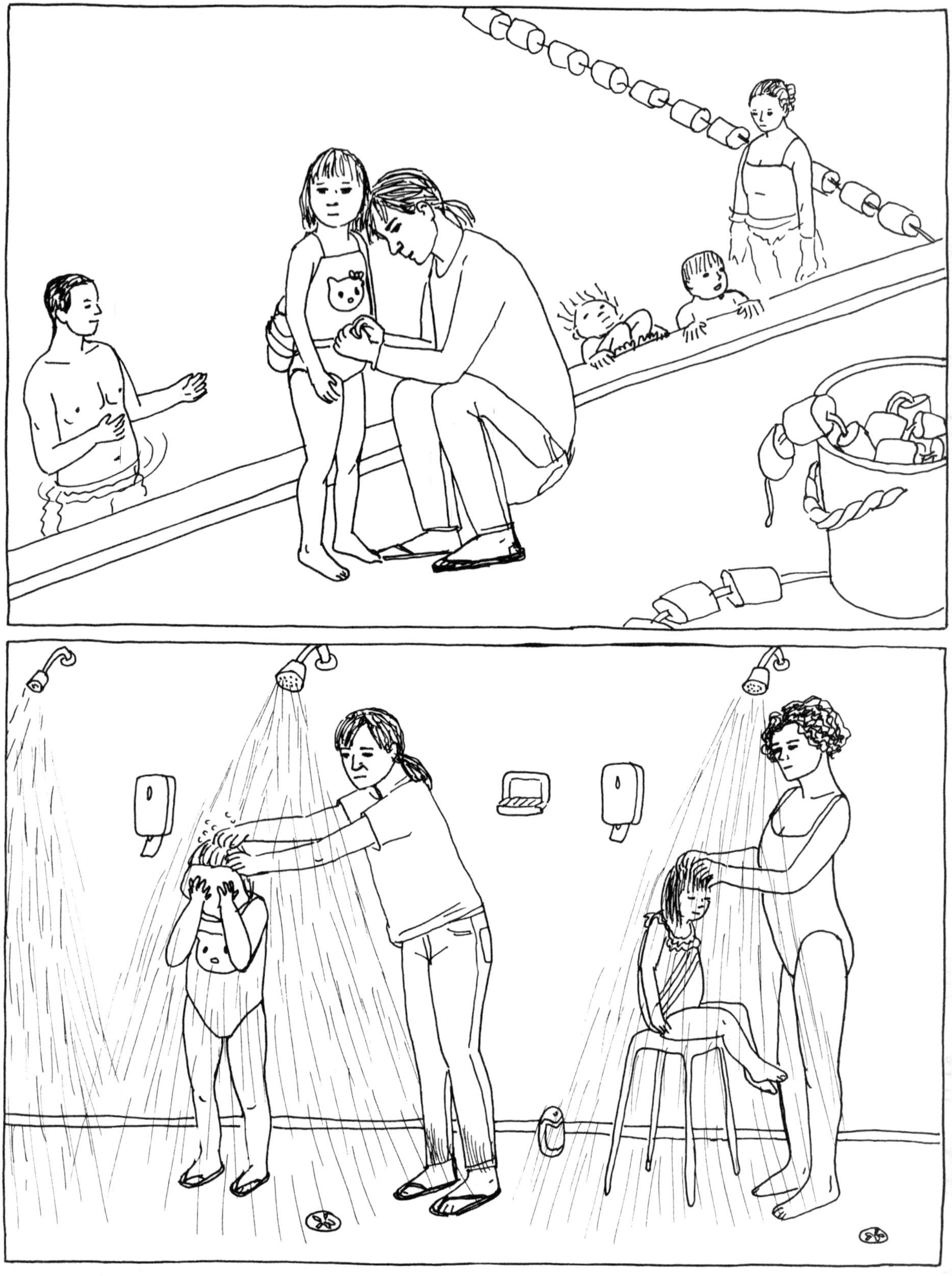

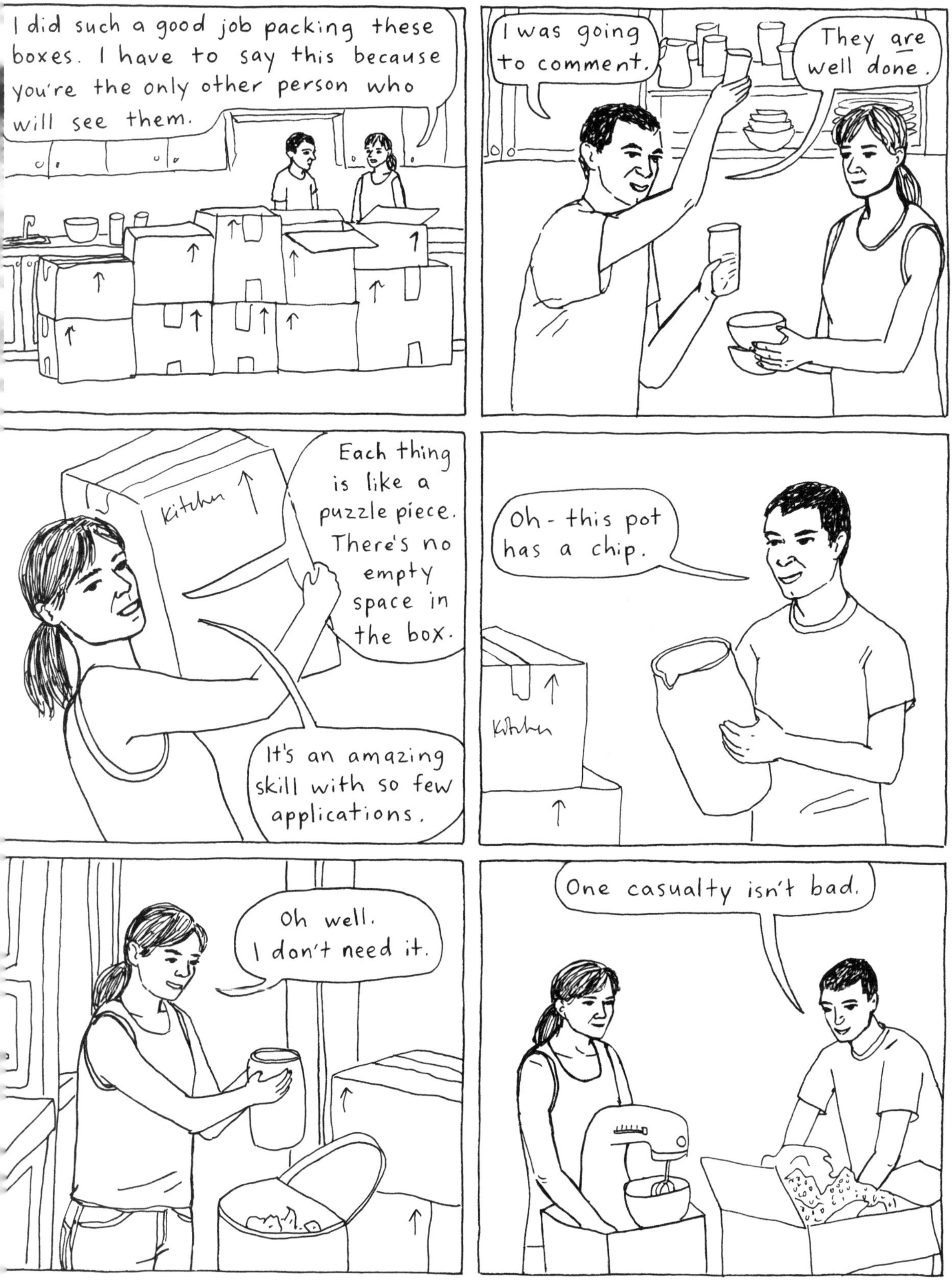
I did such a good job packing these boxes. I have to say this because you're the only other person who will see them.
I was going to comment.
They are well done.
Kitchen
Each thing is like a puzzle piece. There's no empty space in the box.
It's an amazing skill with so few applications.
Oh - this pot has a chip.
Kitchen
Oh well. I don't need it.
One casualty isn't bad.

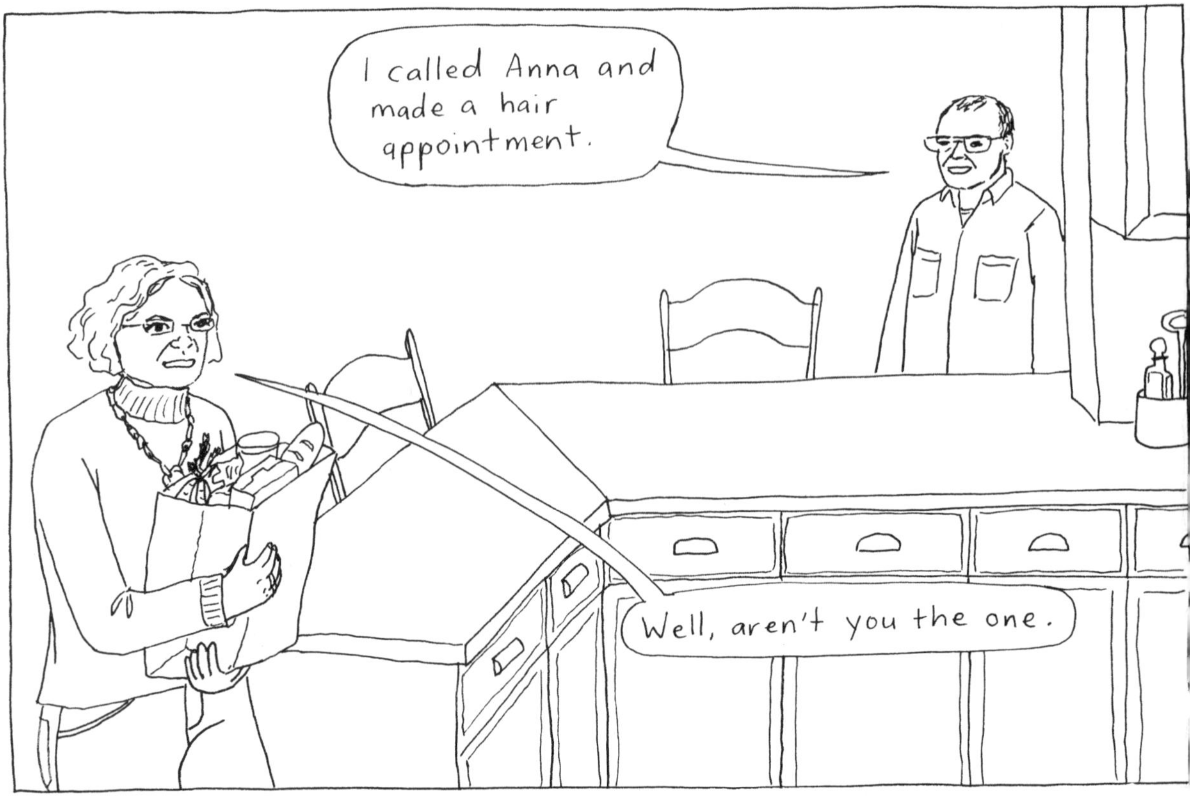
I called Anna and made a hair appointment.
Well, aren't you the one.

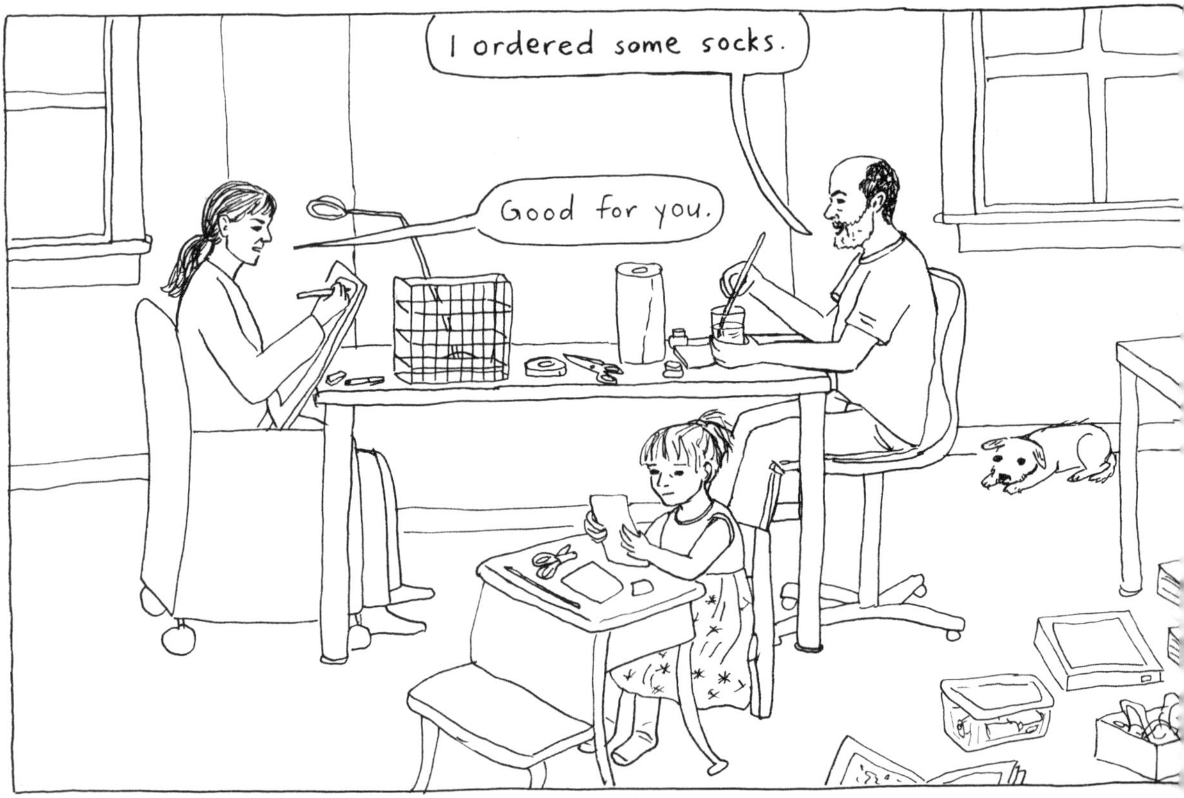
I ordered some socks.
Good for you.

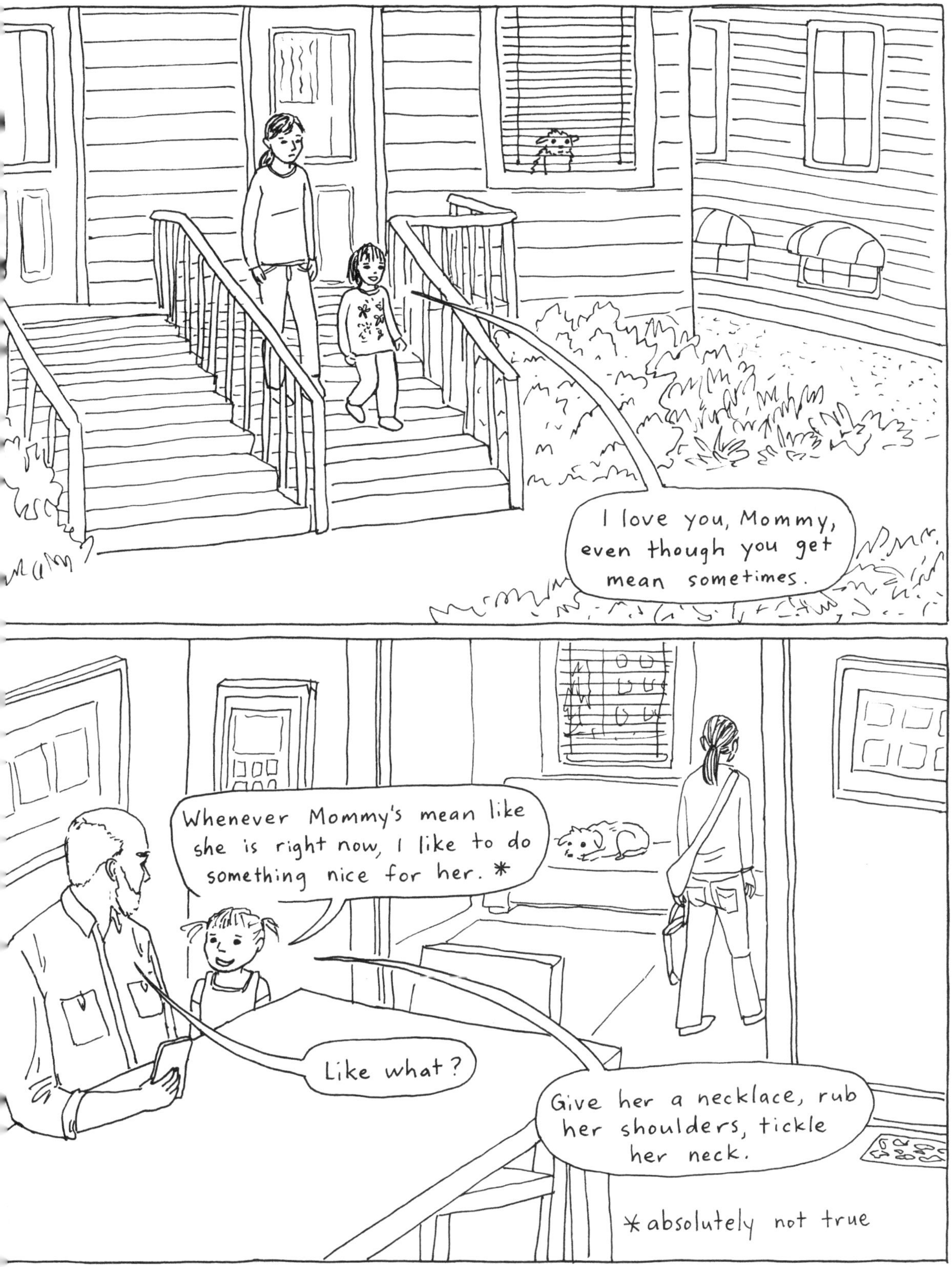
I love you, Mommy, even though you get mean sometimes.
Whenever Mommy's mean like she is right now, I like to do something nice for her. *
Like what?
Give her a necklace, rub her shoulders, tickle her neck.
*absolutely not true

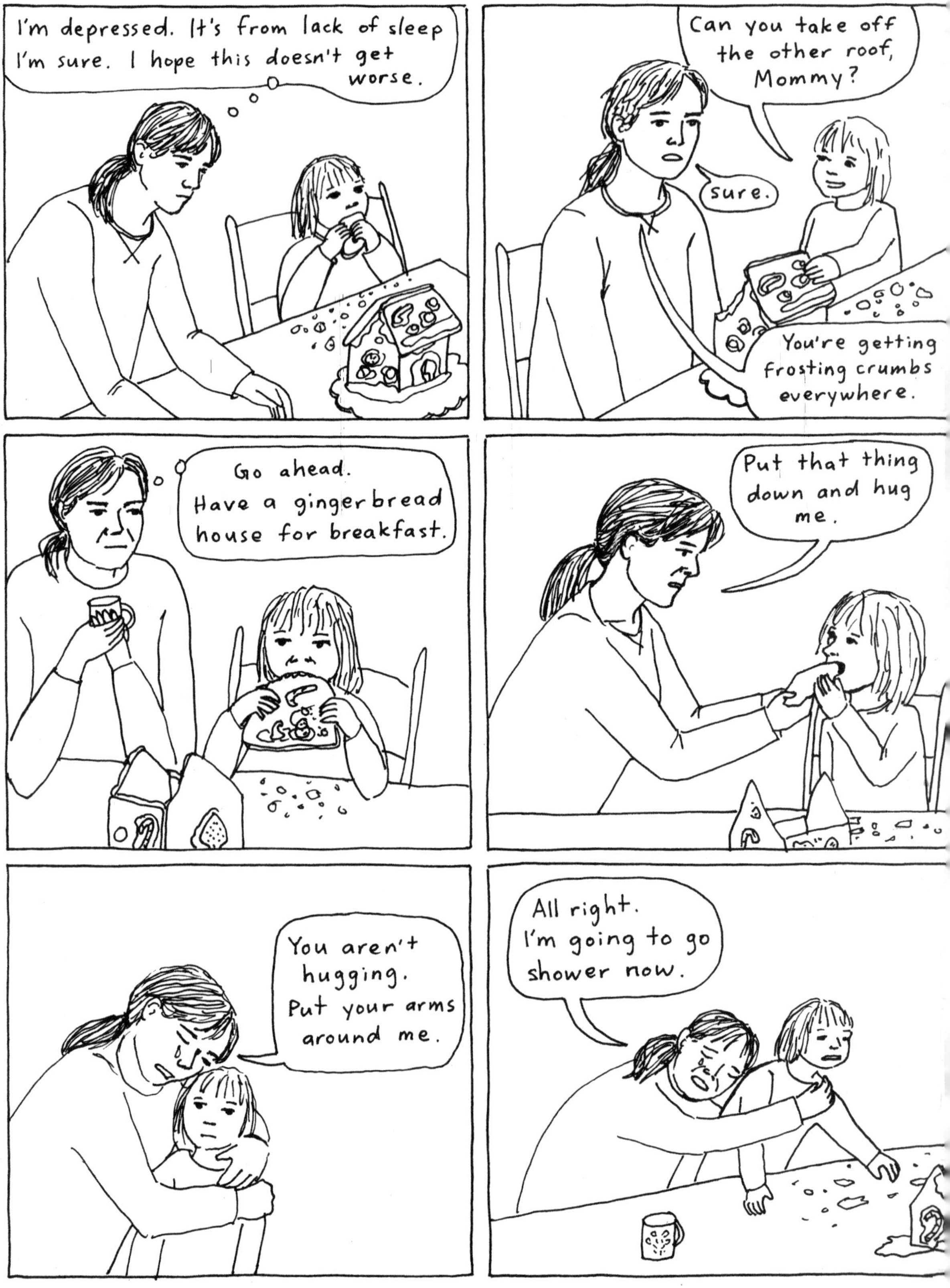
I'm depressed. It's from lack of sleep I'm sure. I hope this doesn't get worse.
Can you take off the other roof, Mommy?
sure.
You're getting frosting crumbs everywhere.
Go ahead. Have a gingerbread house for breakfast.
Put that thing down and hug me.
You aren't hugging. Put your arms around me.
All right. I'm going to go shower now.

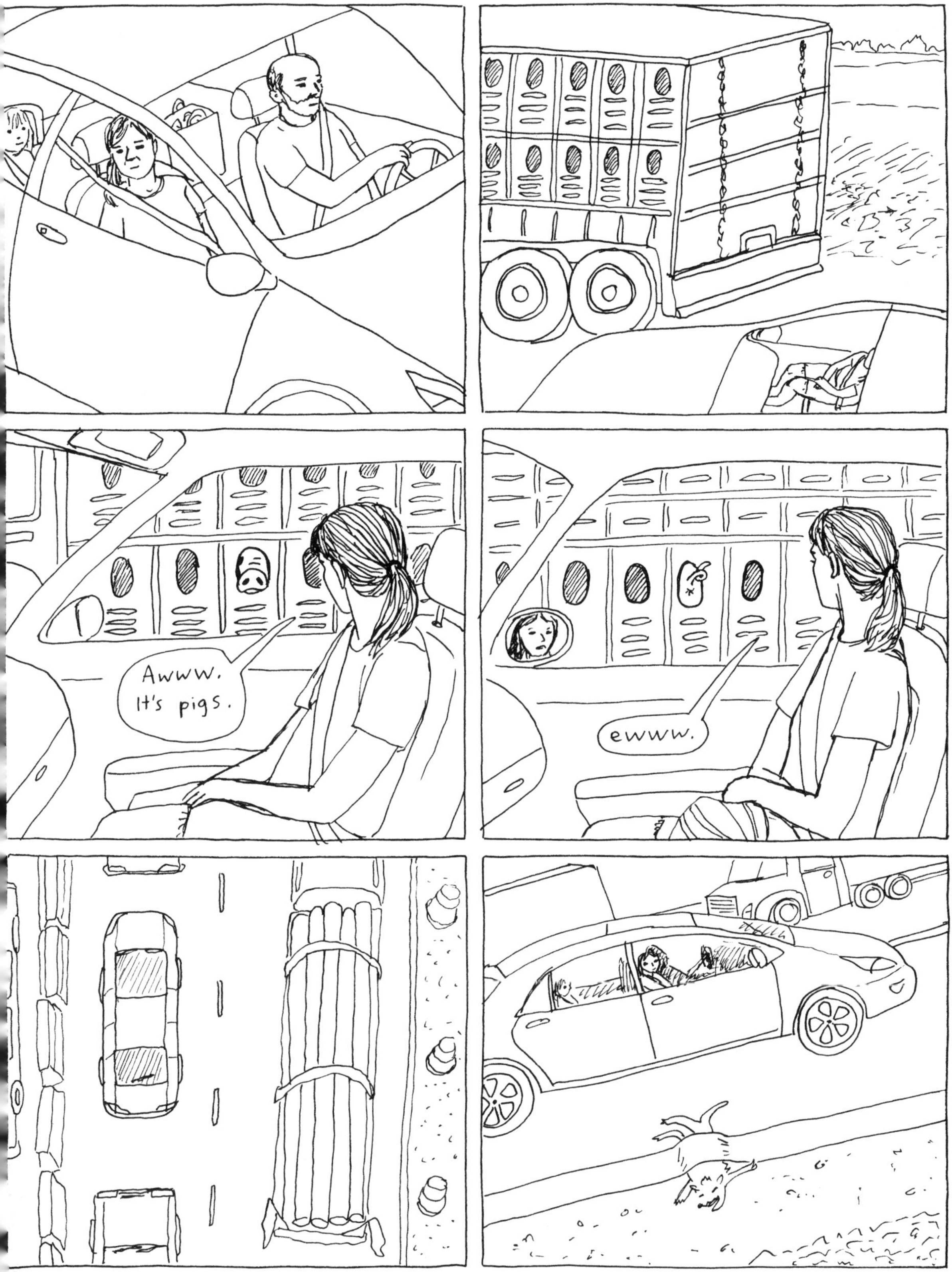
Awww. It's pigs.
ewww.

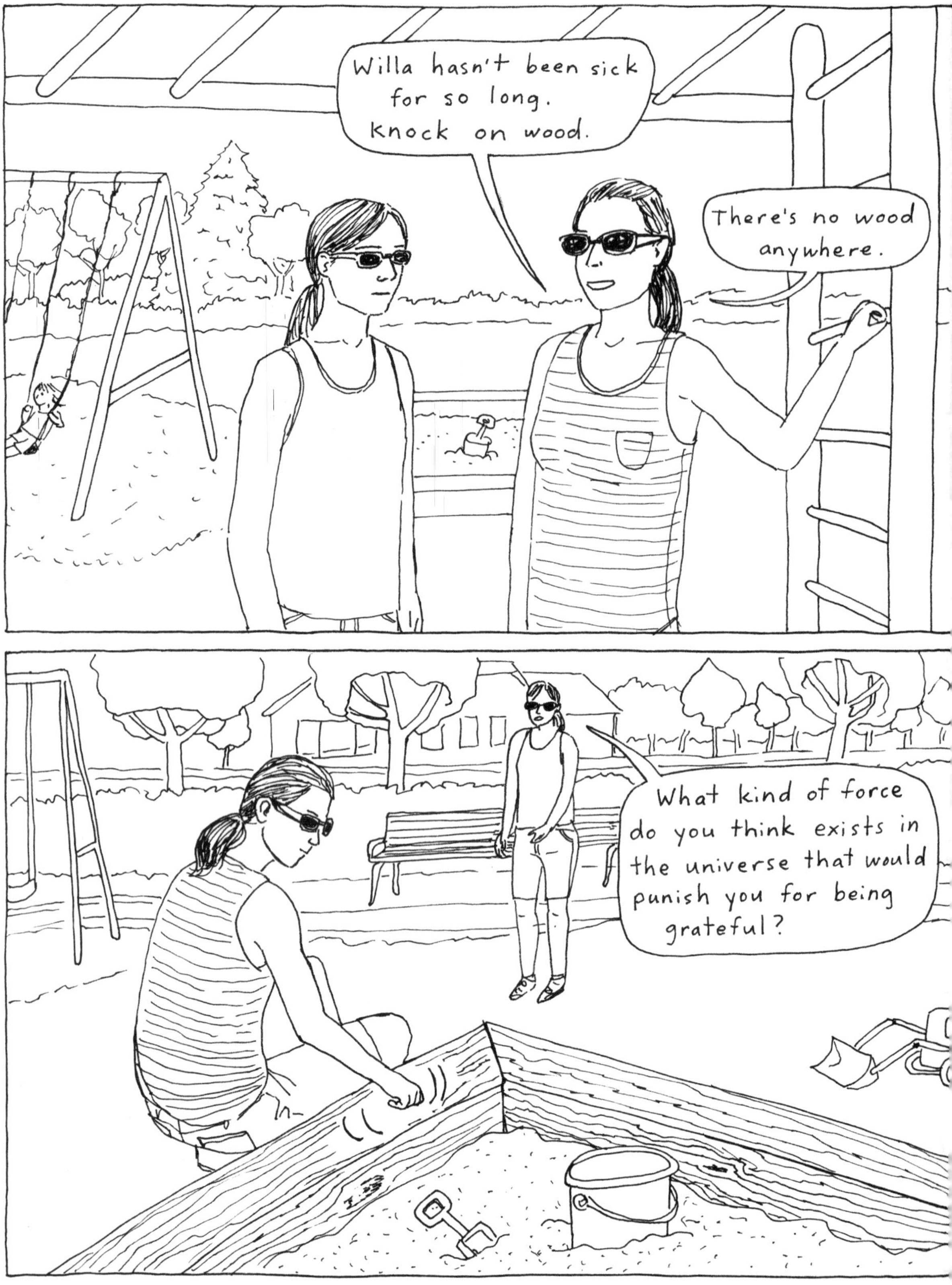
Willa hasn't been sick for so long. Knock on wood.
There's no wood anywhere.
What kind of force do you think exists in the universe that would punish you for being grateful?

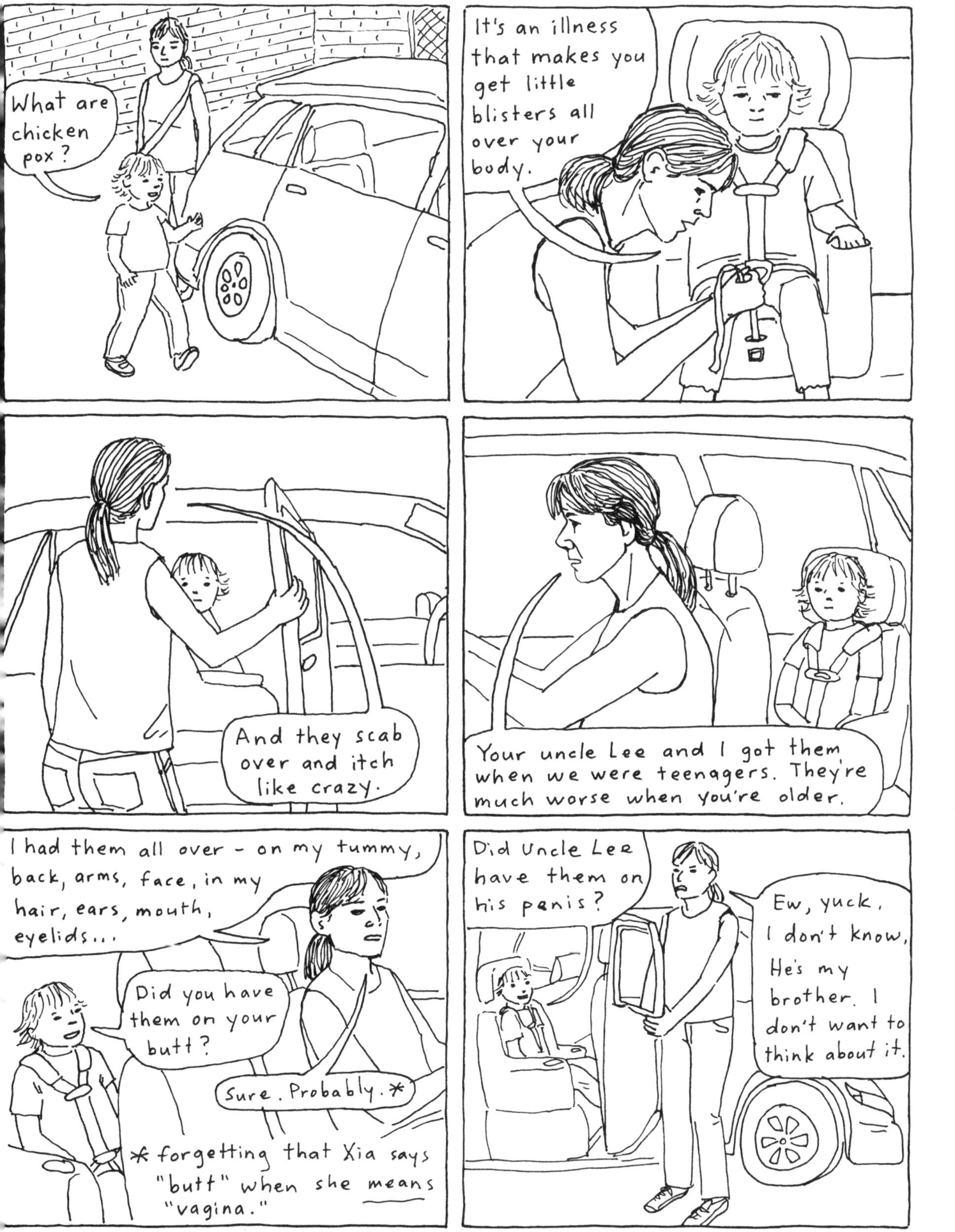
What are chicken pox?
It's an illness that makes you get little blisters all over your body.
And they scab over and itch like crazy.
Your uncle Lee and I got them when we were teenagers. They're much worse when you're older.
I had them all over - on my tummy, back, arms, face, in my hair, ears, mouth, eyelids...
Did you have them on your butt?
Sure. Probably. *
* forgetting that Xia says "butt" when she means "vagina."
Did Uncle Lee have them on his penis?
Ew, yuck. I don't know. He's my brother. I don't want to think about it.

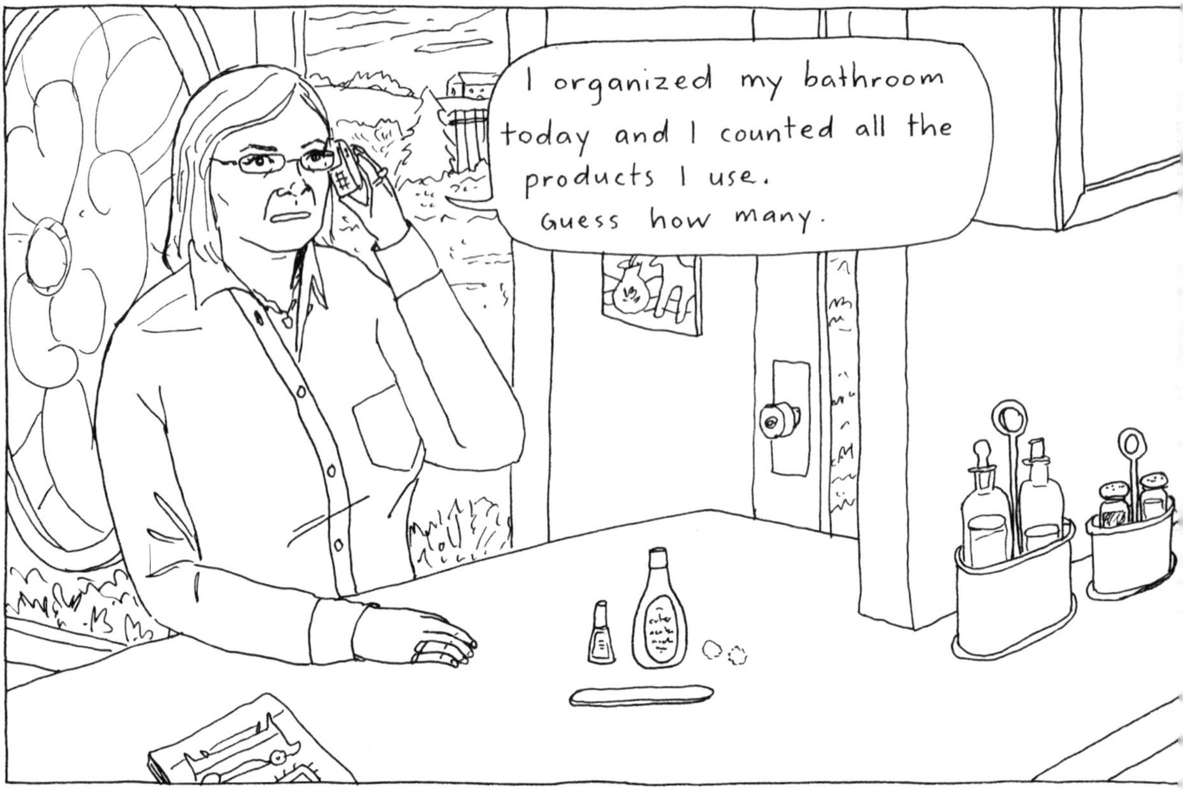
I organized my bathroom today and I counted all the products I use. Guess how many.

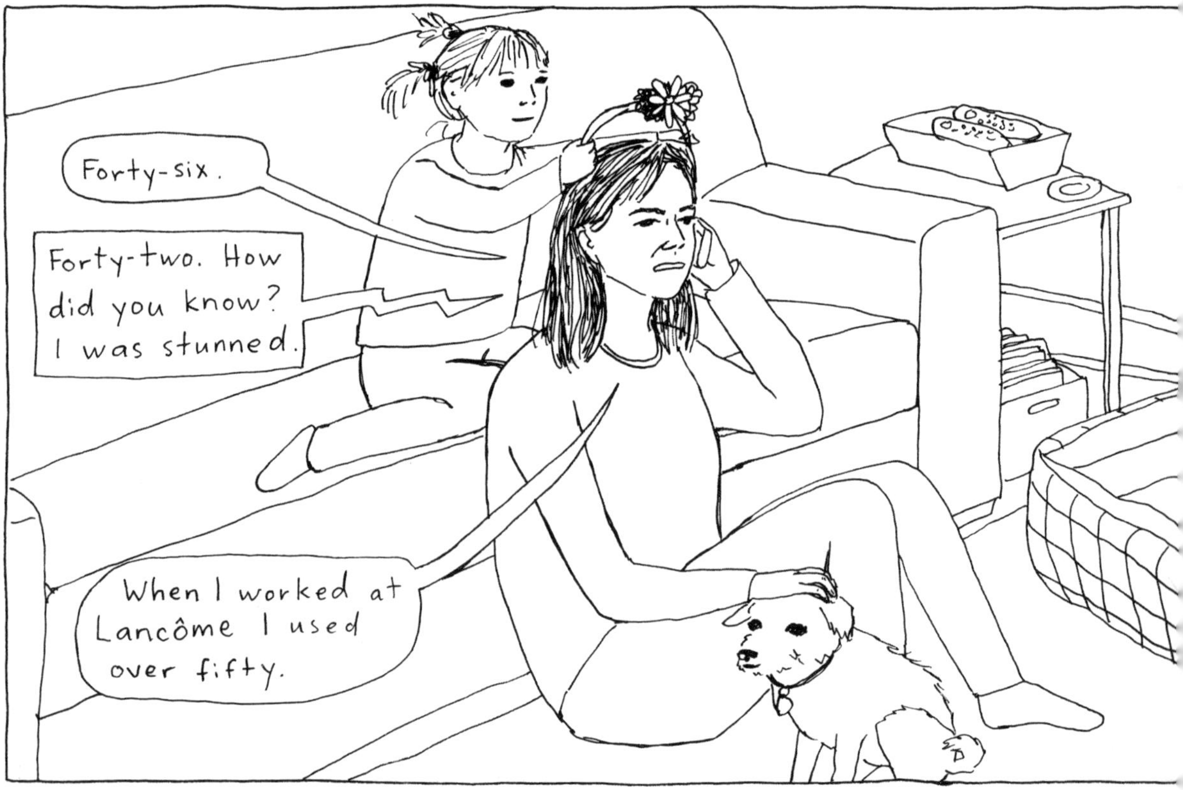
Forty-six.
Forty-two. How did you know? I was stunned.
When I worked at Lancôme I used over fifty.

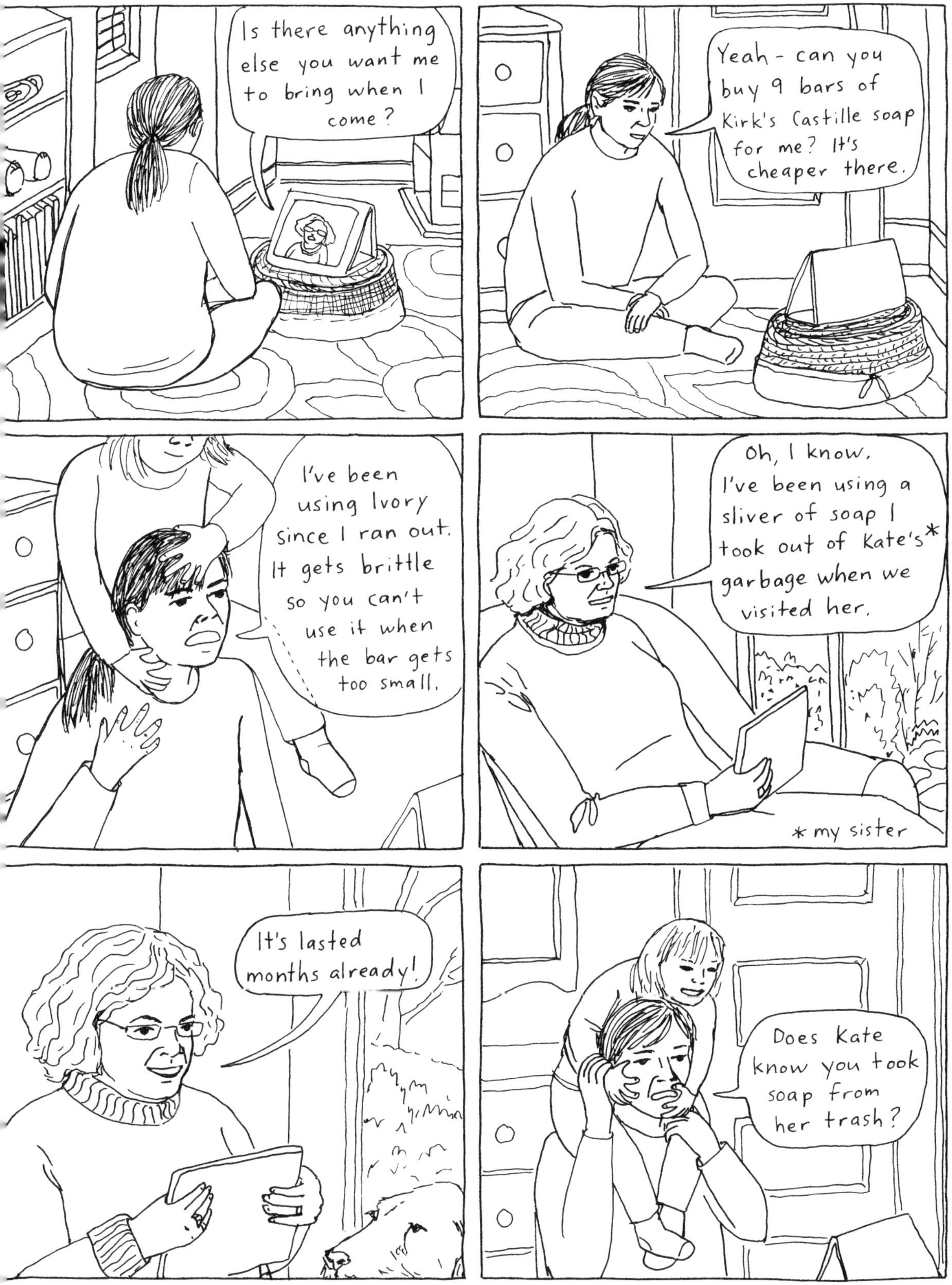
Is there anything else you want me to bring when I come?
Yeah - can you buy 9 bars of Kirk's Castille soap for me? It's cheaper there.
I've been using Ivory since I ran out. It gets brittle so you can't use it when the bar gets too small.
Oh, I know. I've been using a sliver of soap I took out of Kate's* garbage when we visited her.
* my sister
It's lasted months already!
Does Kate know you took soap from her trash?

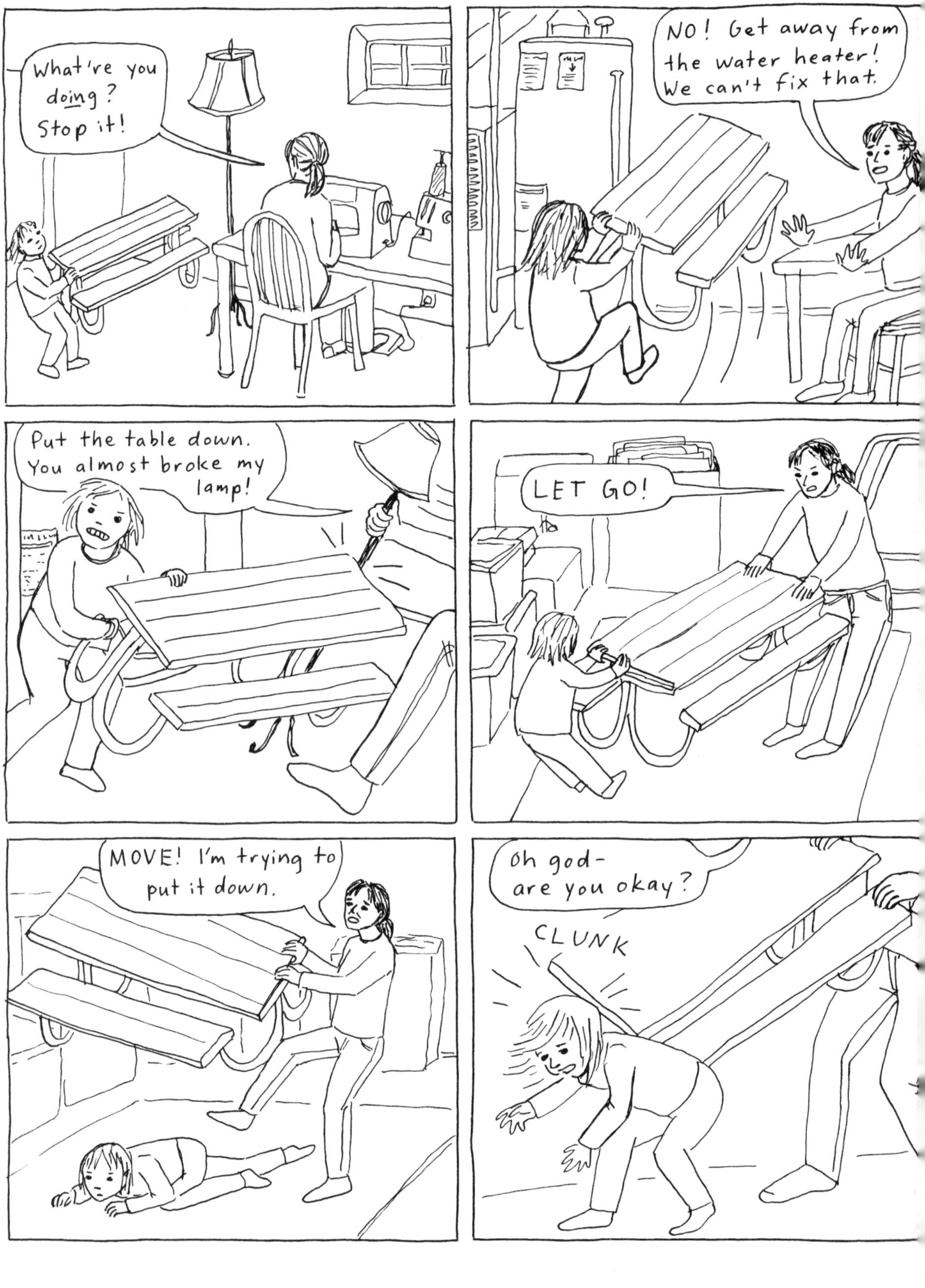
What're you doing? Stop it!
NO! Get away from the water heater! We can't fix that.
Put the table down. You almost broke my lamp!
LET GO!
MOVE! I'm trying to put it down.
Oh god- are you okay?
CLUNK

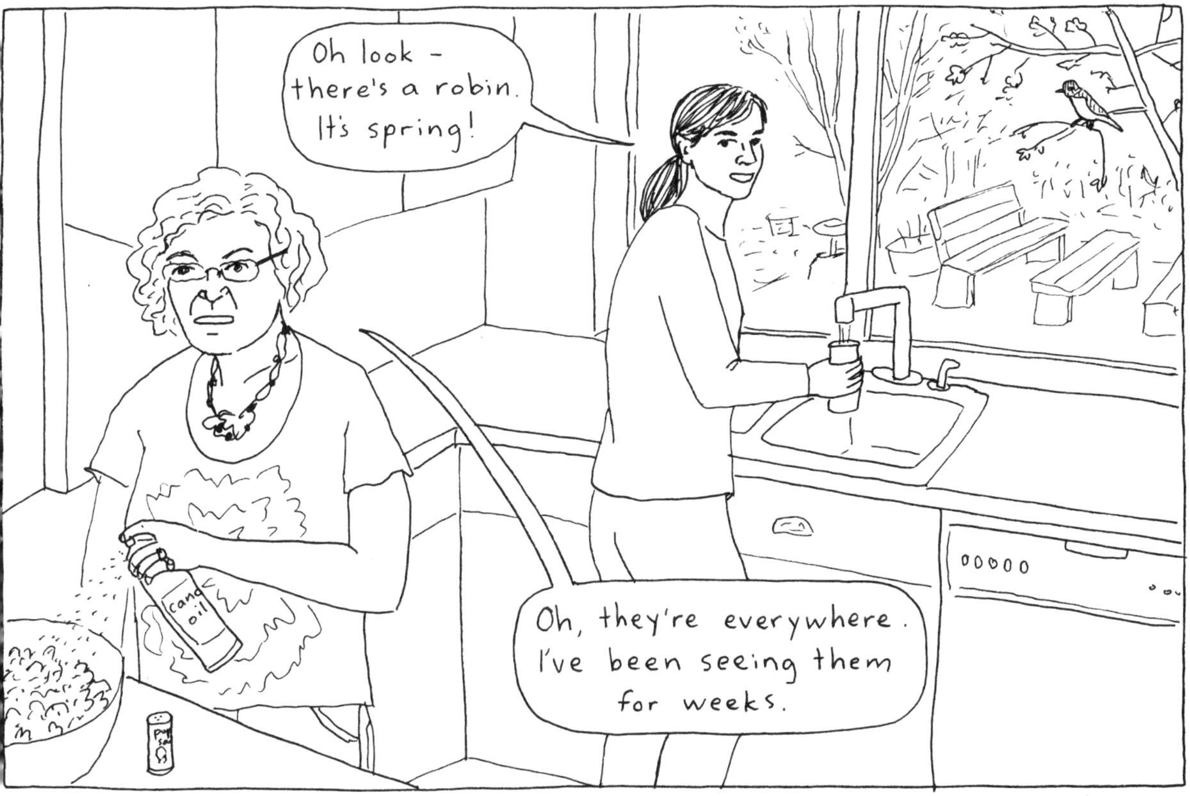

Oh look - there's a robin. It's spring!
Oh, they're everywhere. I've been seeing them for weeks.

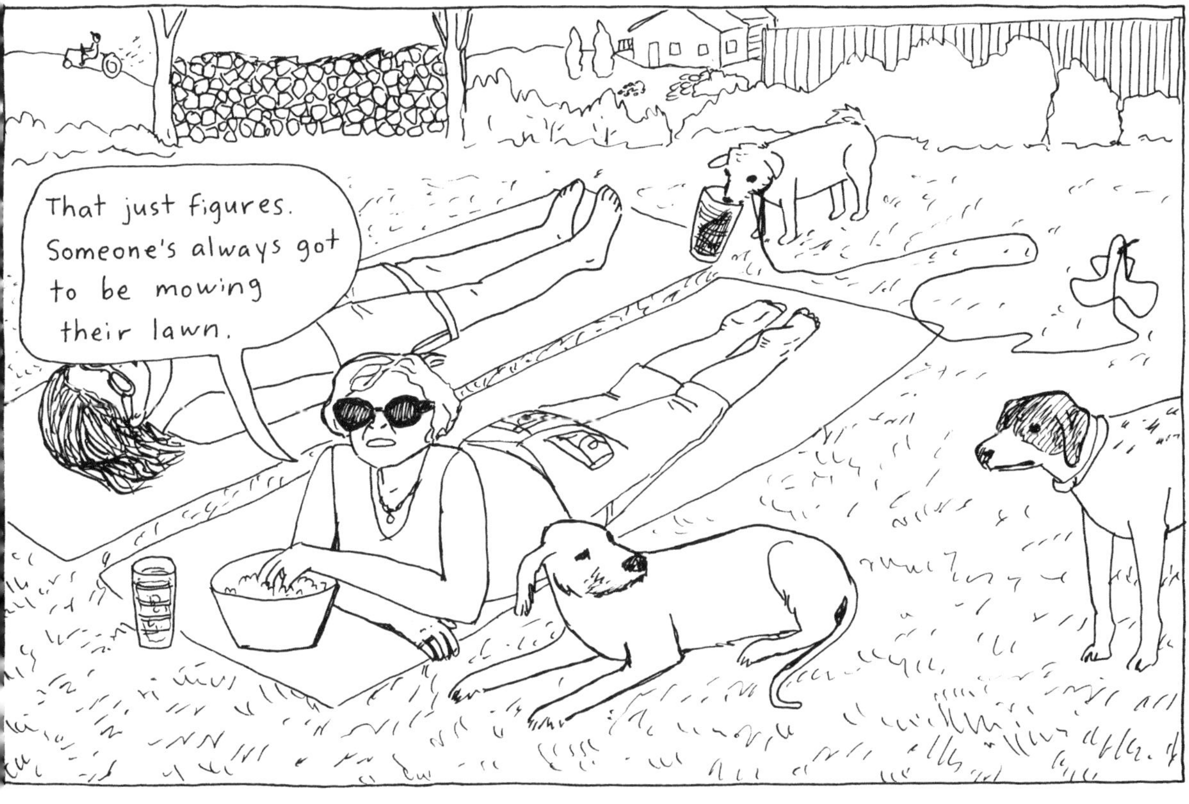

That just figures. Someone's always got to be mowing their lawn.

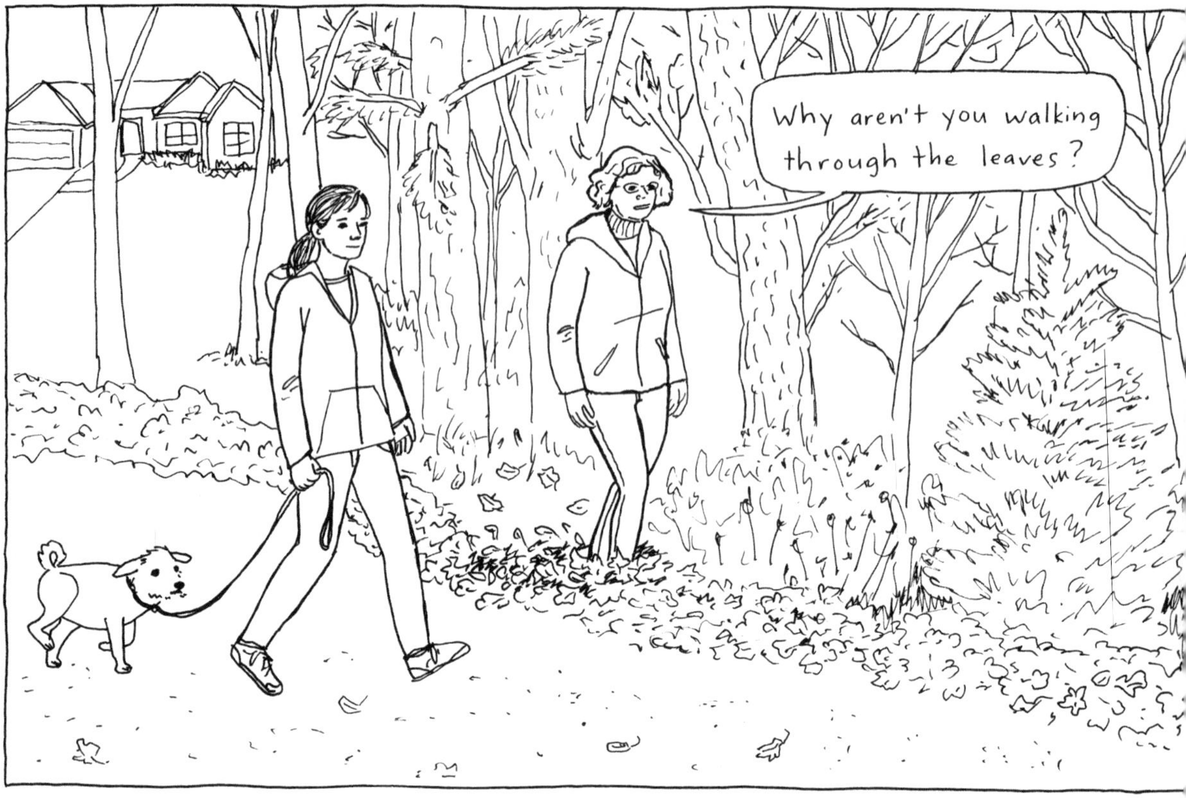
Why aren't you walking through the leaves?

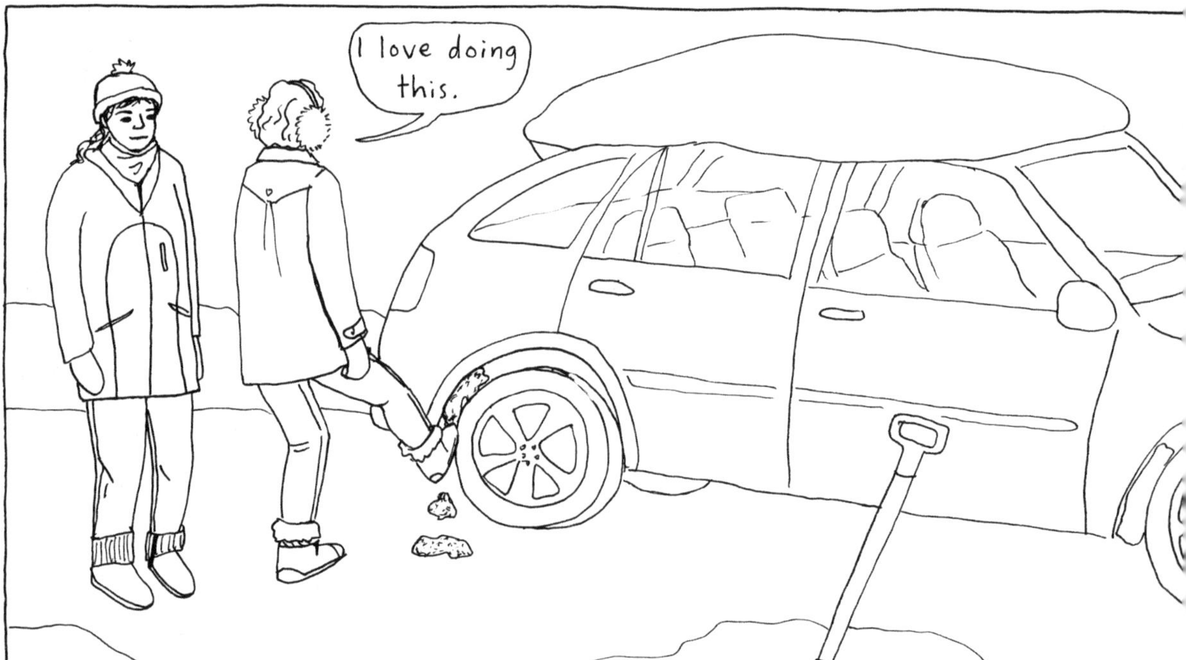
I love doing this.

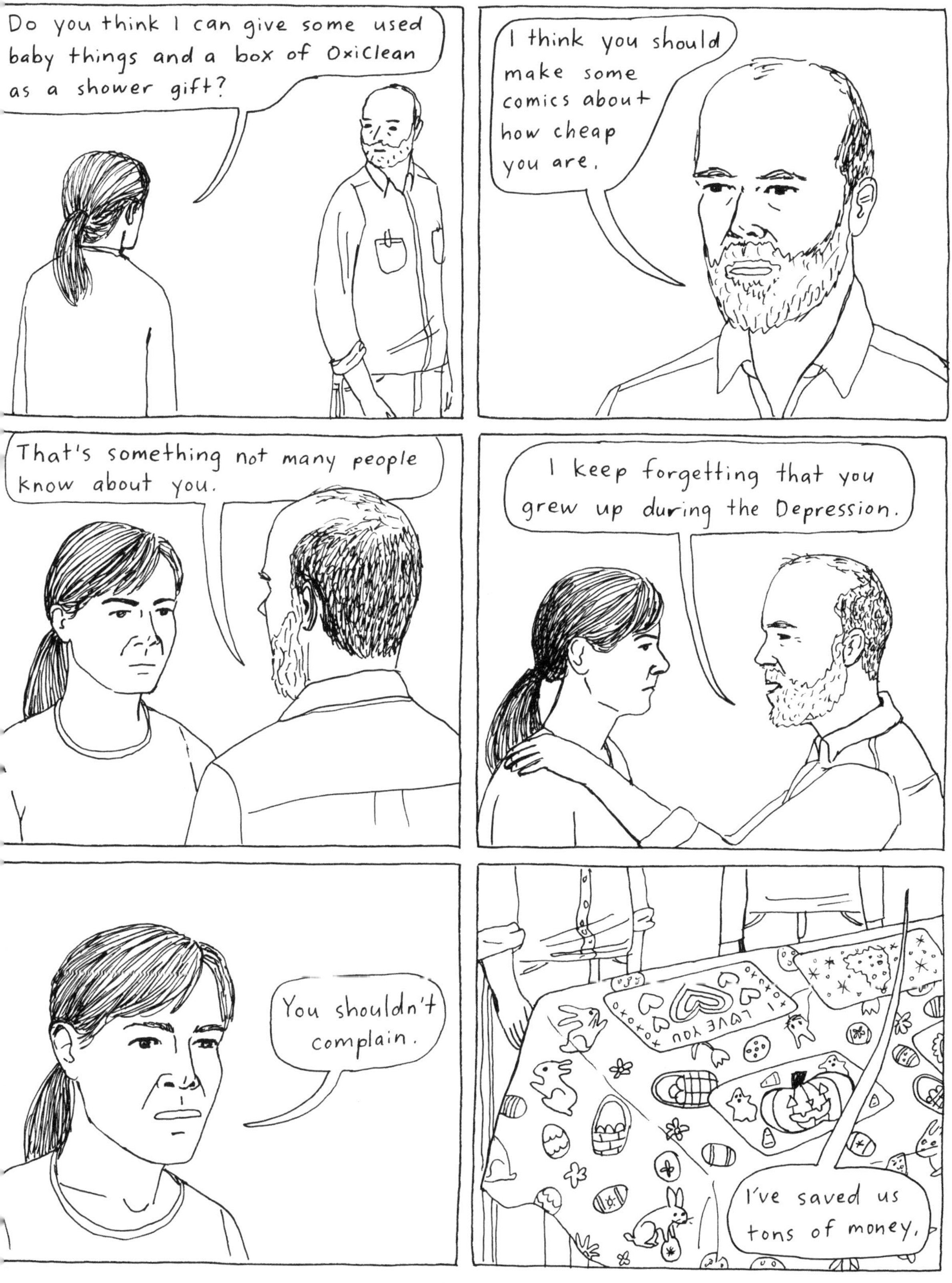
Do you think I can give some used baby things and a box of OxiClean as a shower gift?
I think you should make some comics about how cheap you are.
That's something not many people know about you.
I keep forgetting that you grew up during the Depression.
You shouldn't complain.
I LOVE YOU
I've saved us tons of money.

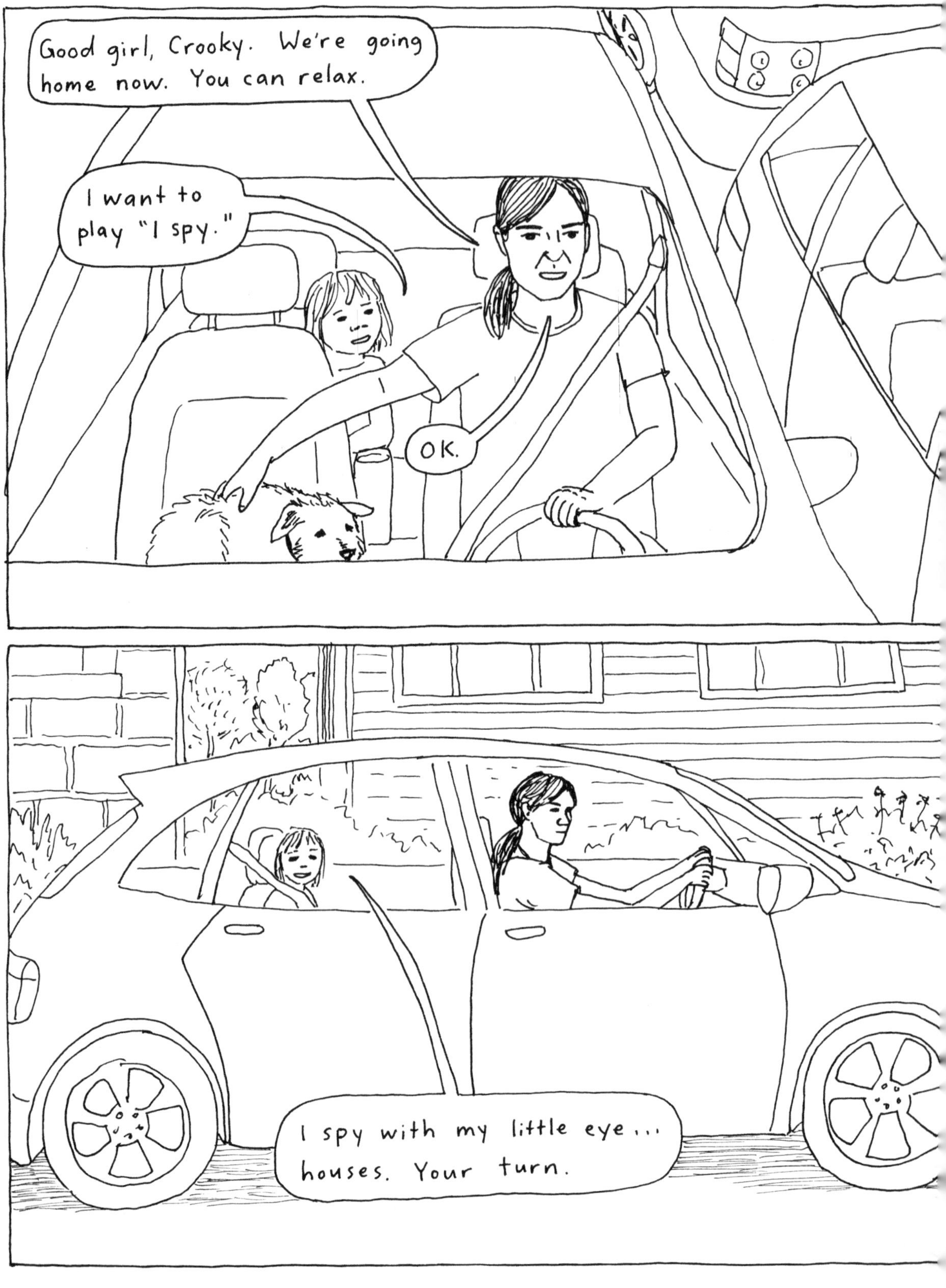
Good girl, Crooky. We're going home now. You can relax.
I want to play "I spy."
OK.
I spy with my little eye... houses. Your turn.

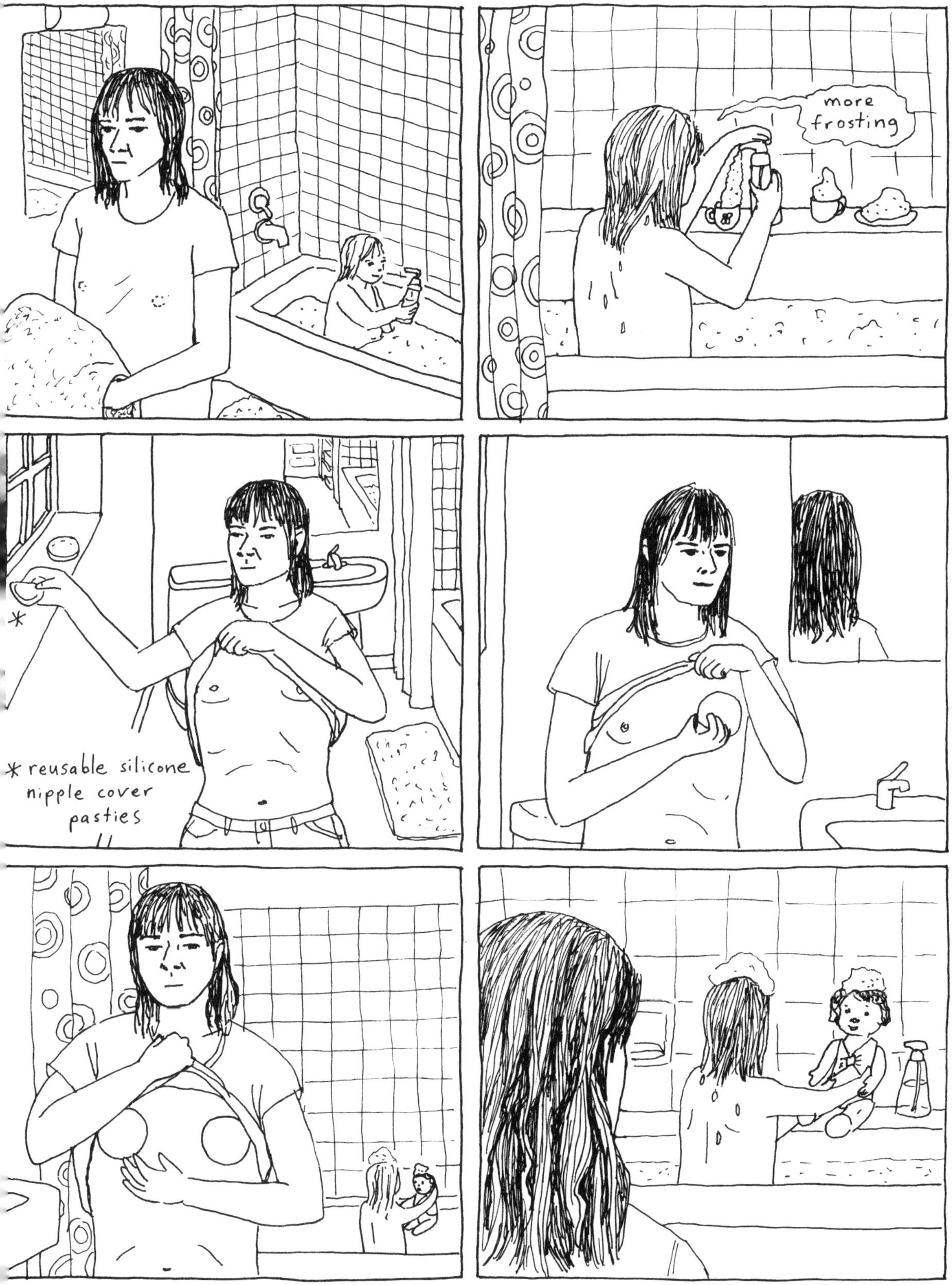
more frosting
* reusable silicone nipple cover pasties

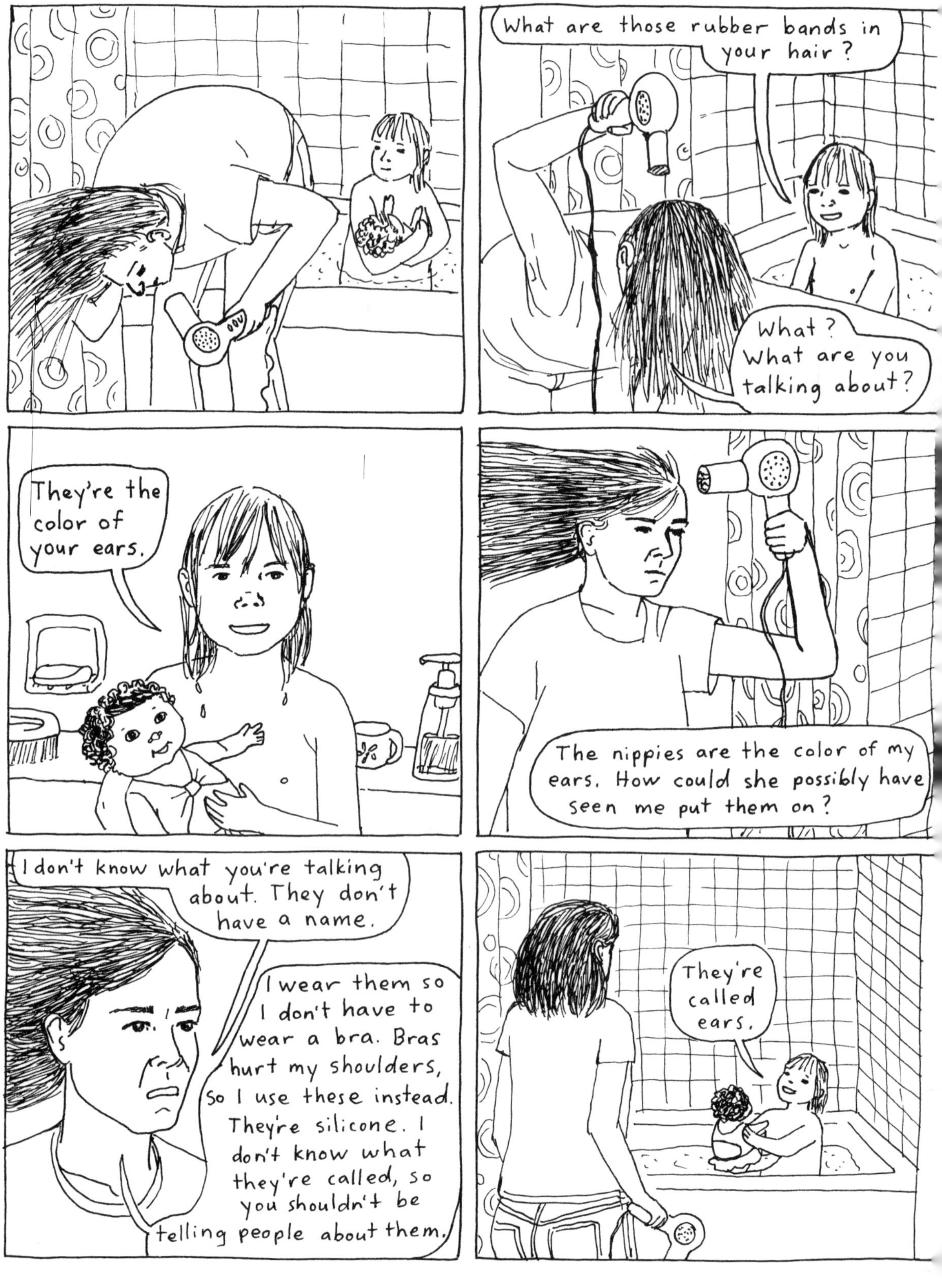
What are those rubber bands in your hair?
What? What are you talking about?
They're the color of your ears.
The nippies are the color of my ears. How could she possibly have seen me put them on?
I don't know what you're talking about. They don't have a name.
I wear them so I don't have to wear a bra. Bras hurt my shoulders, so I use these instead. They're silicone. I don't know what they're called, so you shouldn't be telling people about them.
They're called ears.

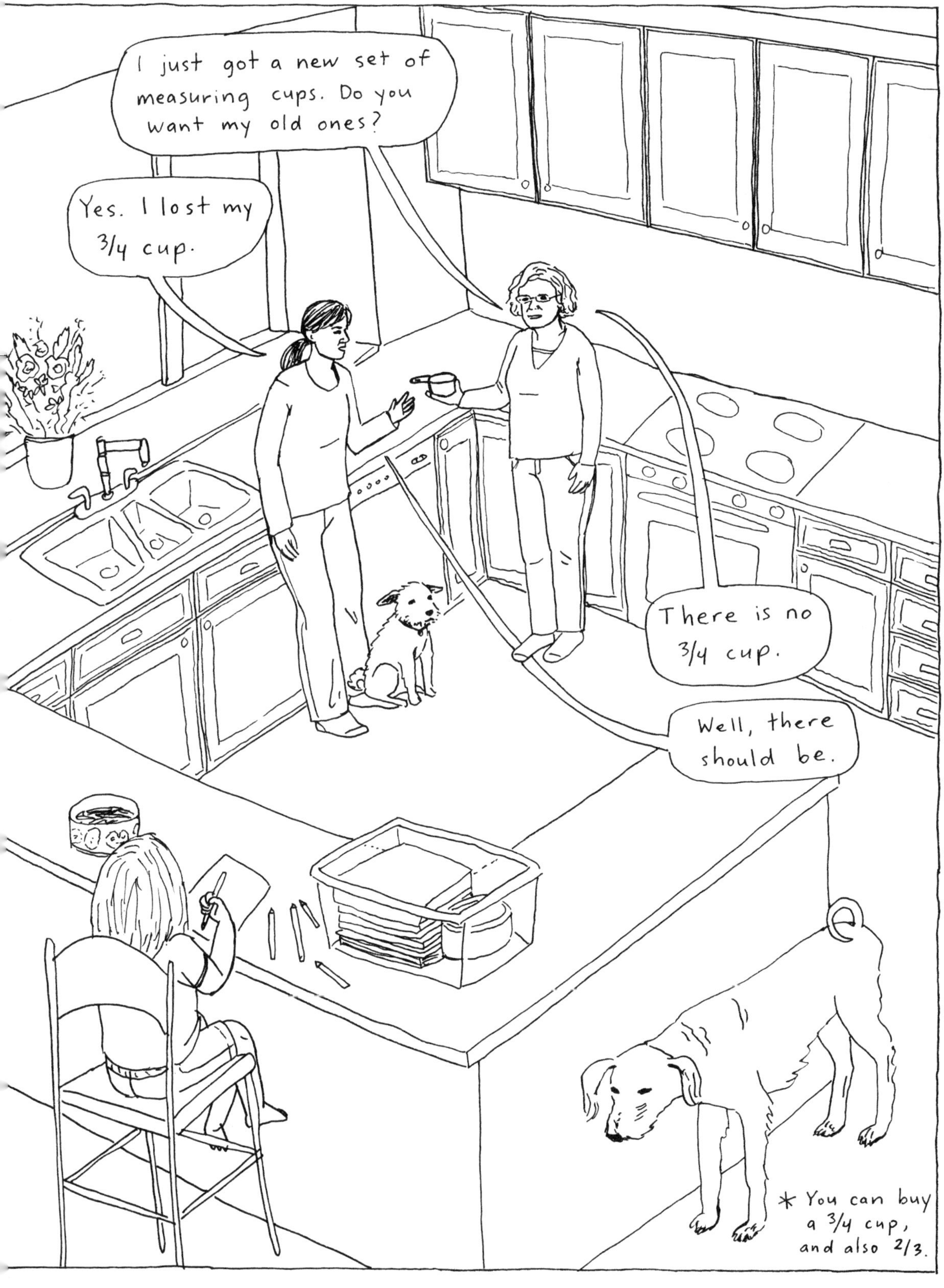
I just got a new set of measuring cups. Do you want my old ones?
Yes. I lost my 3/4 cup.
There is no 3/4 cup.
Well, there should be.
* You can buy a 3/4 cup, and also 2/3.

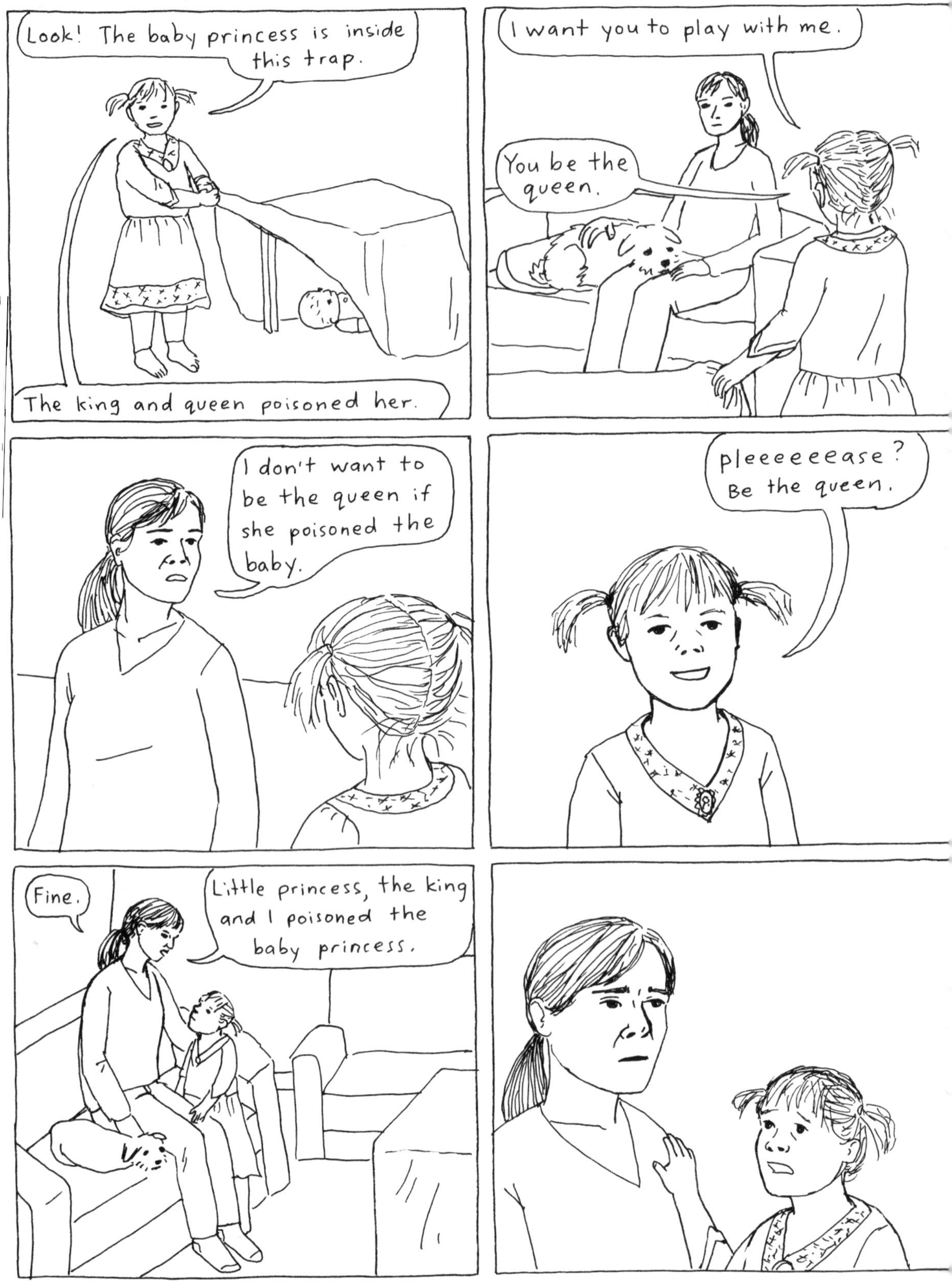

Look! The baby princess is inside this trap.
The king and queen poisoned her.
I want you to play with me.
You be the queen.
I don't want to be the queen if she poisoned the baby.
pleeeeeeease? Be the queen.
Fine.
Little princess, the king and I poisoned the baby princess.

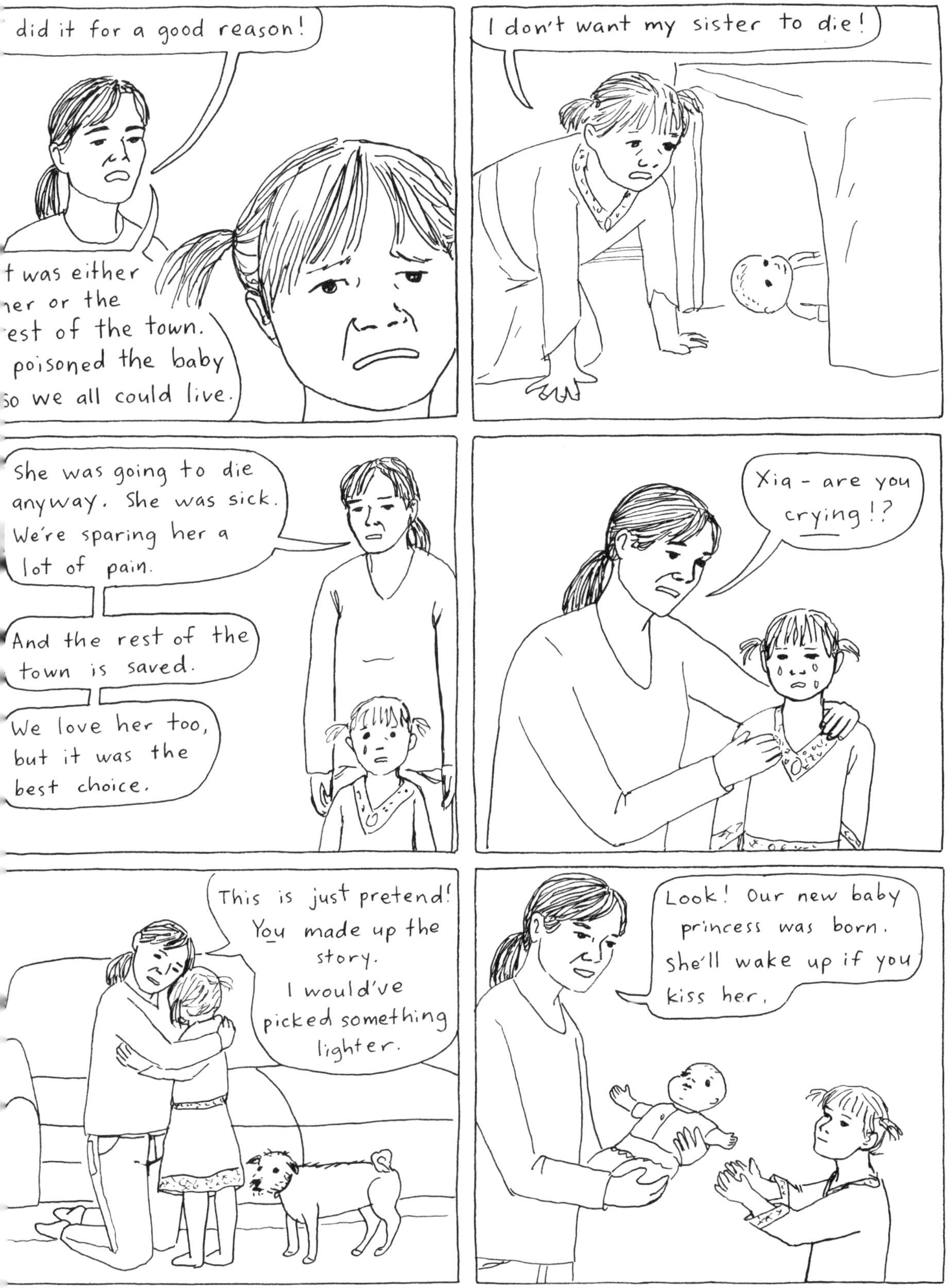
did it for a good reason!
t was either
ner or the
est of the town.
poisoned the baby
so we all could live.
I don't want my sister to die!
She was going to die anyway. She was sick. We're sparing her a lot of pain.
And the rest of the town is saved.
We love her too, but it was the best choice.
Xia - are you crying!?
This is just pretend! You made up the story. I would've picked something lighter.
Look! Our new baby princess was born. She'll wake up if you kiss her.

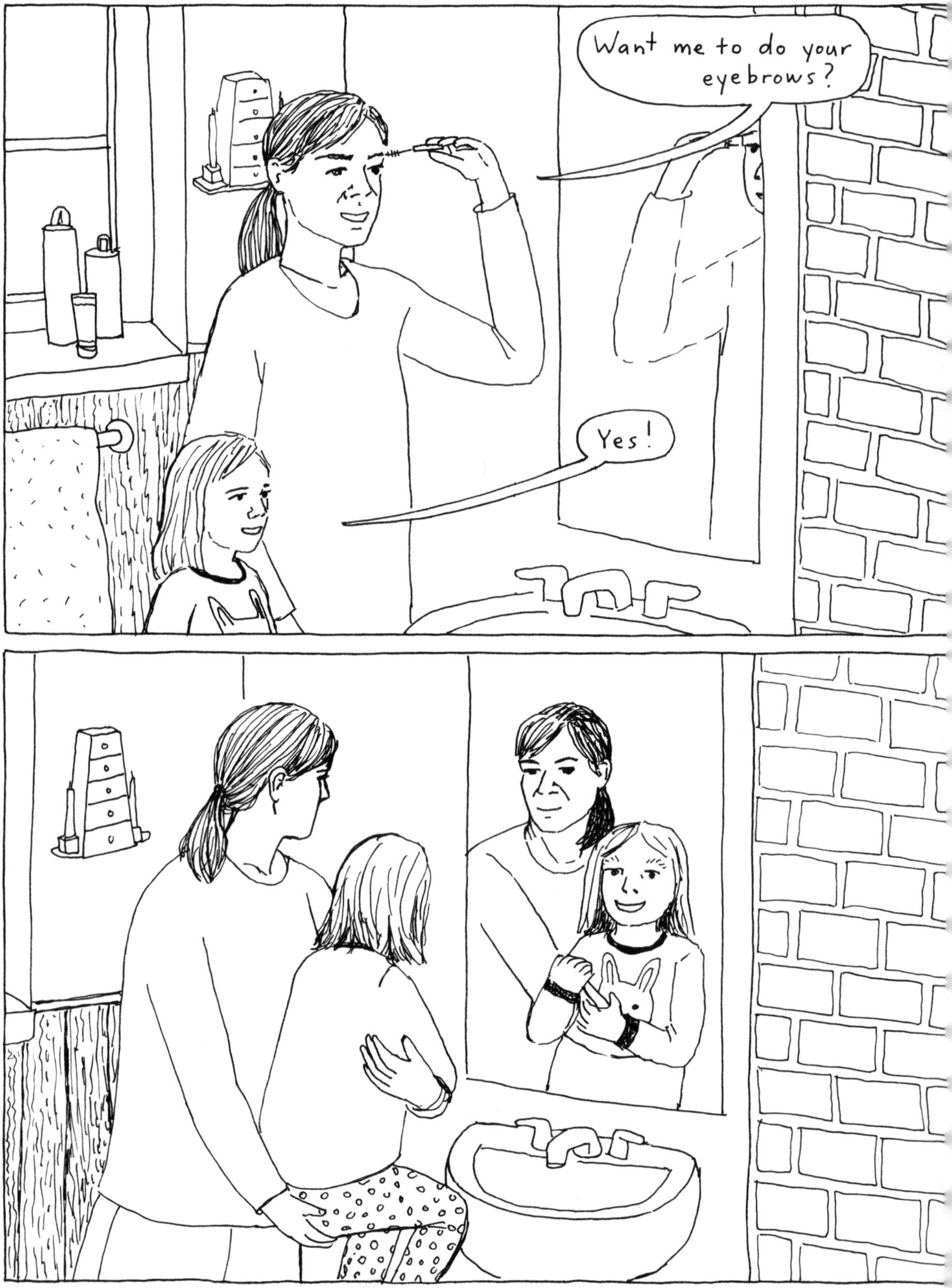
Want me to do your eyebrows?
Yes!

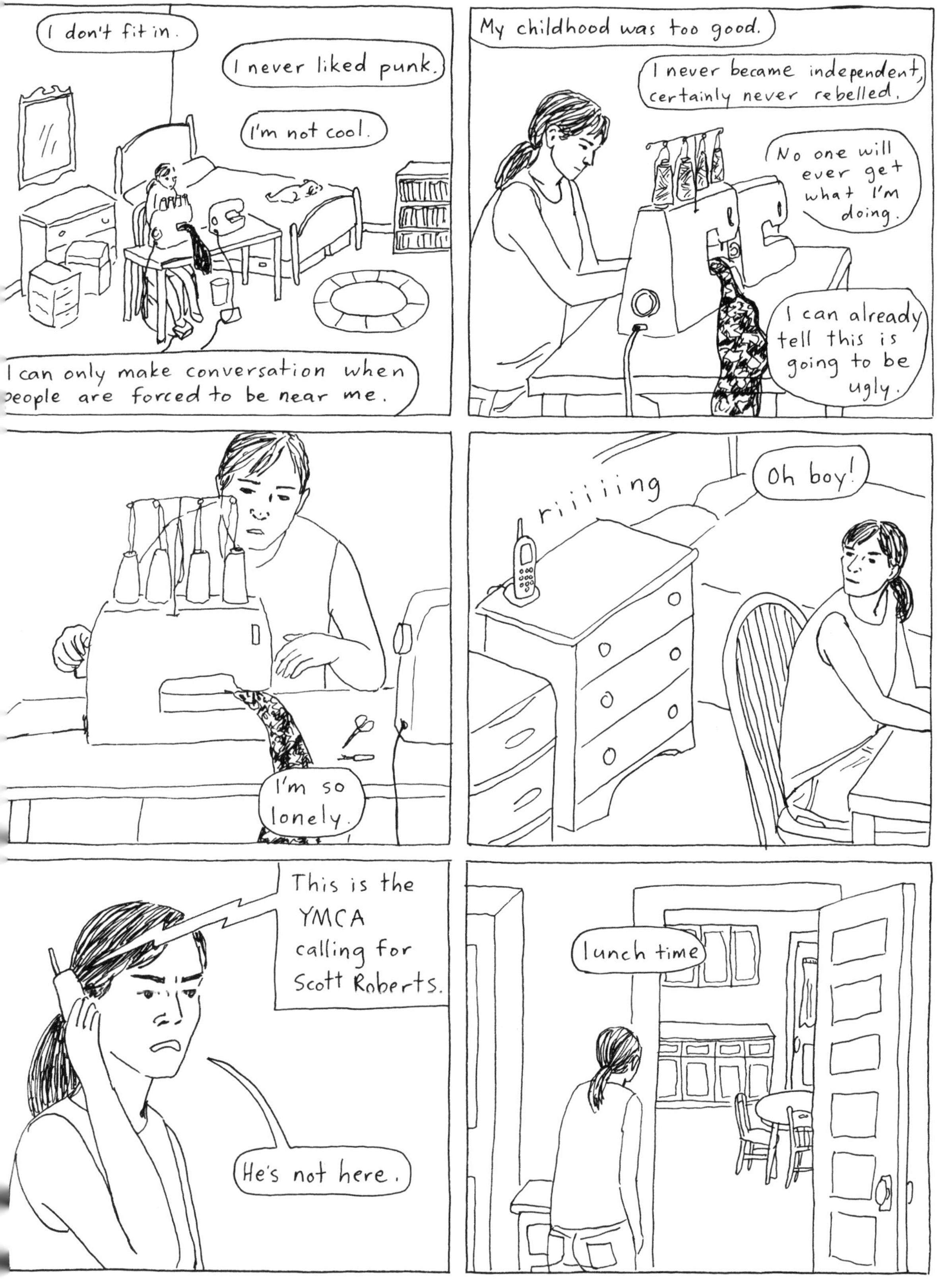
I don't fit in.
I never liked punk.
I'm not cool.
I can only make conversation when people are forced to be near me.
My childhood was too good.
I never became independent, certainly never rebelled.
No one will ever get what I'm doing.
I can already tell this is going to be ugly.
I'm so lonely.
riiiiiing
Oh boy!
This is the YMCA calling for Scott Roberts.
He's not here.
lunch time

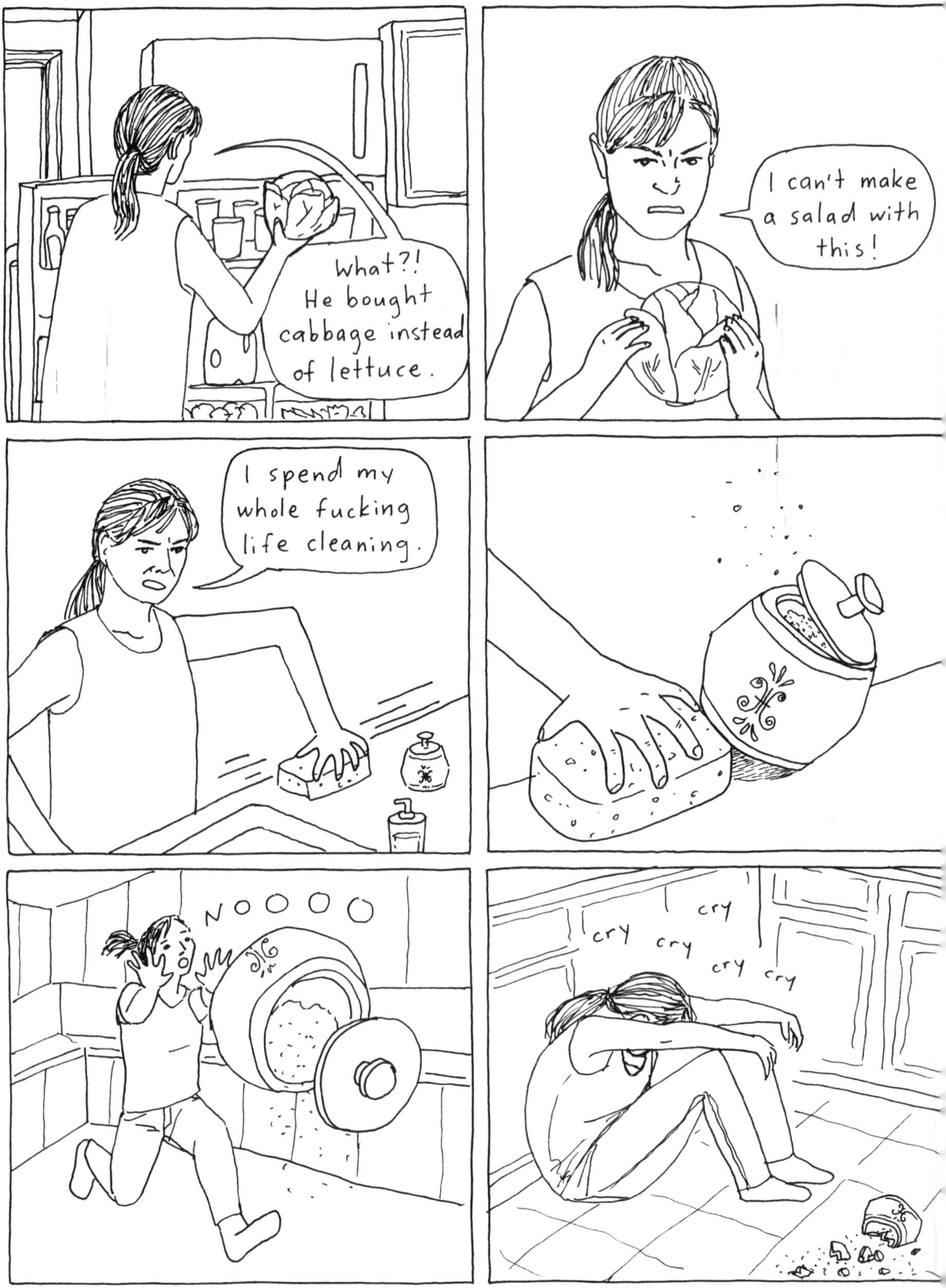
What?! He bought cabbage instead of lettuce.
I can't make a salad with this!
I spend my whole fucking life cleaning.
NOOOOO
cry cry cry cry cry

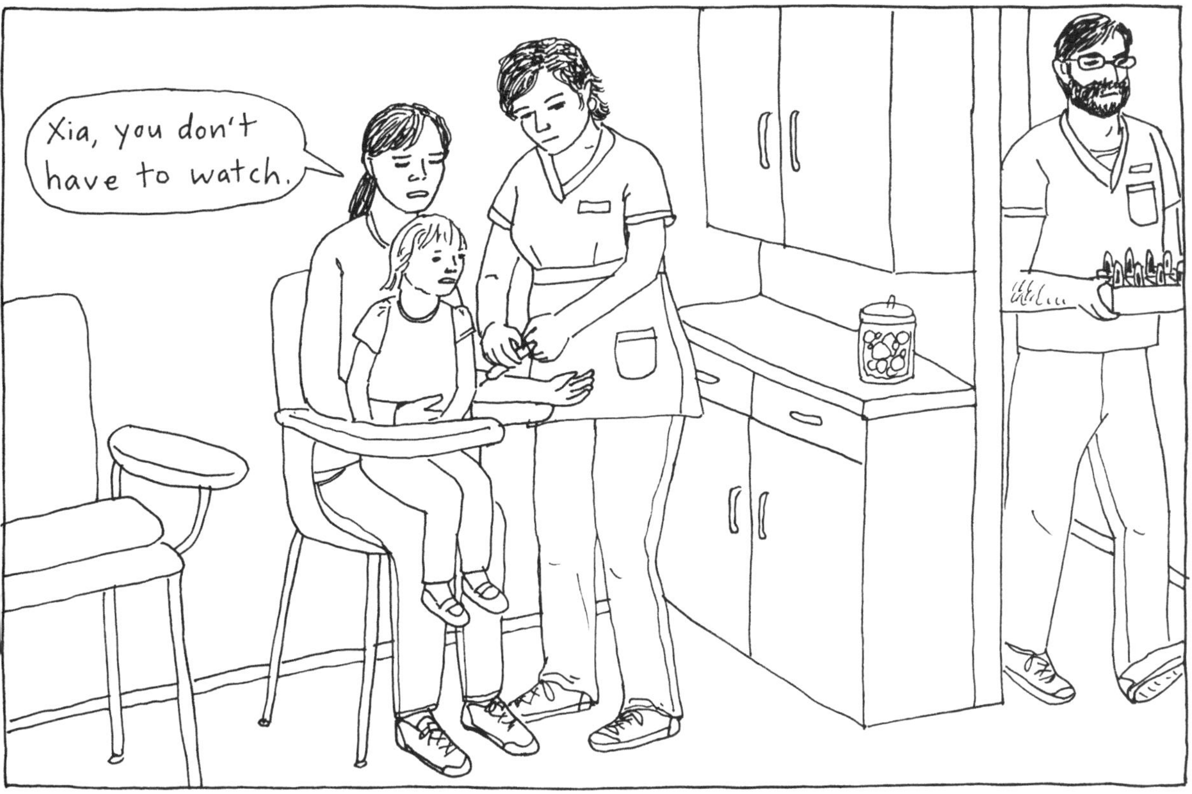
Xia, you don't have to watch.

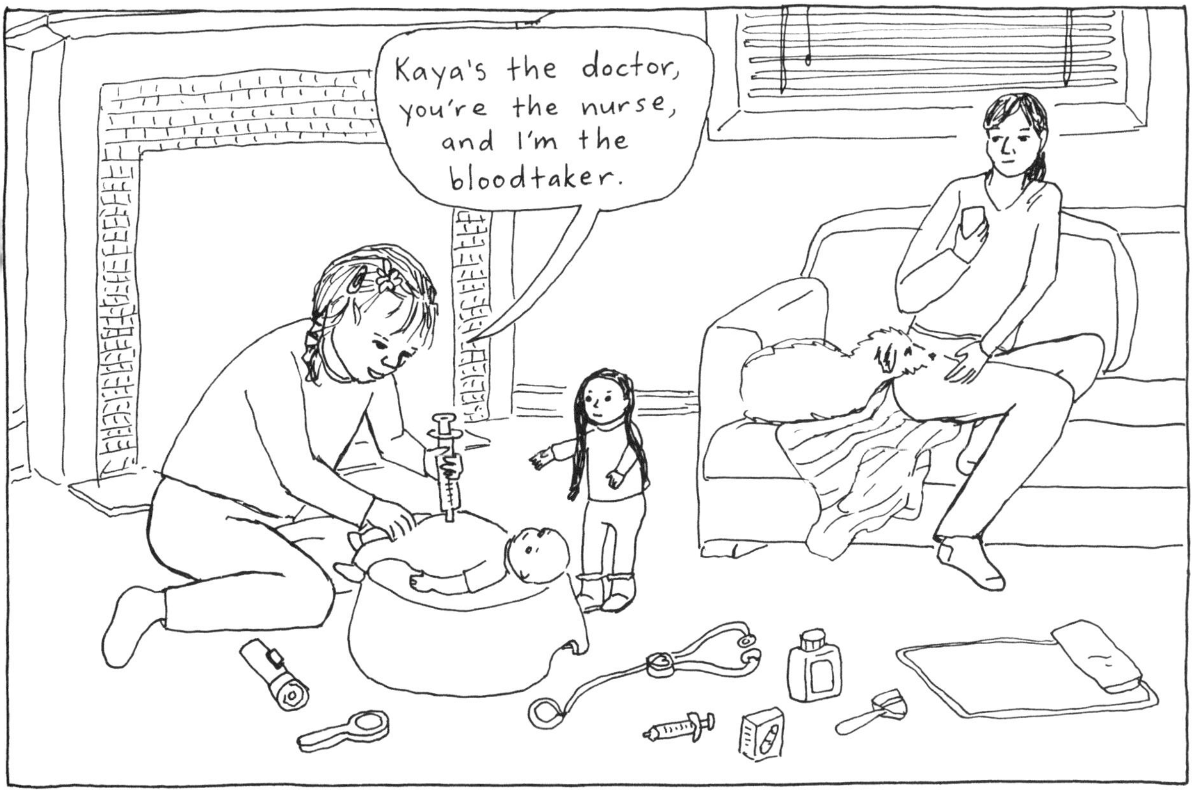
Kaya's the doctor, you're the nurse, and I'm the bloodtaker.

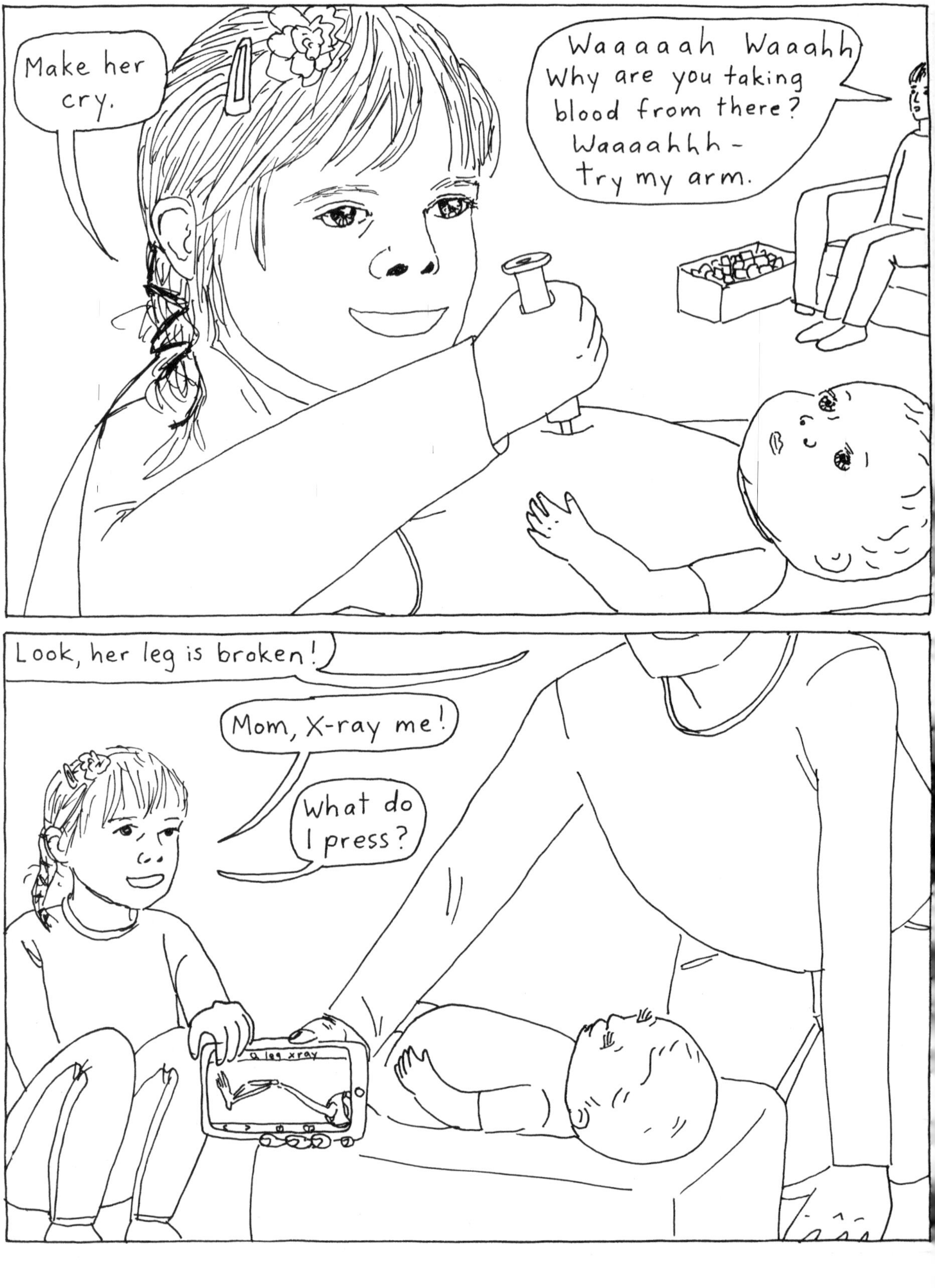
Make her cry.
Waaaaah Waaahh Why are you taking blood from there? Waaaahhh - try my arm.
Look, her leg is broken!
Mom, X-ray me!
What do I press?
leg xray

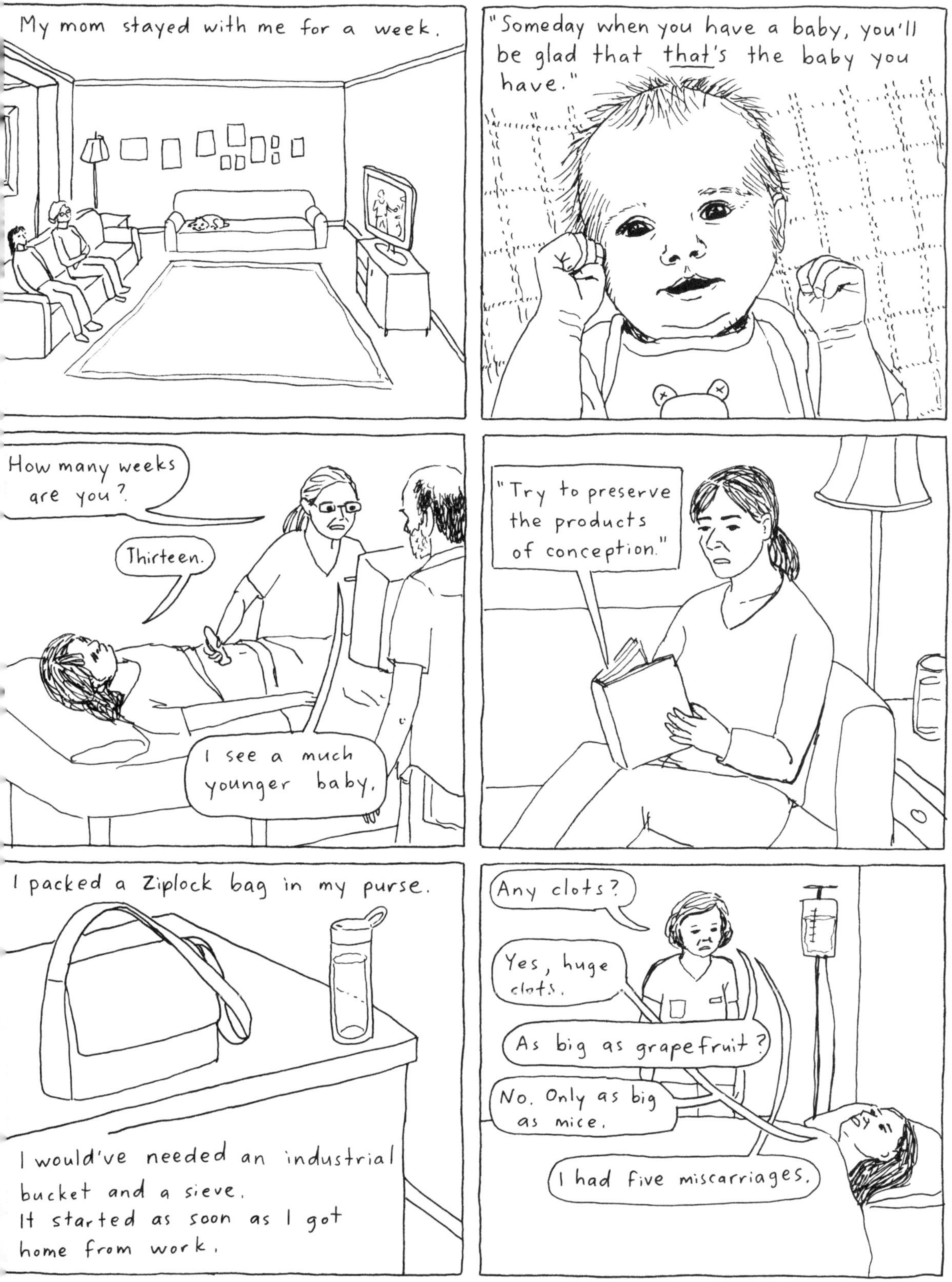
My mom stayed with me for a week.
"Someday when you have a baby, you'll be glad that that's the baby you have."
How many weeks are you?
Thirteen.
I see a much younger baby.
"Try to preserve the products of conception."
I packed a Ziplock bag in my purse.
I would've needed an industrial bucket and a sieve.
It started as soon as I got home from work.
Any clots?
Yes, huge clots.
As big as grapefruit?
No. Only as big as mice.
I had five miscarriages.

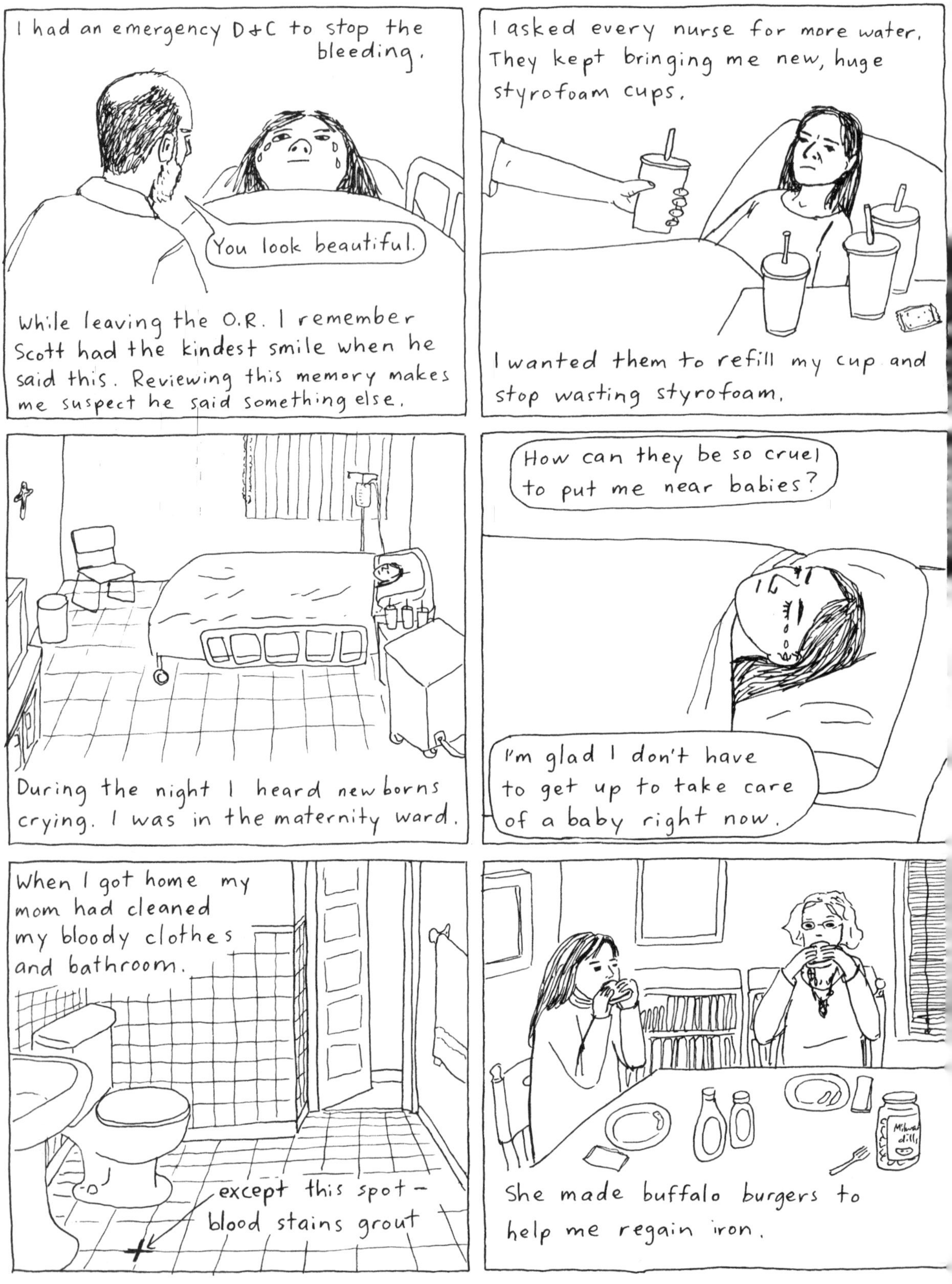
I had an emergency D&C to stop the bleeding.
You look beautiful.
While leaving the O.R. I remember Scott had the kindest smile when he said this. Reviewing this memory makes me suspect he said something else.
I asked every nurse for more water. They kept bringing me new, huge styrofoam cups.
I wanted them to refill my cup and stop wasting styrofoam.
During the night I heard newborns crying. I was in the maternity ward.
How can they be so cruel to put me near babies?
I'm glad I don't have to get up to take care of a baby right now.
When I got home my mom had cleaned my bloody clothes and bathroom.
except this spot - blood stains grout
She made buffalo burgers to help me regain iron.

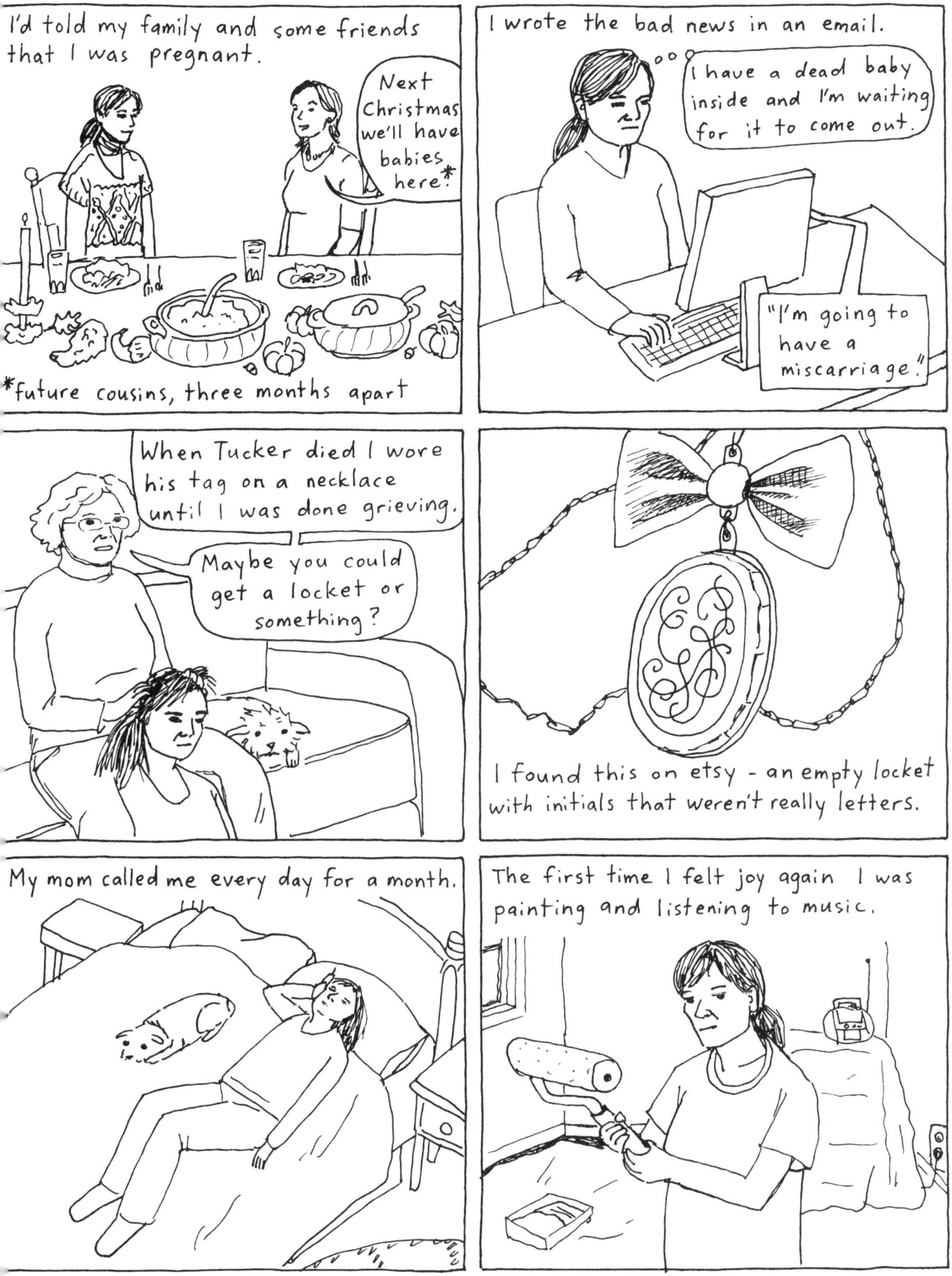
I'd told my family and some friends that I was pregnant.
Next Christmas we'll have babies here*
*future cousins, three months apart
I wrote the bad news in an email.
I have a dead baby inside and I'm waiting for it to come out.
"I'm going to have a miscarriage."
When Tucker died I wore his tag on a necklace until I was done grieving.
Maybe you could get a locket or something?
I found this on etsy - an empty locket with initials that weren't really letters.
My mom called me every day for a month.
The first time I felt joy again I was painting and listening to music.

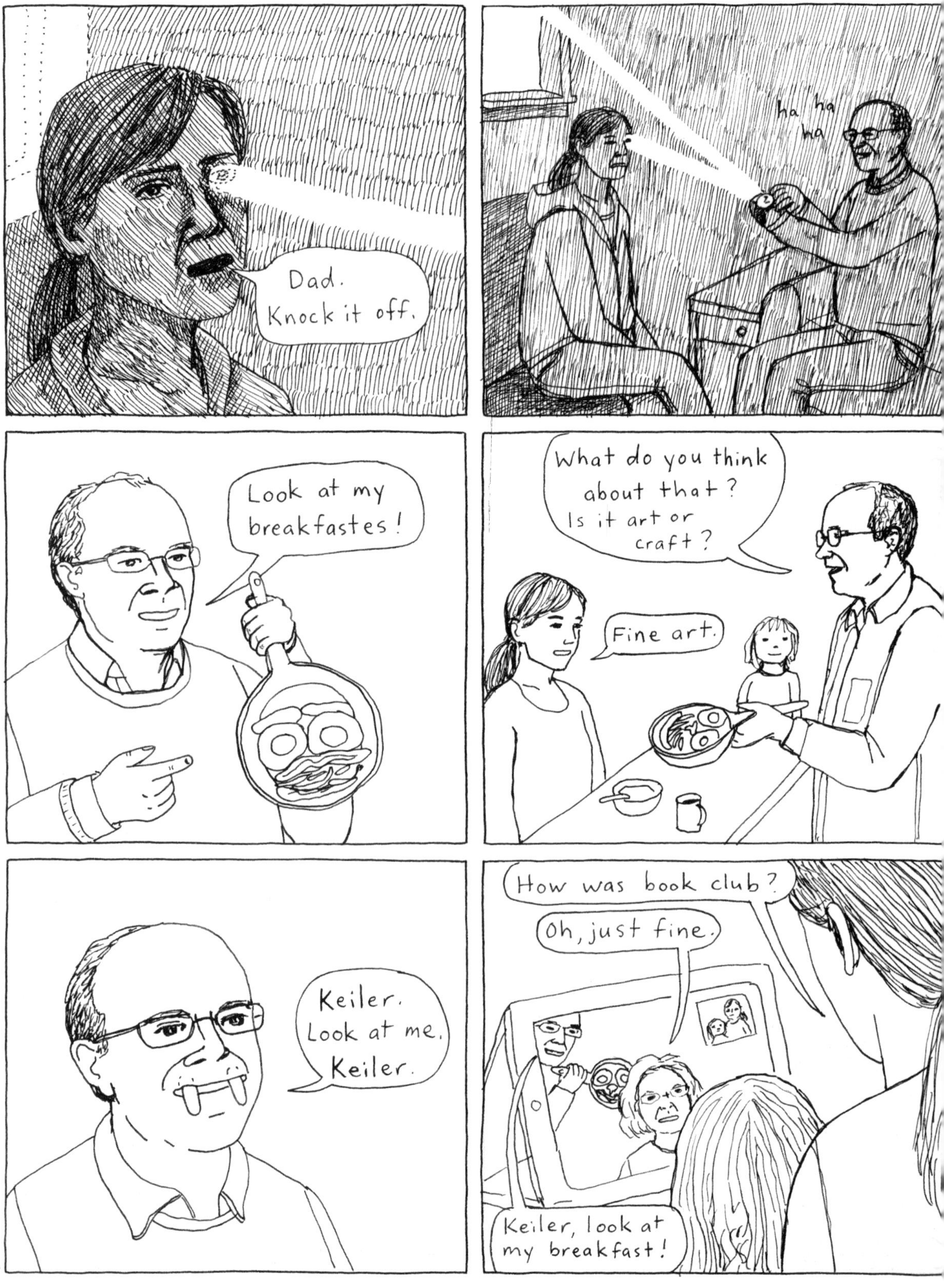
Dad.
Knock it off.
ha ha
ha
Look at my breakfastes!
What do you think about that? Is it art or craft?
Fine art.
Keiler. Look at me. Keiler.
How was book club?
Oh, just fine.
Keiler, look at my breakfast!

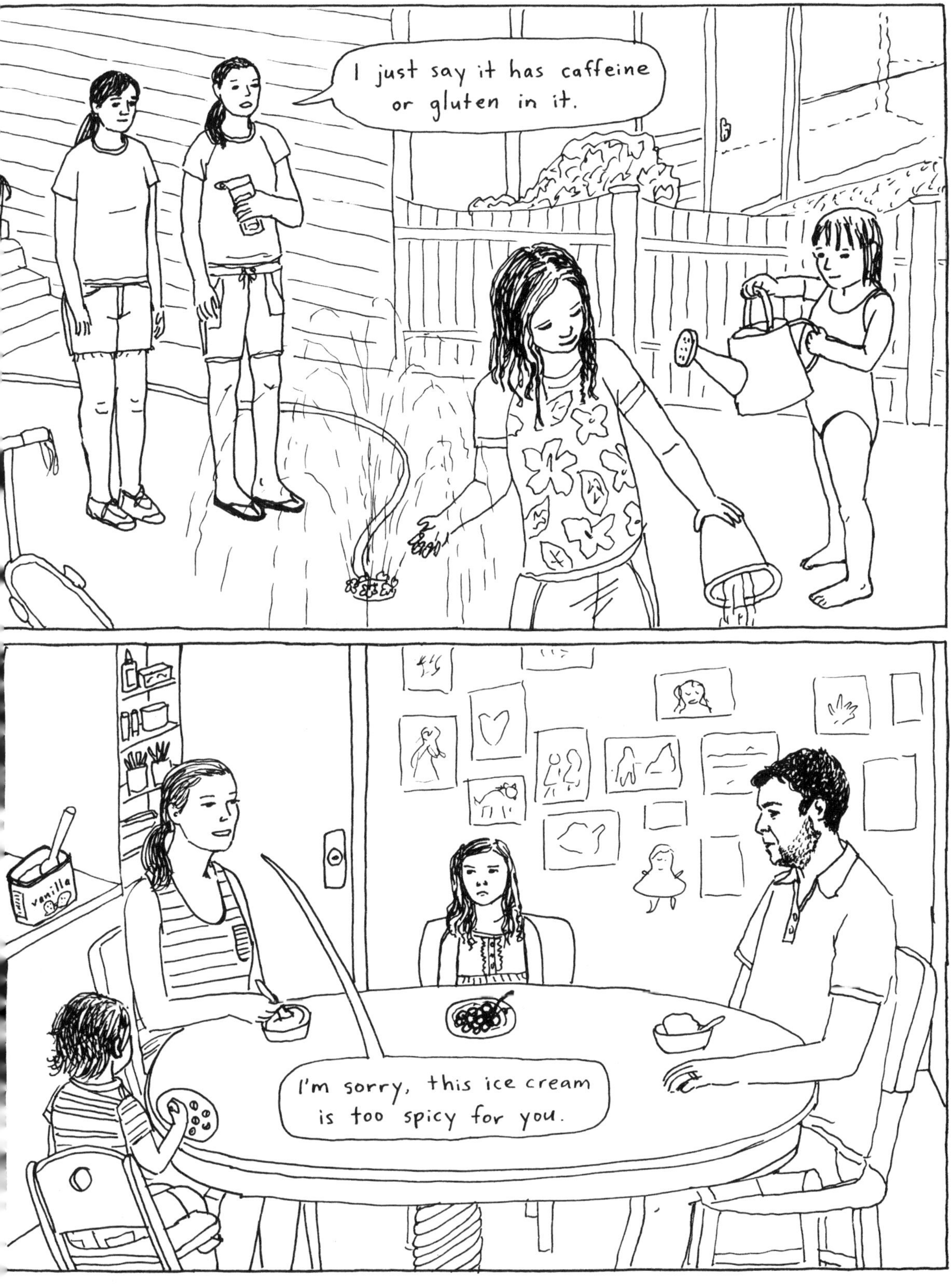
I just say it has caffeine or gluten in it.
vanilla
I'm sorry, this ice cream is too spicy for you.

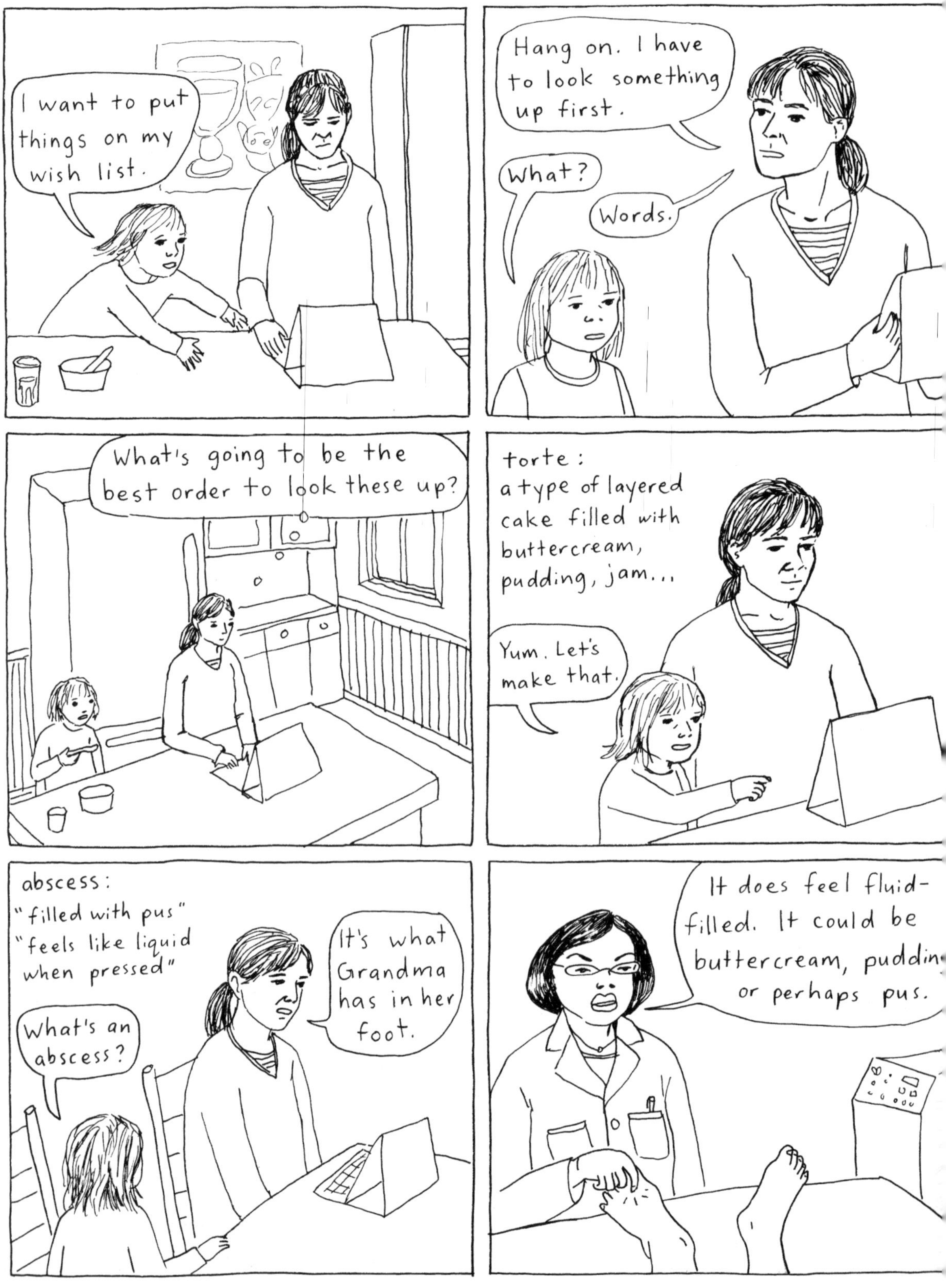
I want to put things on my wish list.
Hang on. I have to look something up first.
What?
Words.
What's going to be the best order to look these up?
torte: a type of layered cake filled with buttercream, pudding, jam...
Yum. Let's make that.
abscess: "filled with pus" "feels like liquid when pressed"
What's an abscess?
It's what Grandma has in her foot.
It does feel fluid-filled. It could be buttercream, puddin or perhaps pus.

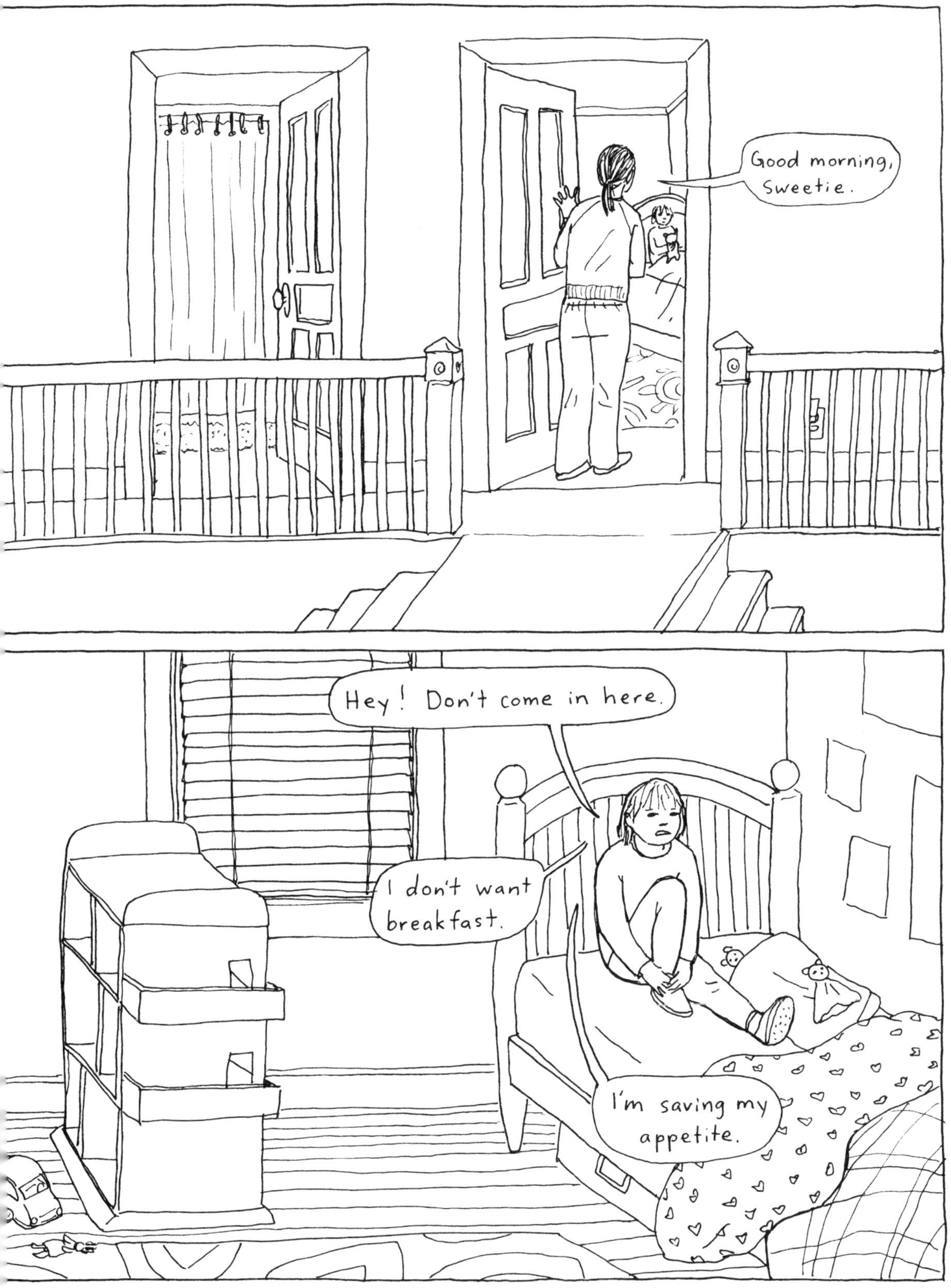
Good morning, Sweetie.
Hey! Don't come in here.
I don't want breakfast.
I'm saving my appetite.

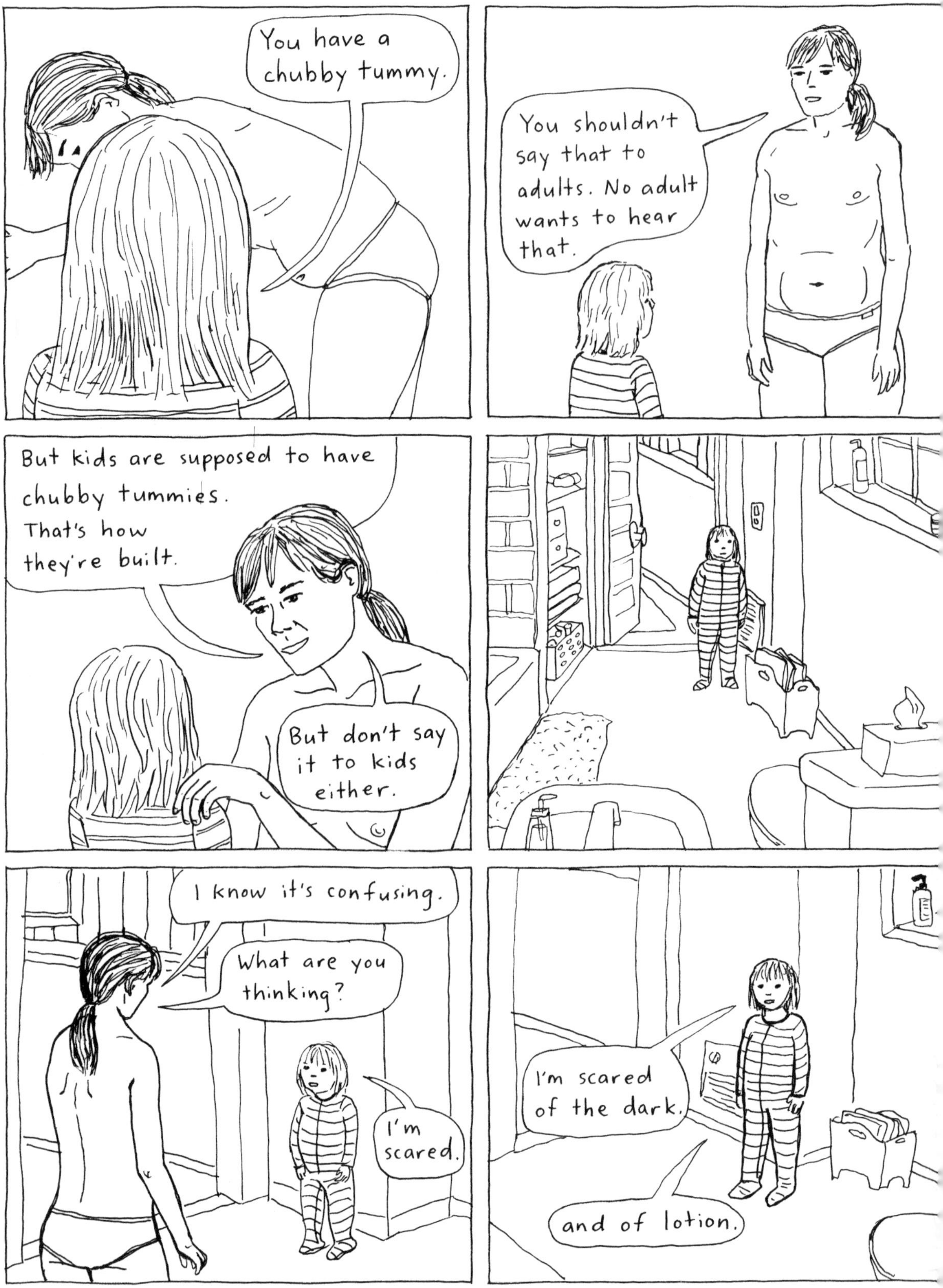
You have a chubby tummy.
You shouldn't say that to adults. No adult wants to hear that.
But kids are supposed to have chubby tummies. That's how they're built.
But don't say it to kids either.
I know it's confusing.
What are you thinking?
I'm scared.
I'm scared of the dark.
and of lotion.

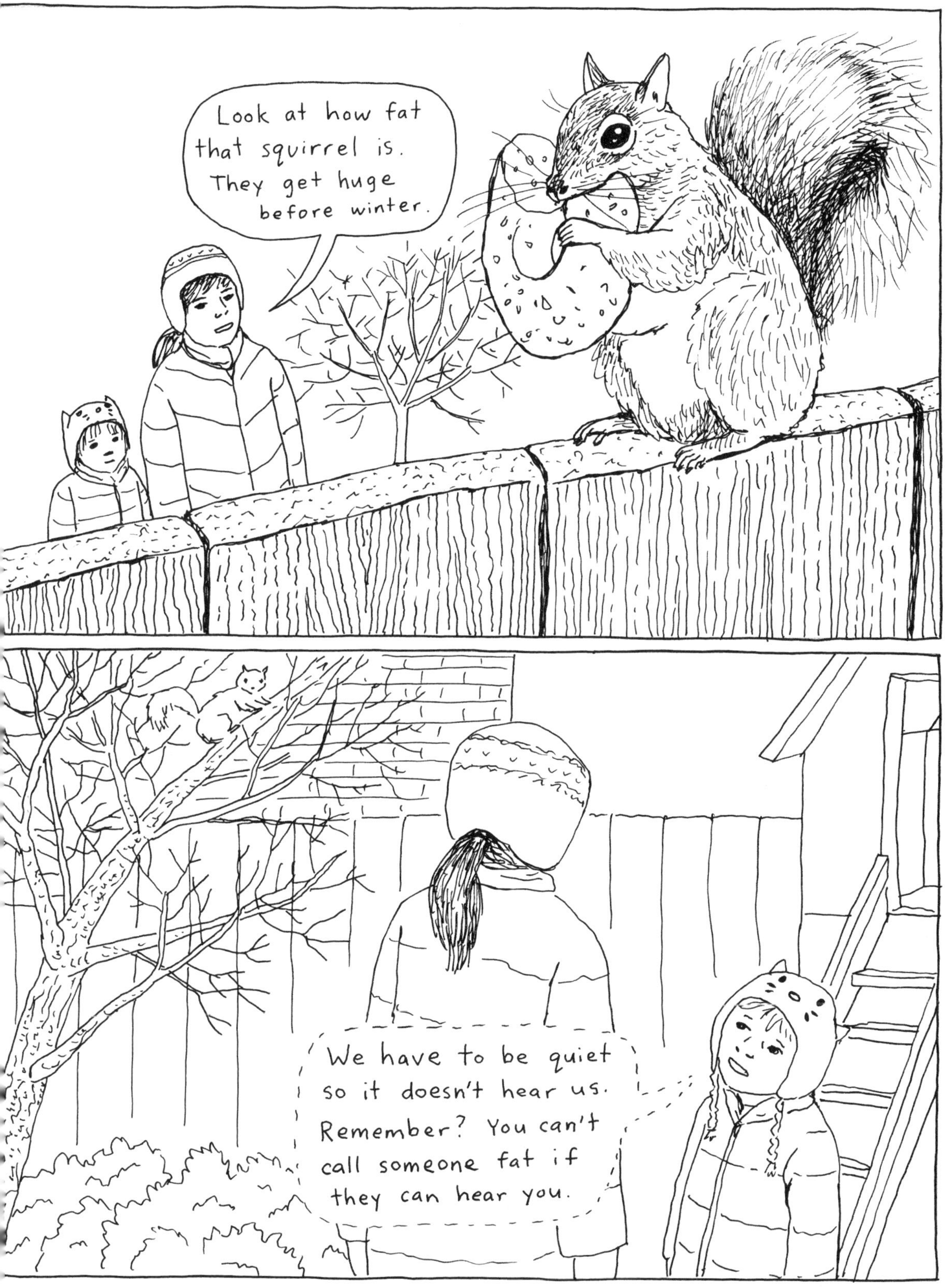
Look at how fat that squirrel is. They get huge before winter.
We have to be quiet so it doesn't hear us. Remember? You can't call someone fat if they can hear you.

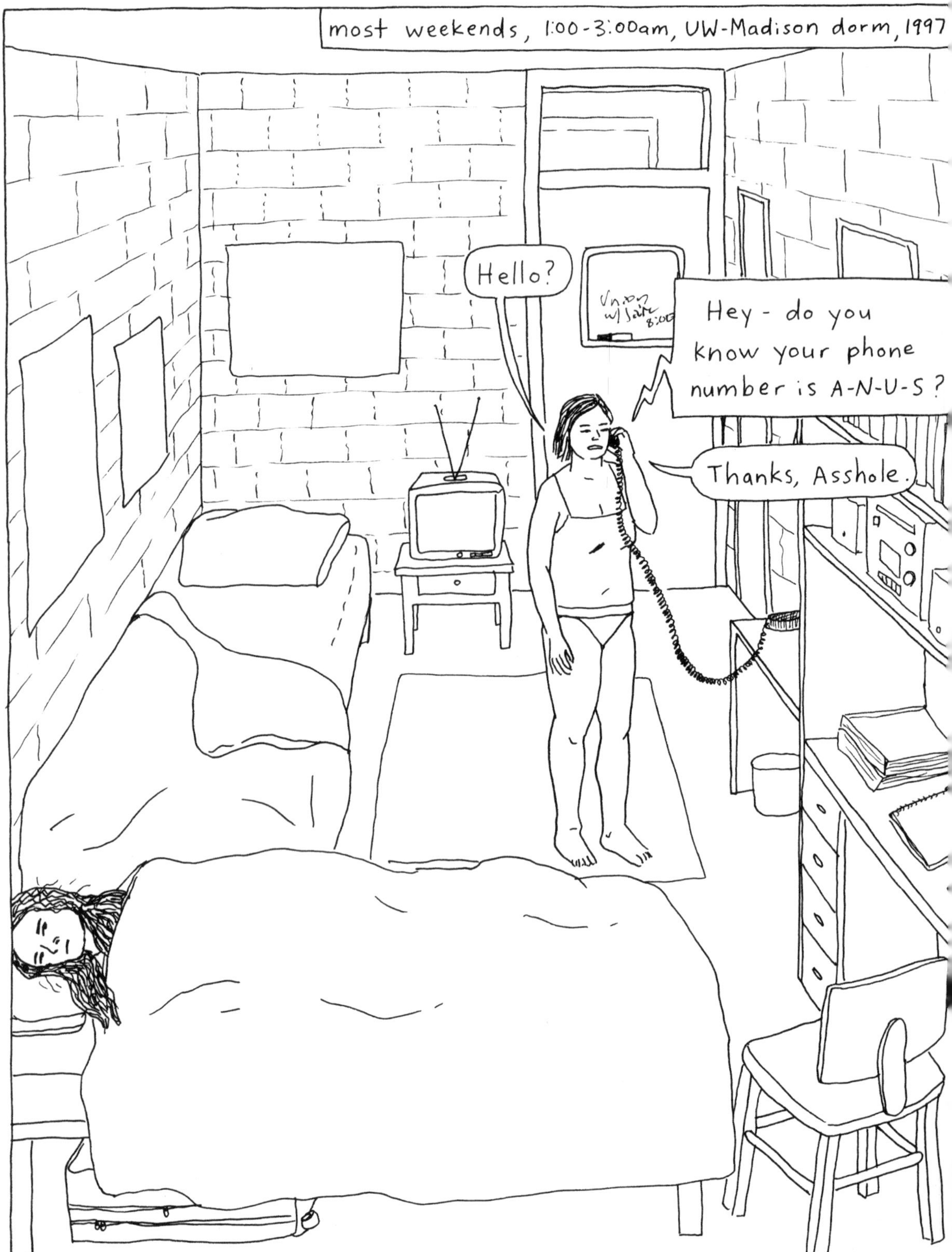
most weekends, 1:00-3:00am, UW-Madison dorm, 1997
Hello?
Hey - do you know your phone number is A-N-U-S?
Thanks, Asshole.

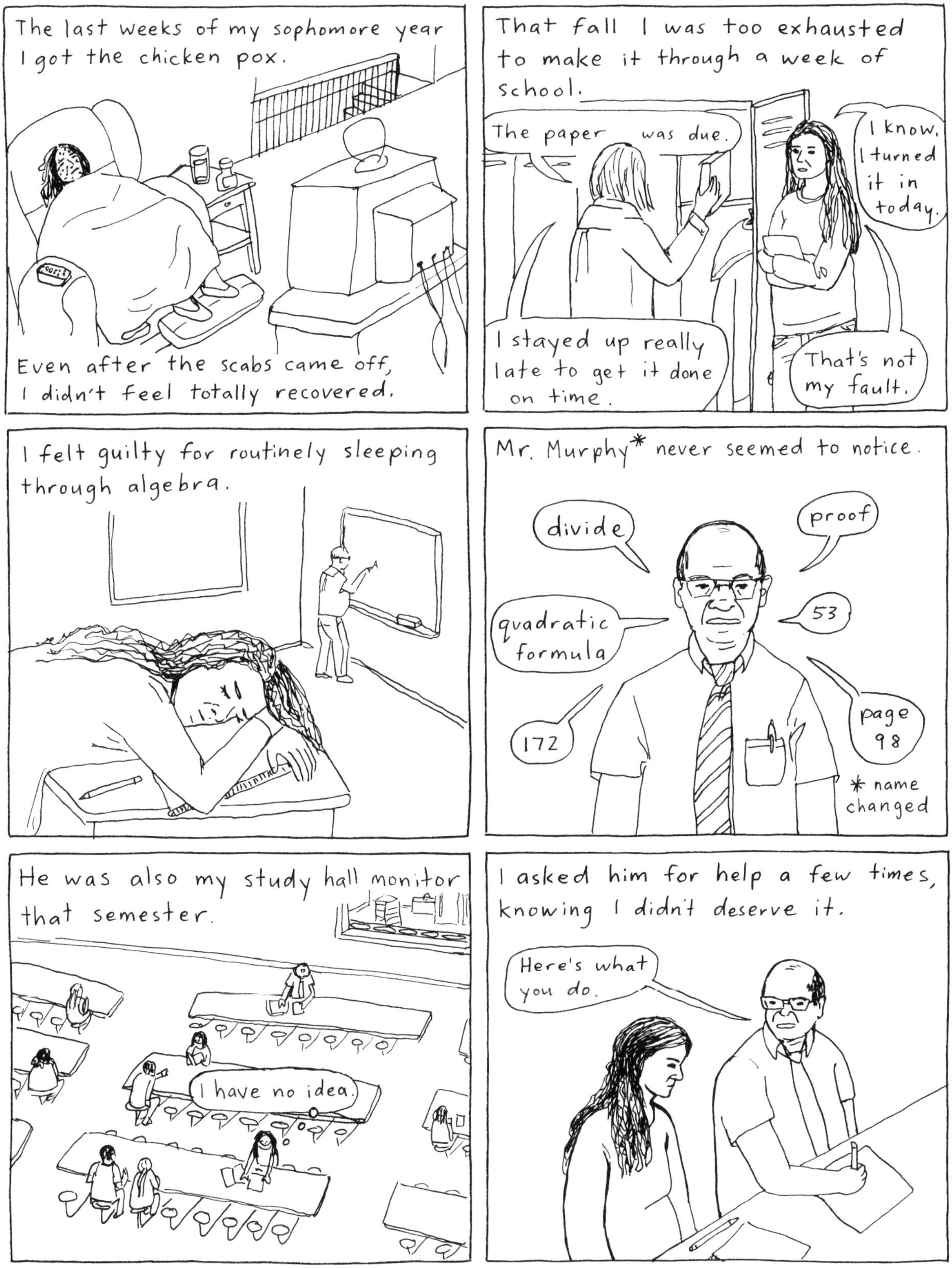
The last weeks of my sophomore year I got the chicken pox.
Even after the scabs came off, I didn't feel totally recovered.
That fall I was too exhausted to make it through a week of school.
The paper was due.
I know. I turned it in today.
I stayed up really late to get it done on time.
That's not my fault.
I felt guilty for routinely sleeping through algebra.
Mr. Murphy* never seemed to notice.
divide
proof
quadratic formula
53
172
page 98
* name changed
He was also my study hall monitor that semester.
I have no idea.
I asked him for help a few times, knowing I didn't deserve it.
Here's what you do.

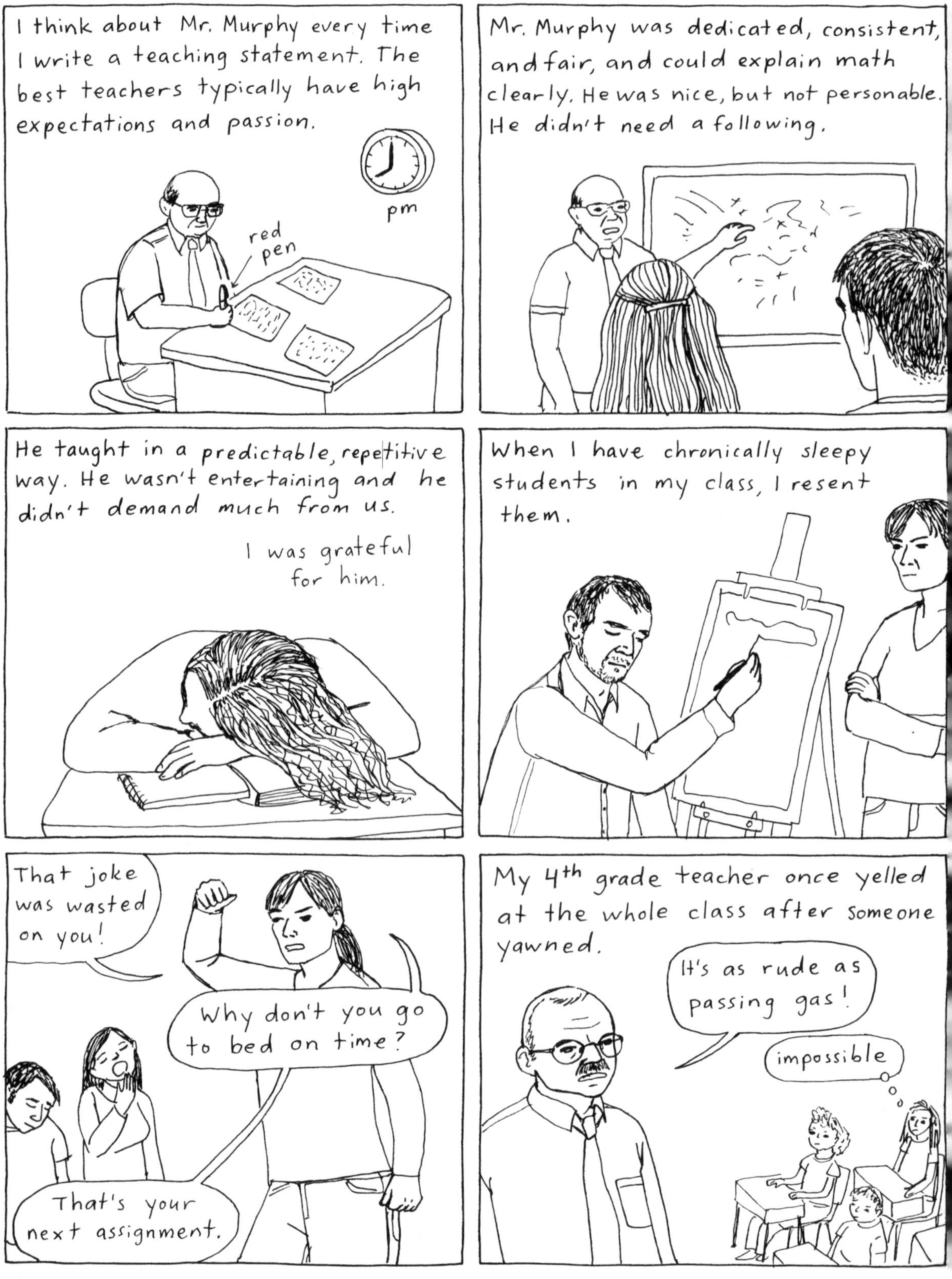
I think about Mr. Murphy every time I write a teaching statement. The best teachers typically have high expectations and passion.
pm
red pen
Mr. Murphy was dedicated, consistent, and fair, and could explain math clearly. He was nice, but not personable. He didn't need a following.
He taught in a predictable, repetitive way. He wasn't entertaining and he didn't demand much from us.
I was grateful for him.
When I have chronically sleepy students in my class, I resent them.
That joke was wasted on you!
Why don't you go to bed on time?
That's your next assignment.
My 4th grade teacher once yelled at the whole class after someone yawned.
It's as rude as passing gas!
impossible

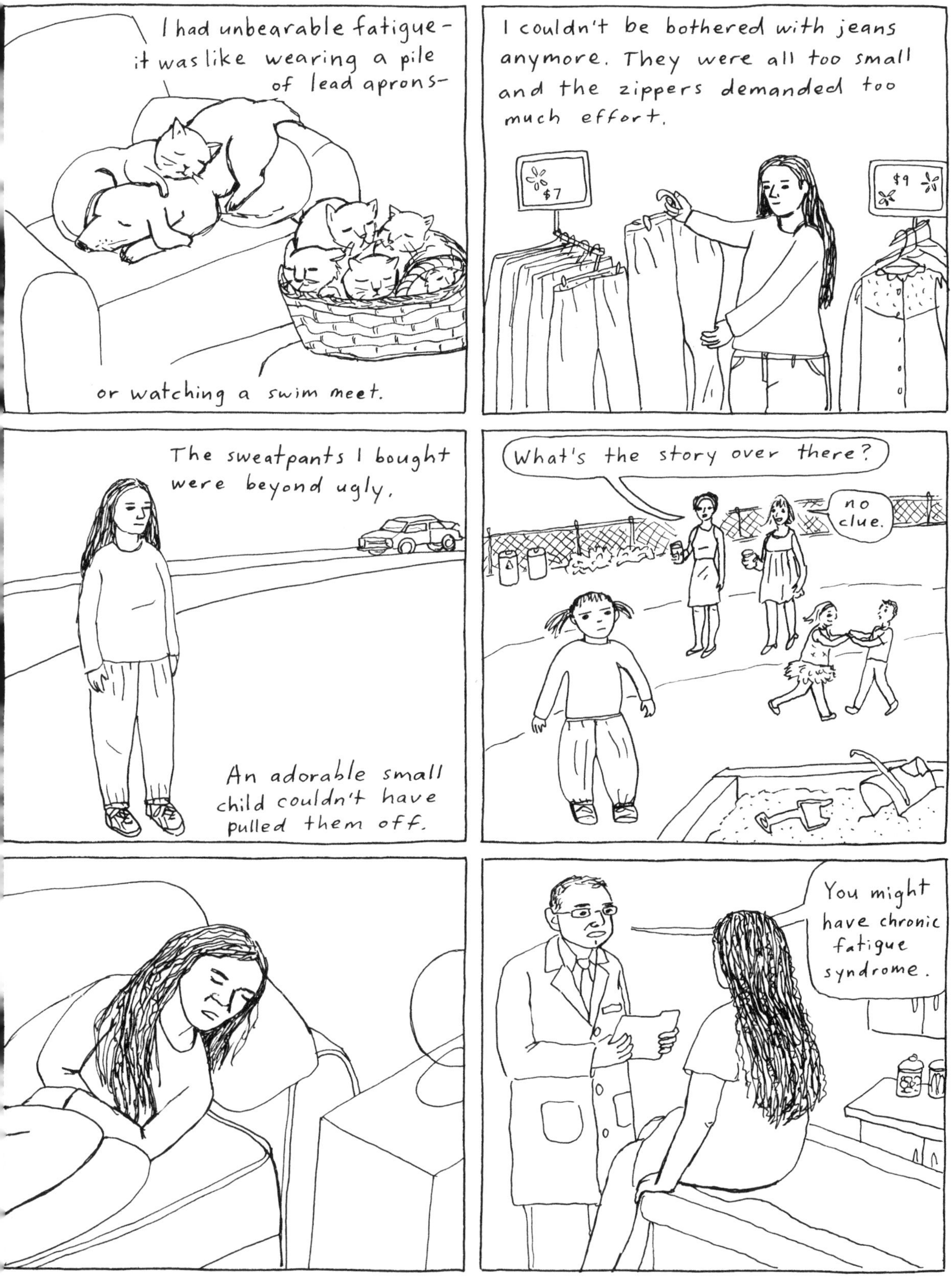
I had unbearable fatigue-
it was like wearing a pile of lead aprons-
or watching a swim meet.
I couldn't be bothered with jeans anymore. They were all too small and the zippers demanded too much effort.
$7
$9
The sweatpants I bought were beyond ugly.
An adorable small child couldn't have pulled them off.
What's the story over there?
no clue.
You might have chronic fatigue syndrome.

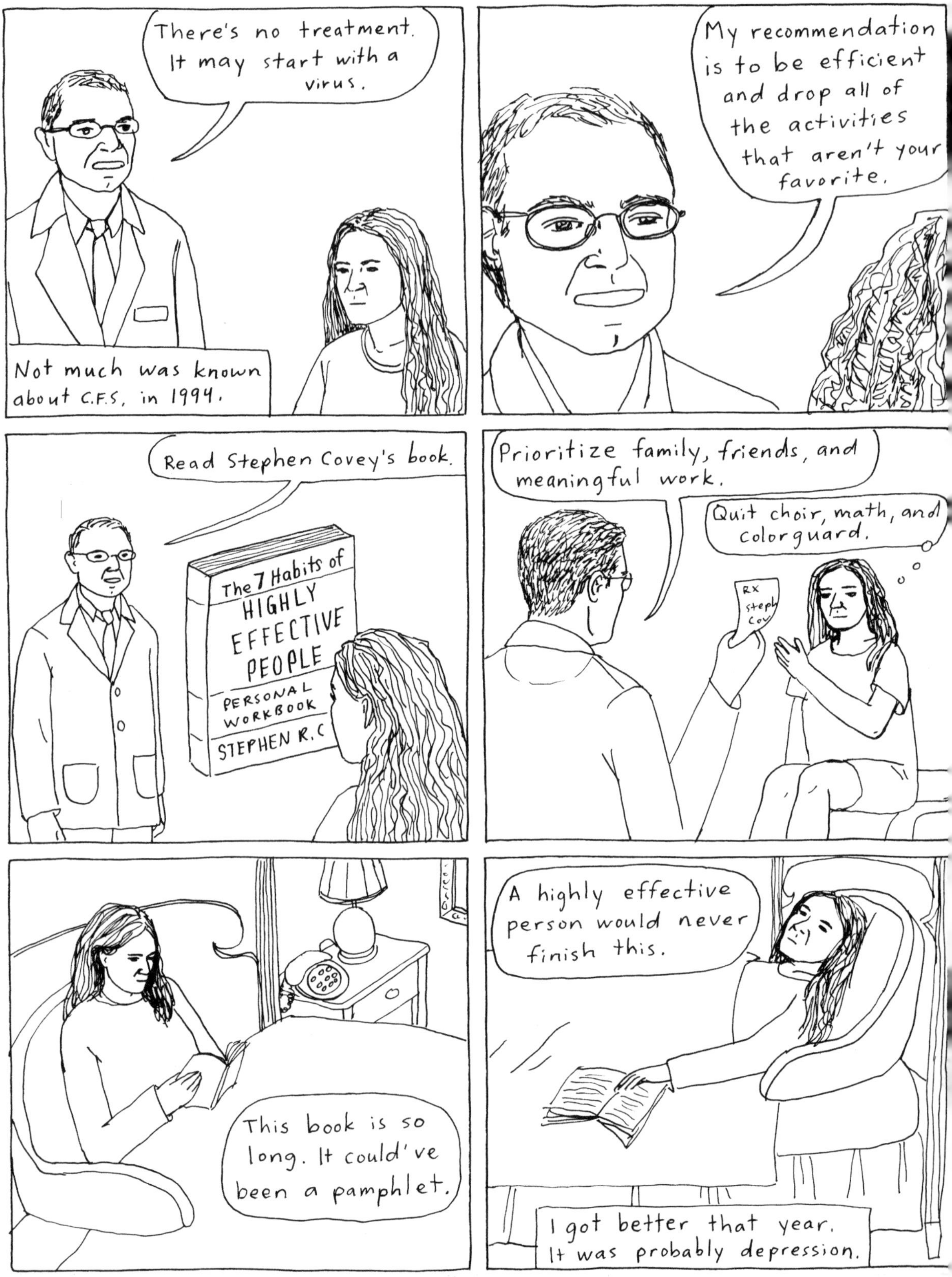
There's no treatment. It may start with a virus.
Not much was known about C.F.S. in 1994.
My recommendation is to be efficient and drop all of the activities that aren't your favorite.
Read Stephen Covey's book.
The 7 Habits of HIGHLY EFFECTIVE PEOPLE PERSONAL WORKBOOK STEPHEN R. C
Prioritize family, friends, and meaningful work.
Quit choir, math, and colorguard.
RX steph Cov
This book is so long. It could've been a pamphlet.
A highly effective person would never finish this.
I got better that year. It was probably depression.

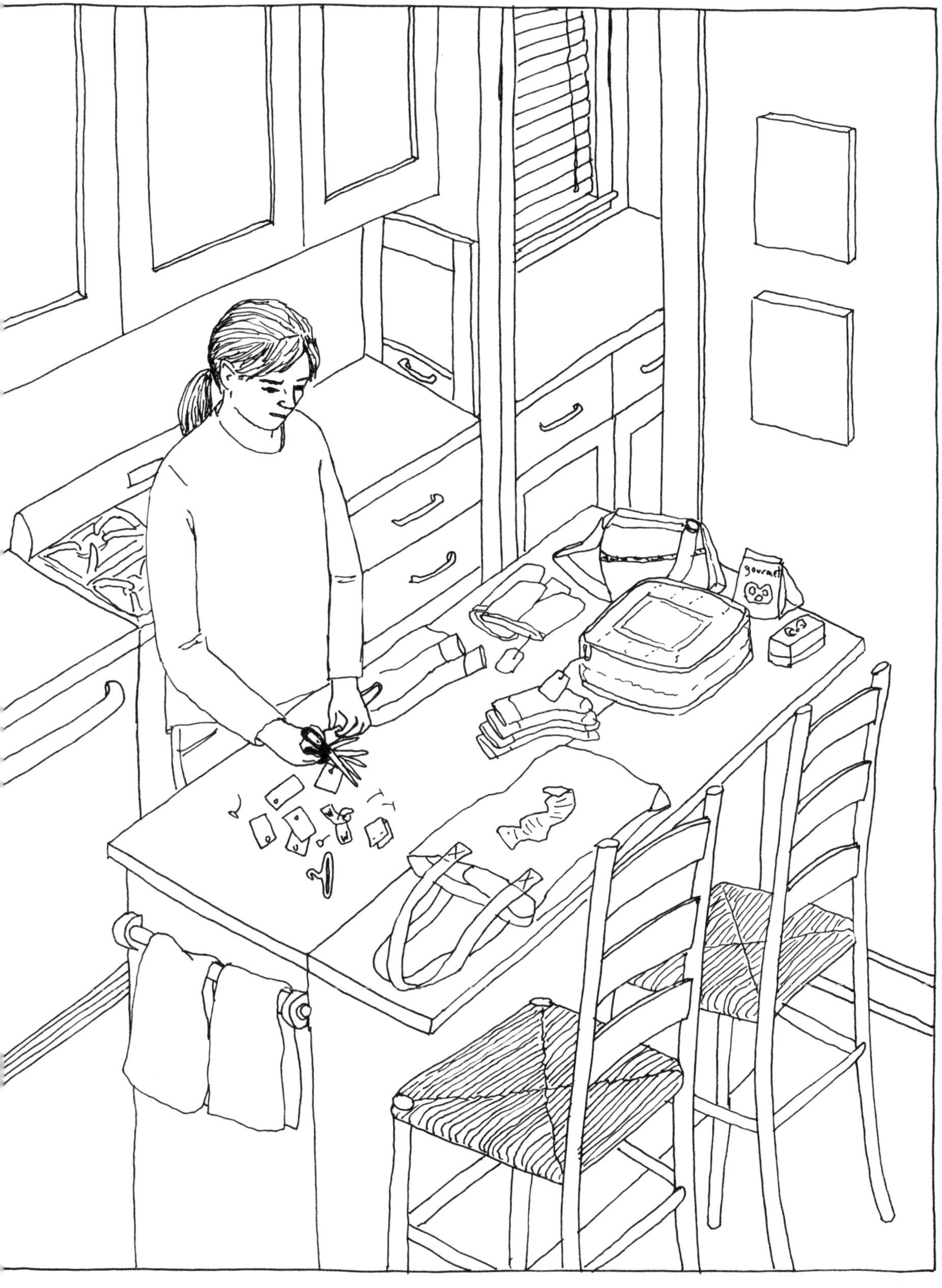
gourmet

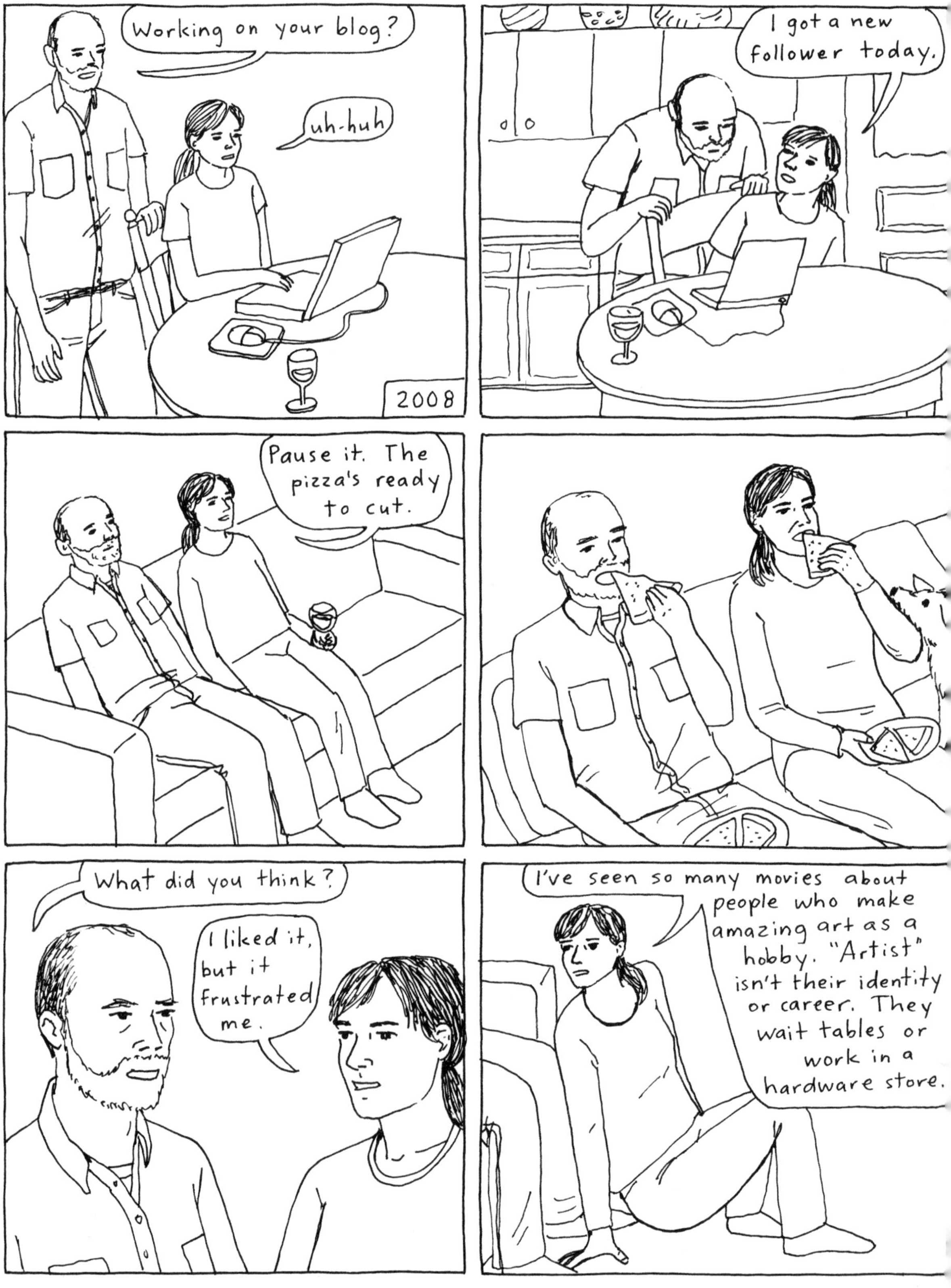

Working on your blog?
uh-huh
2008
I got a new follower today.
Pause it. The pizza's ready to cut.
What did you think?
I liked it, but it frustrated me.
I've seen so many movies about people who make amazing art as a hobby. "Artist" isn't their identity or career. They wait tables or work in a hardware store.

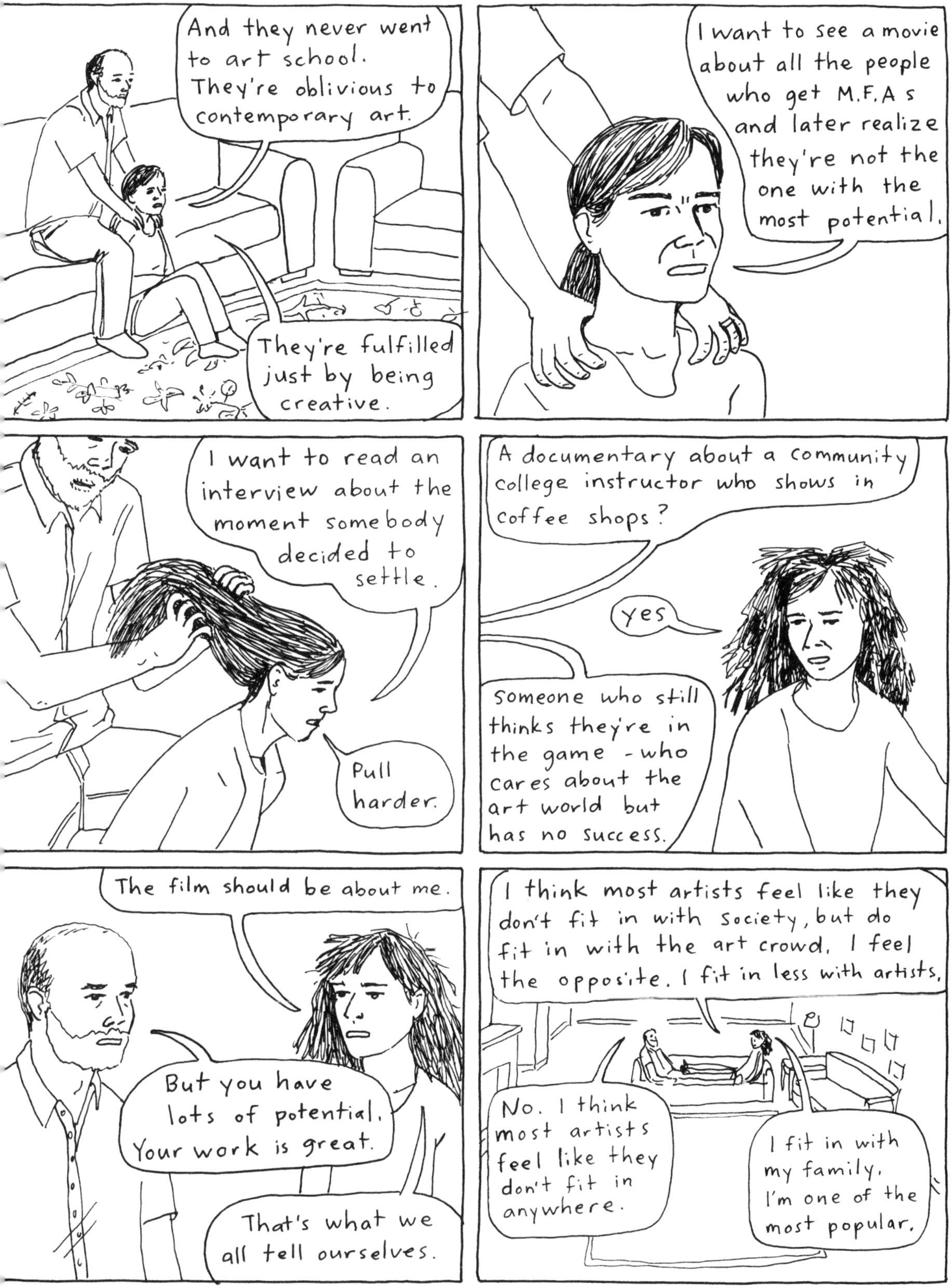
And they never went to art school. They're oblivious to contemporary art.
They're fulfilled just by being creative.
I want to see a movie about all the people who get M.F.A s and later realize they're not the one with the most potential.
I want to read an interview about the moment somebody decided to settle.
Pull harder.
A documentary about a community college instructor who shows in coffee shops?
yes
Someone who still thinks they're in the game - who cares about the art world but has no success.
The film should be about me.
But you have lots of potential. Your work is great.
That's what we all tell ourselves.
I think most artists feel like they don't fit in with society, but do fit in with the art crowd. I feel the opposite. I fit in less with artists.
No. I think most artists feel like they don't fit in anywhere.
I fit in with my family. I'm one of the most popular.

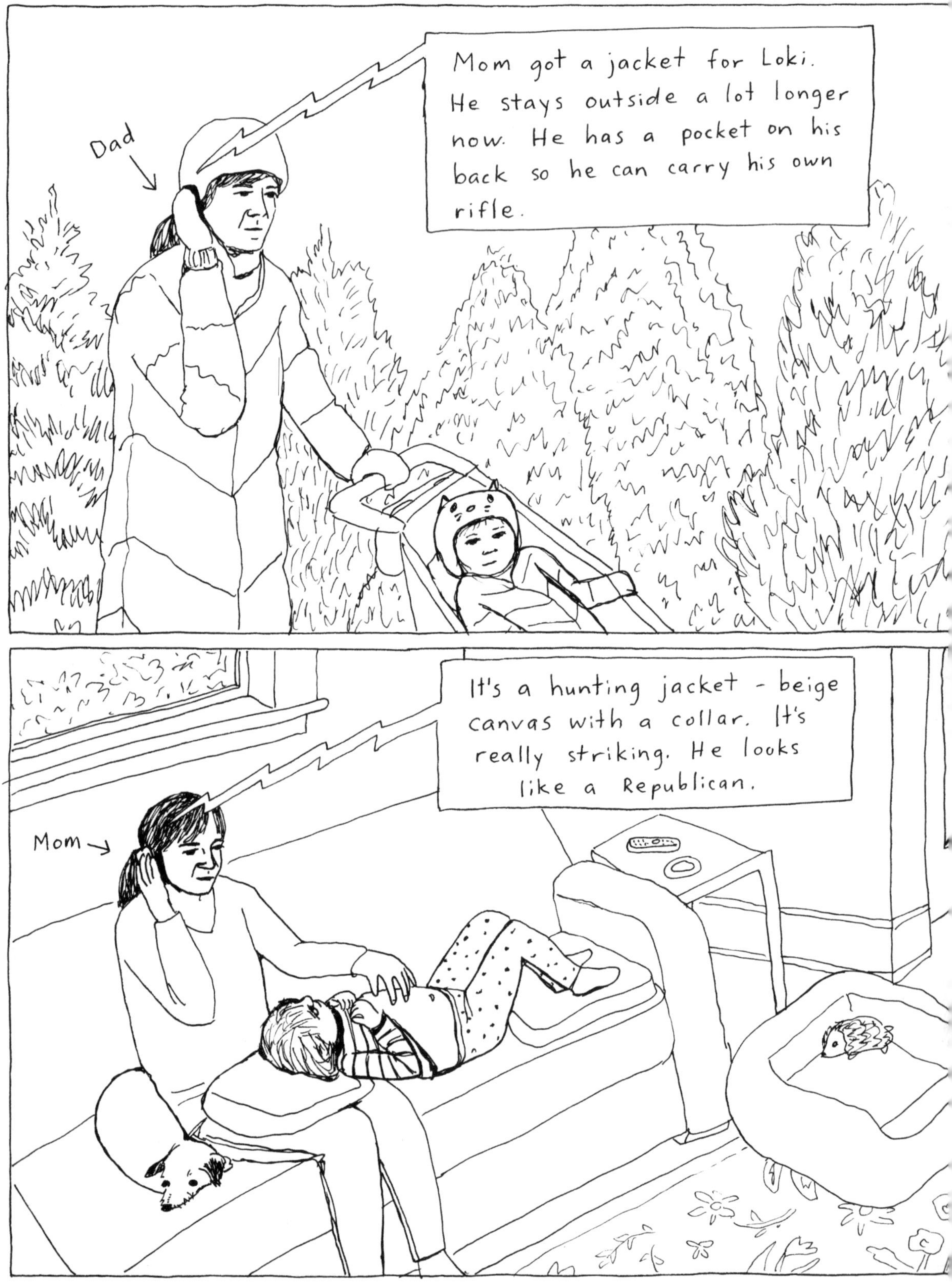
Dad
Mom got a jacket for Loki. He stays outside a lot longer now. He has a pocket on his back so he can carry his own rifle.
Mom
It's a hunting jacket - beige canvas with a collar. It's really striking. He looks like a Republican.

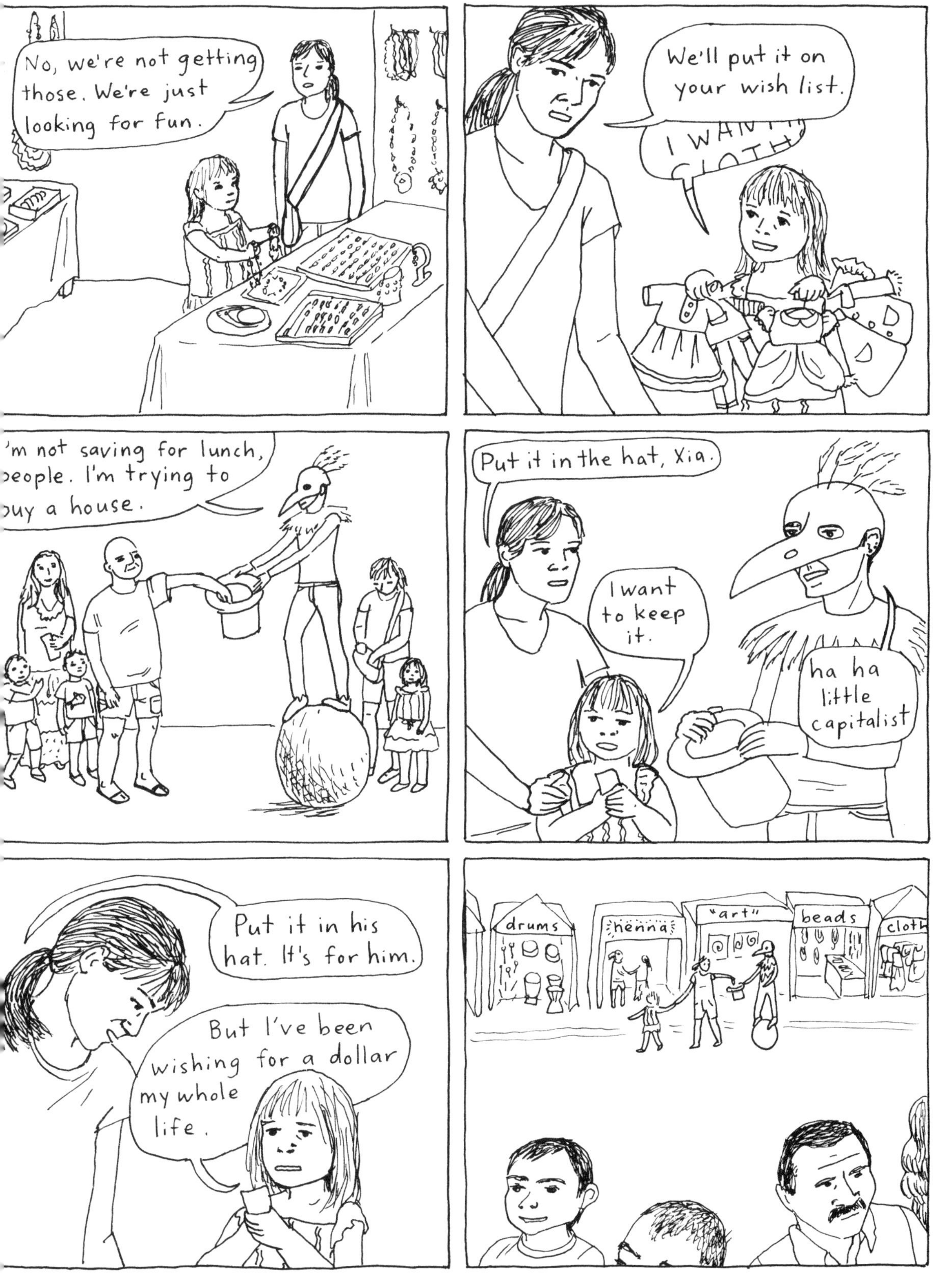
No, we're not getting those. We're just looking for fun.
We'll put it on your wish list.
'm not saving for lunch, eople. I'm trying to uy a house.
Put it in the hat, Xia.
I want to keep it.
ha ha little capitalist
Put it in his hat. It's for him.
But I've been wishing for a dollar my whole life.
drums
henna
"art"
beads
cloth

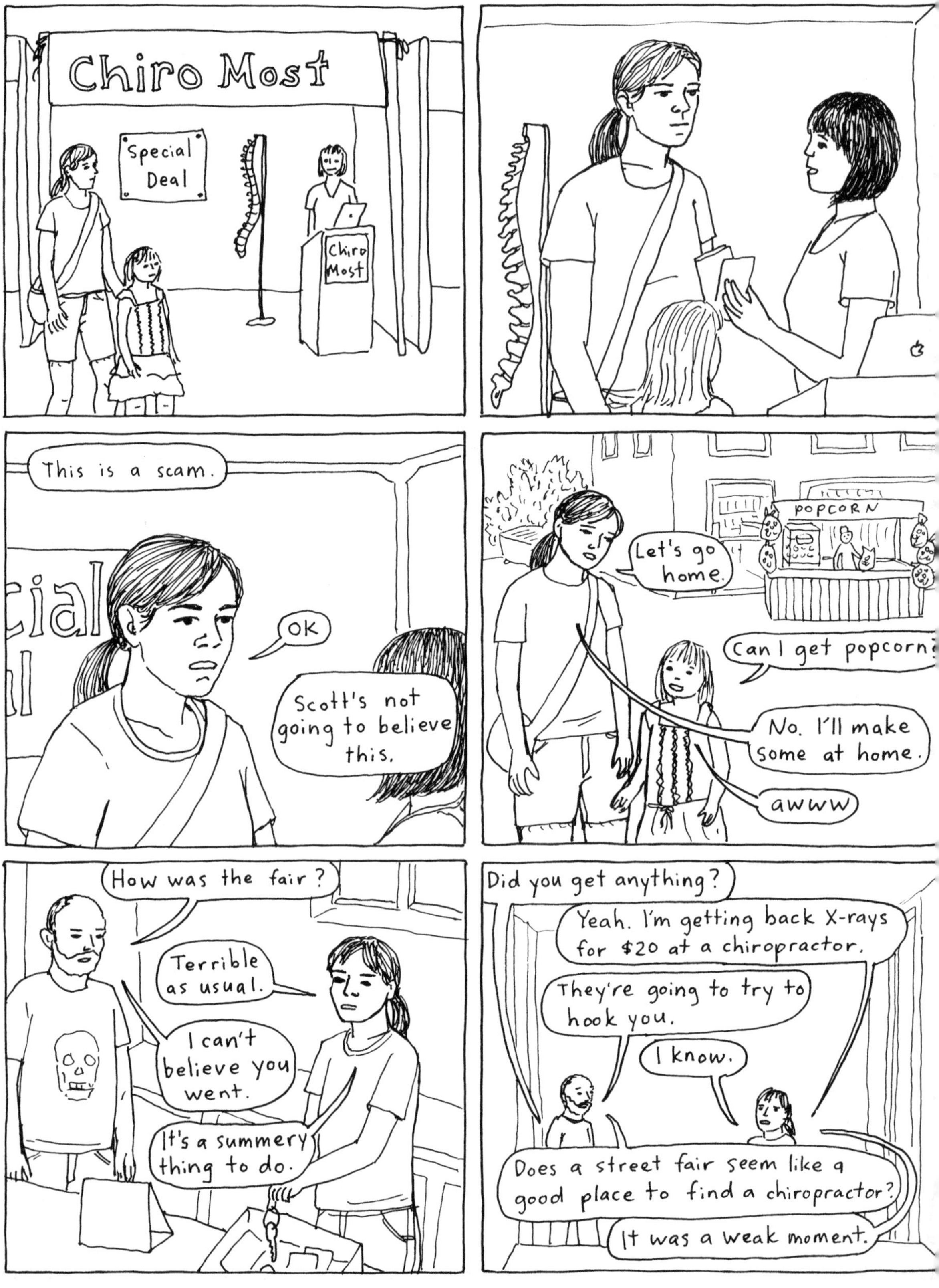
Chiro Most
Special Deal
Chiro Most
This is a scam.
OK
Scott's not going to believe this.
Let's go home.
POPCORN
Can I get popcorn
No. I'll make some at home.
awww
How was the fair?
Terrible as usual.
I can't believe you went.
It's a summery thing to do.
Did you get anything?
Yeah. I'm getting back X-rays for $20 at a chiropractor.
They're going to try to hook you.
I know.
Does a street fair seem like a good place to find a chiropractor?
It was a weak moment.

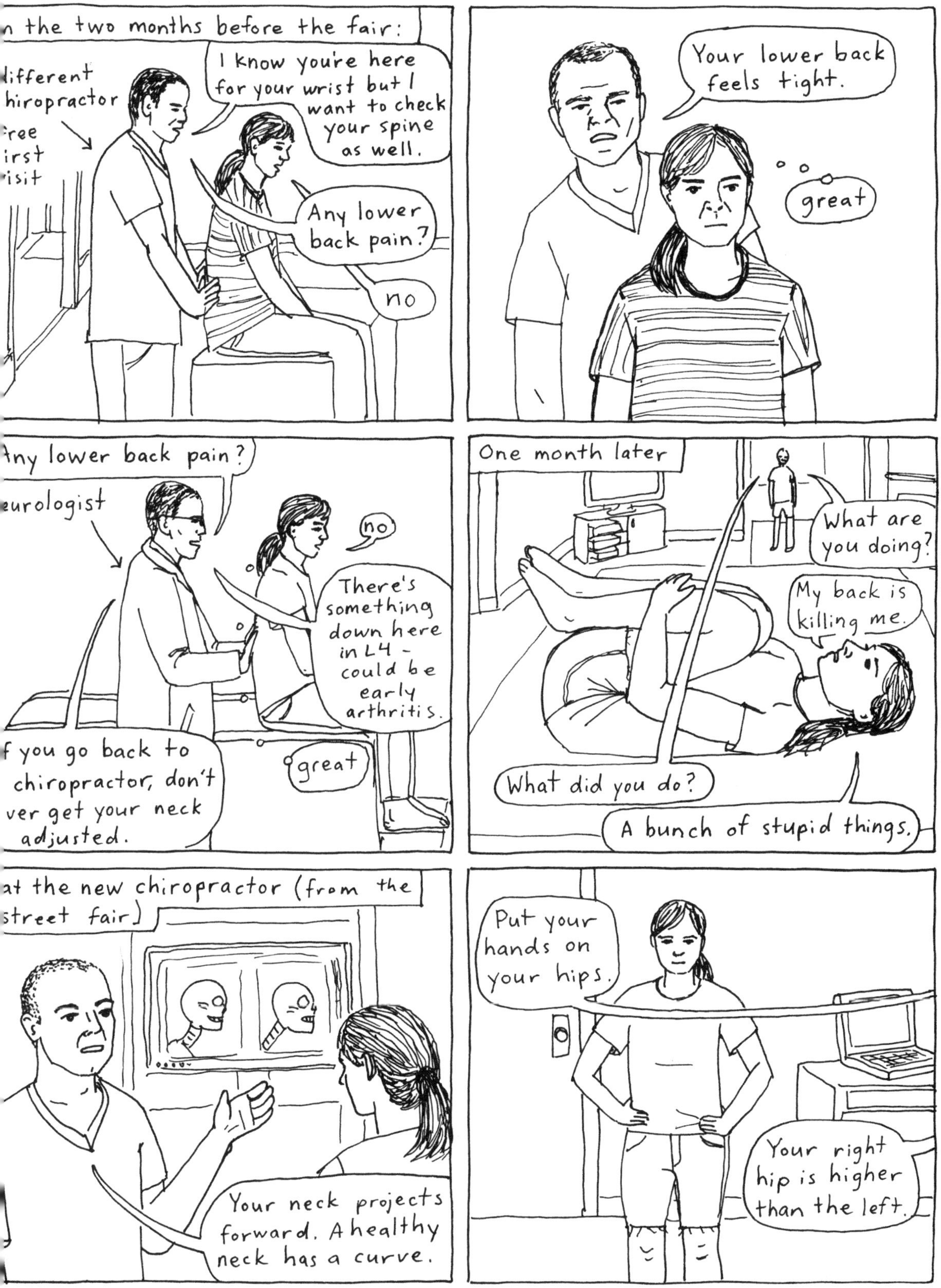
n the two months before the fair:
lifferent hiropractor free irst isit
I know you're here for your wrist but I want to check your spine as well.
Any lower back pain?
no
Your lower back feels tight.
great
Any lower back pain?
eurologist
no
There's something down here in L4 - could be early arthritis.
great
f you go back to chiropractor, don't ver get your neck adjusted.
One month later
What are you doing?
My back is killing me.
What did you do?
A bunch of stupid things.
at the new chiropractor (from the street fair)
Your neck projects forward. A healthy neck has a curve.
Put your hands on your hips.
Your right hip is higher than the left.

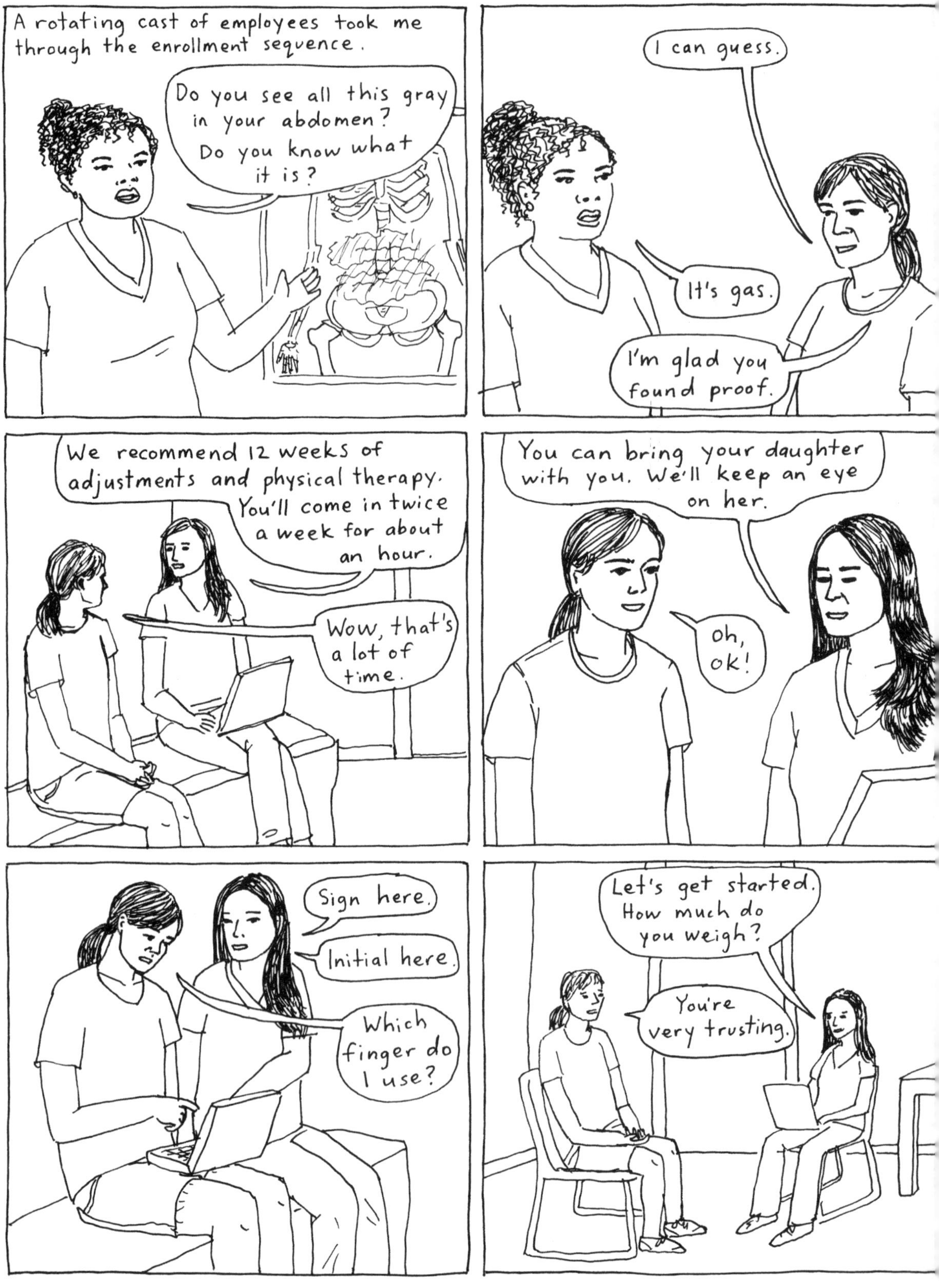
A rotating cast of employees took me through the enrollment sequence.
Do you see all this gray in your abdomen? Do you know what it is?
I can guess.
It's gas.
I'm glad you found proof.
We recommend 12 weeks of adjustments and physical therapy. You'll come in twice a week for about an hour.
Wow, that's a lot of time.
You can bring your daughter with you. We'll keep an eye on her.
Oh, ok!
Sign here.
Initial here.
Which finger do I use?
Let's get started. How much do you weigh?
You're very trusting.

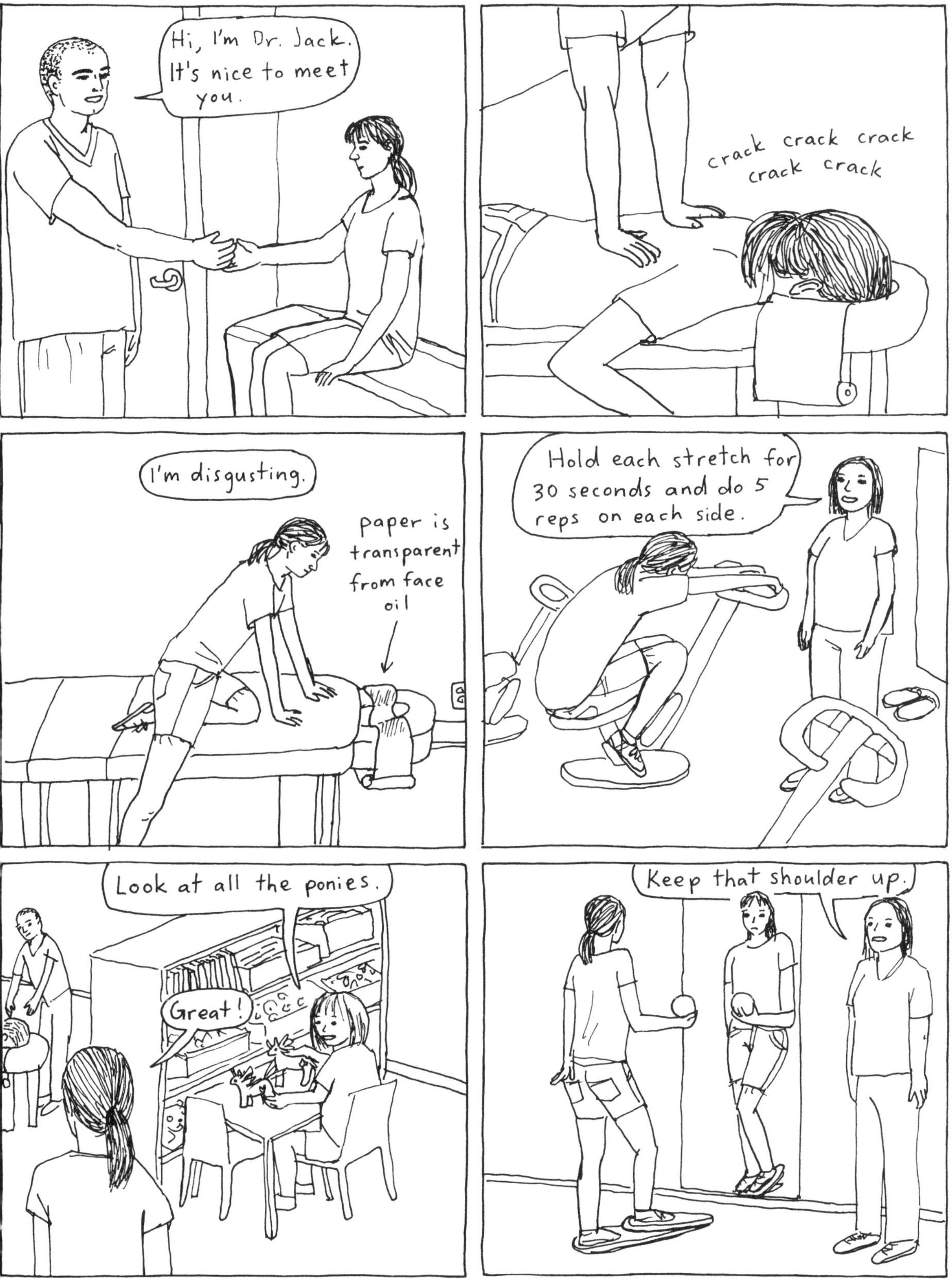
Hi, I'm Dr. Jack. It's nice to meet you.
crack crack crack crack crack
I'm disgusting.
paper is transparent from face oil
Hold each stretch for 30 seconds and do 5 reps on each side.
Look at all the ponies.
Great!
Keep that shoulder up.

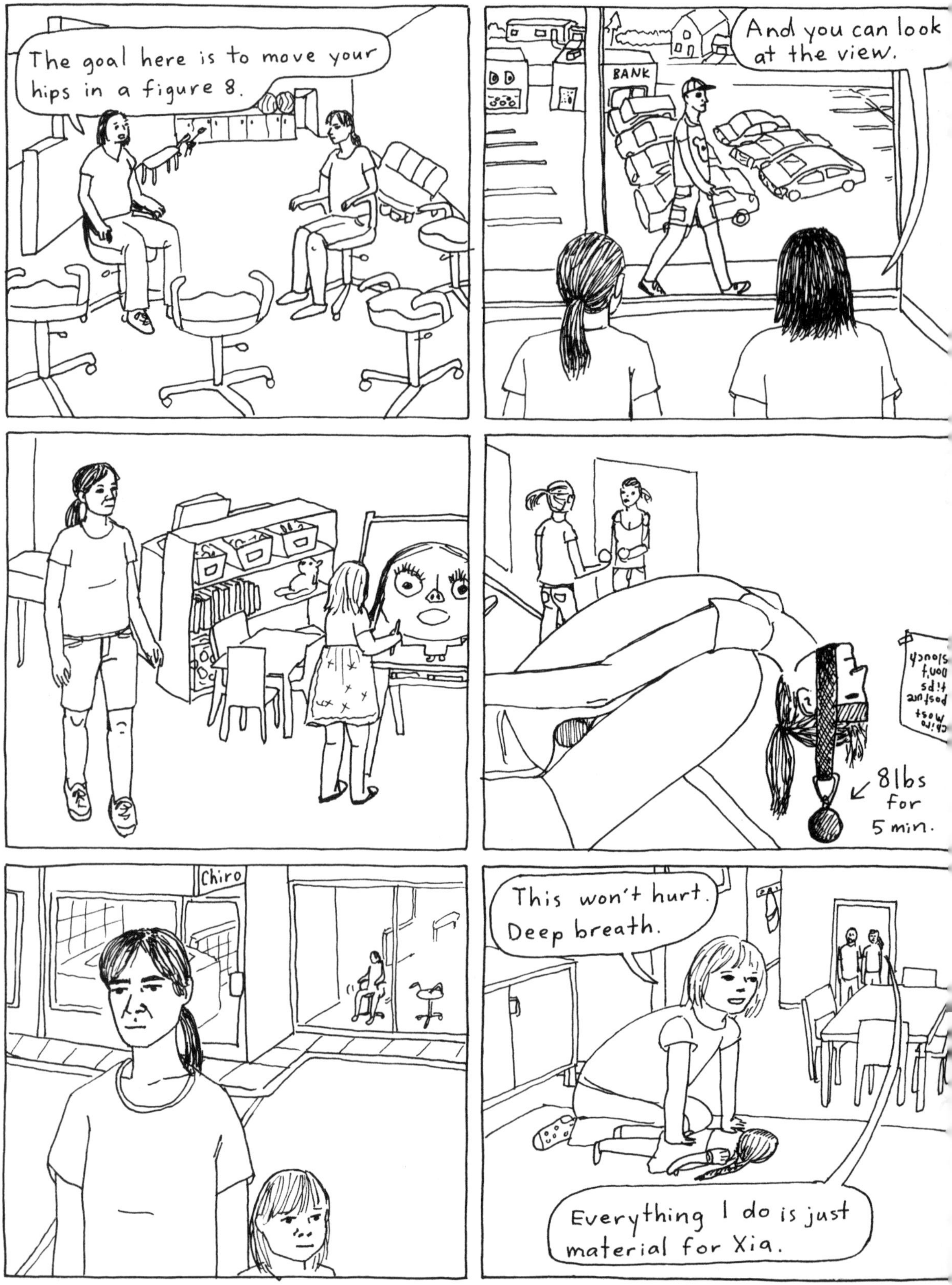
The goal here is to move your hips in a figure 8.
And you can look at the view.
BANK
Chiro
Most
posture
tips
Don't
slouch
8lbs for 5 min.
Chiro
This won't hurt. Deep breath.
Everything I do is just material for Xia.

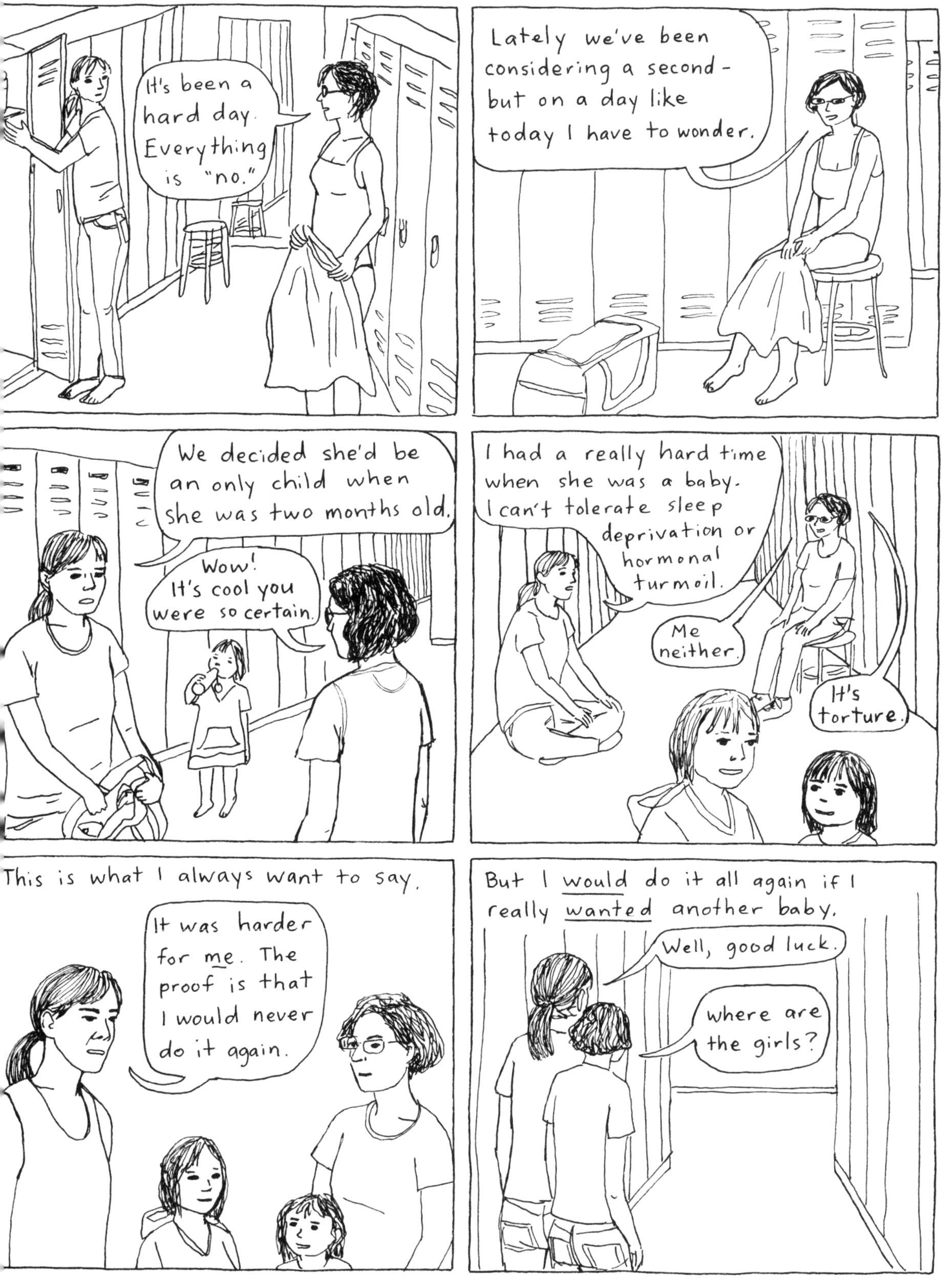
It's been a hard day. Everything is "no."
Lately we've been considering a second - but on a day like today I have to wonder.
We decided she'd be an only child when she was two months old.
Wow! It's cool you were so certain.
I had a really hard time when she was a baby. I can't tolerate sleep deprivation or hormonal turmoil.
Me neither.
It's torture.
This is what I always want to say.
It was harder for me. The proof is that I would never do it again.
But I would do it all again if I really wanted another baby.
Well, good luck.
where are the girls?

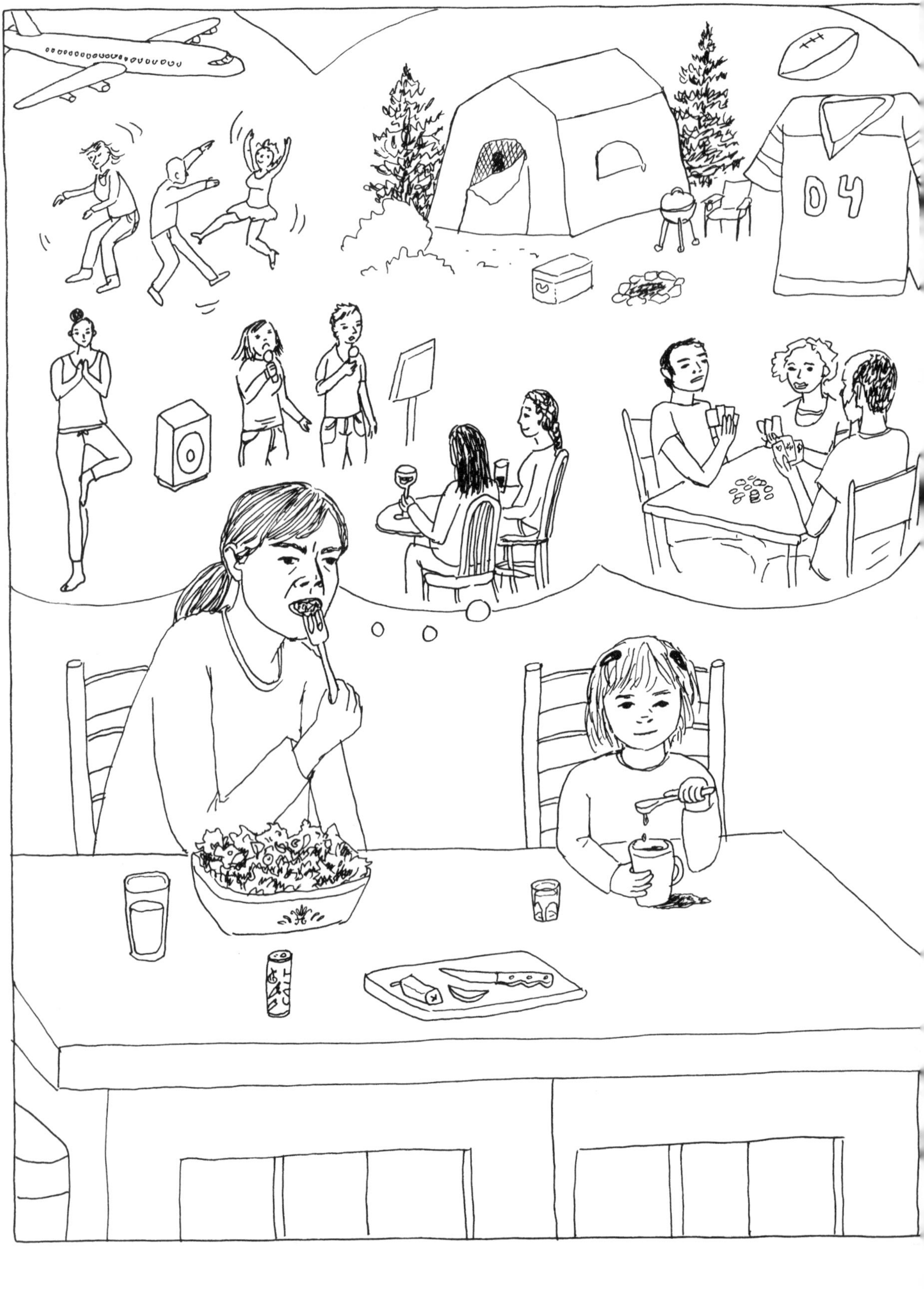
04

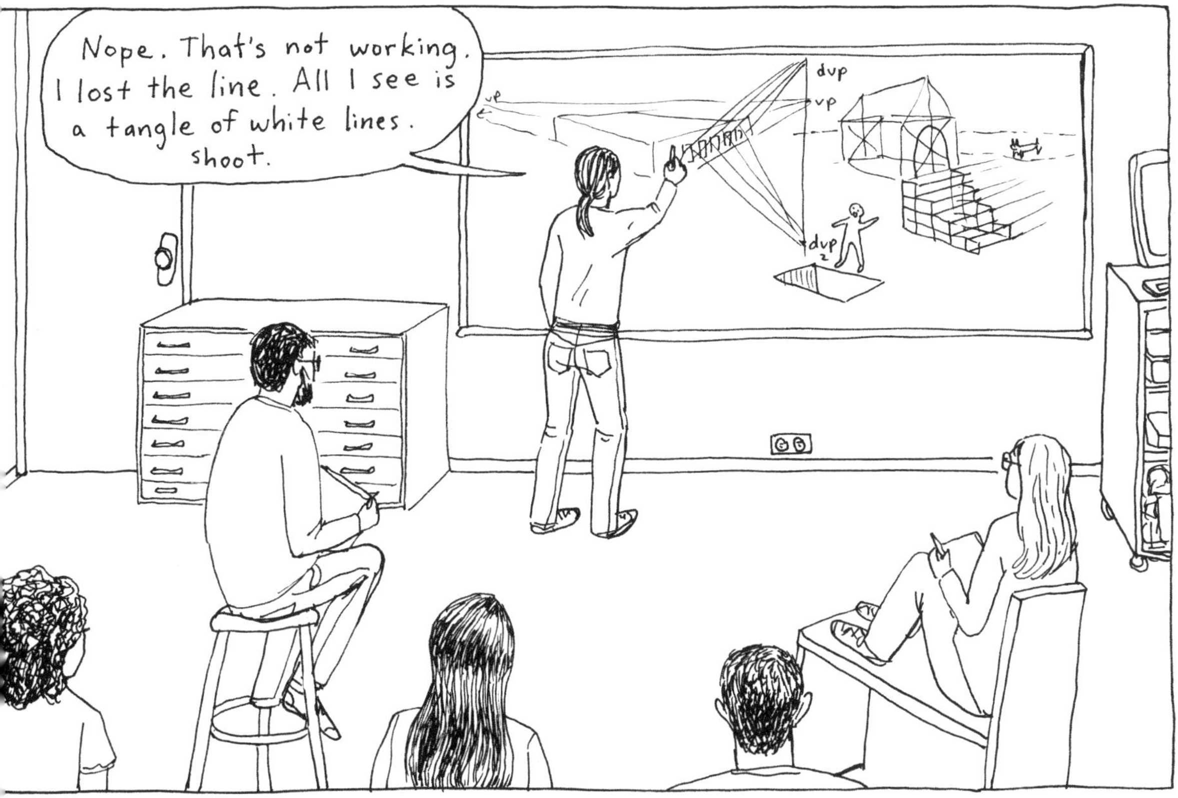
Nope. That's not working. I lost the line. All I see is a tangle of white lines. shoot.
dvp
vp
dvp

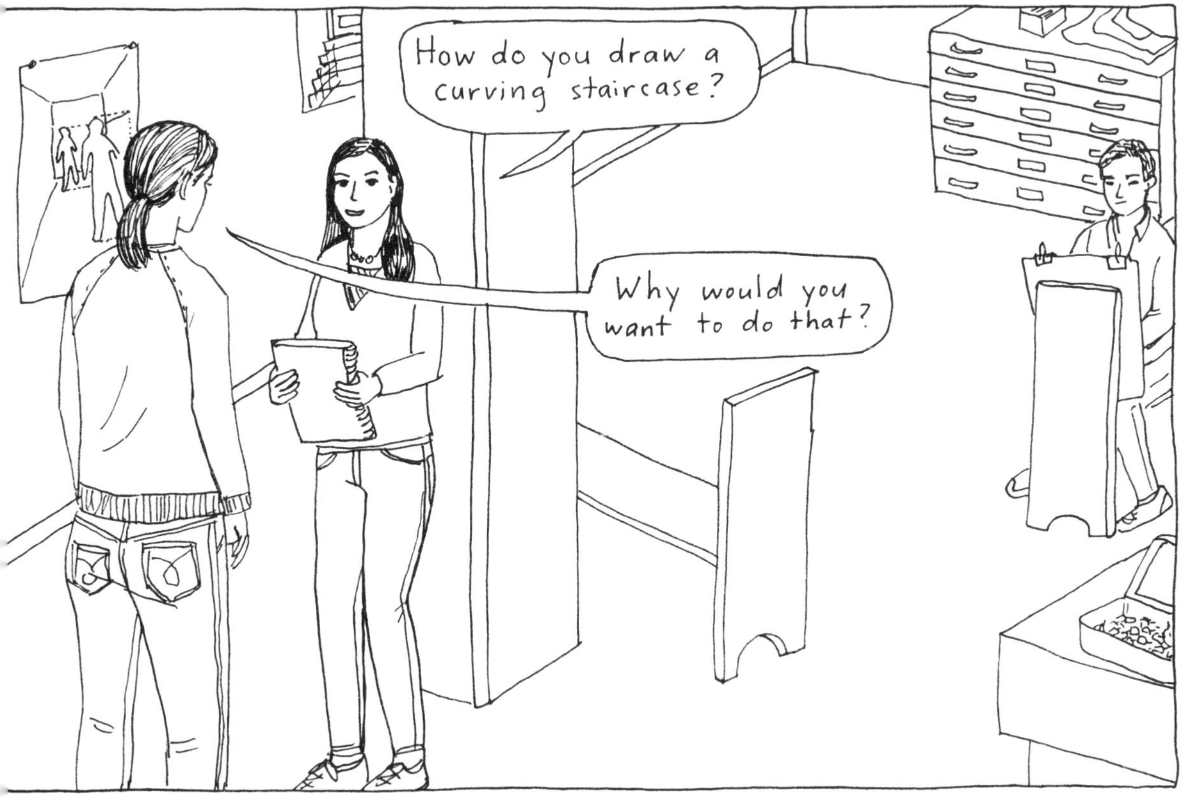
How do you draw a curving staircase?
Why would you want to do that?

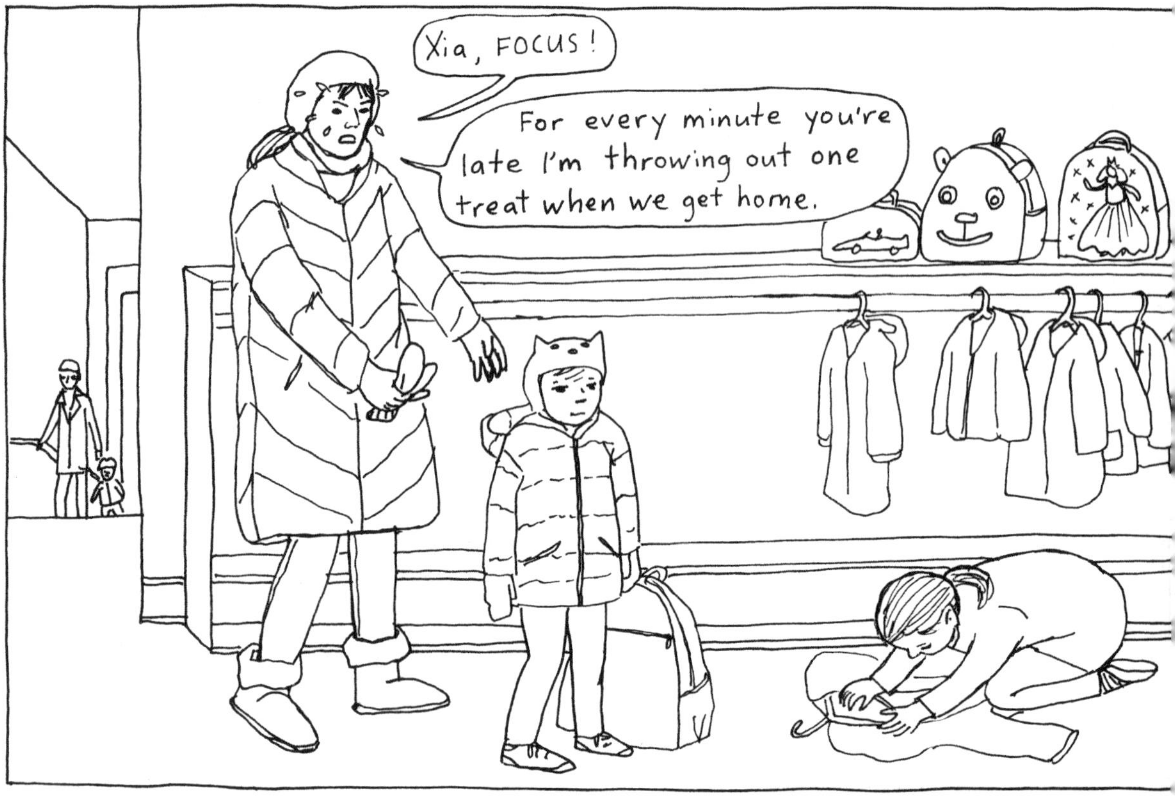
Xia, FOCUS!
For every minute you're late I'm throwing out one treat when we get home.

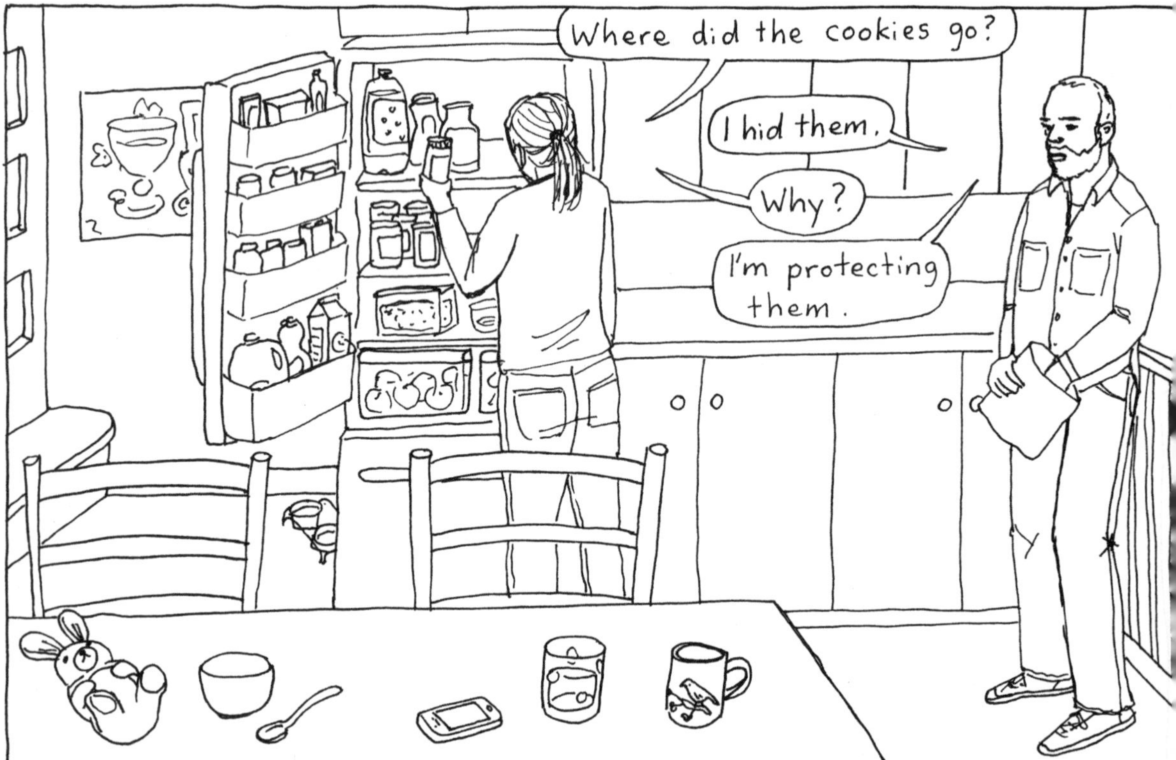
Where did the cookies go?
I hid them.
Why?
I'm protecting them.

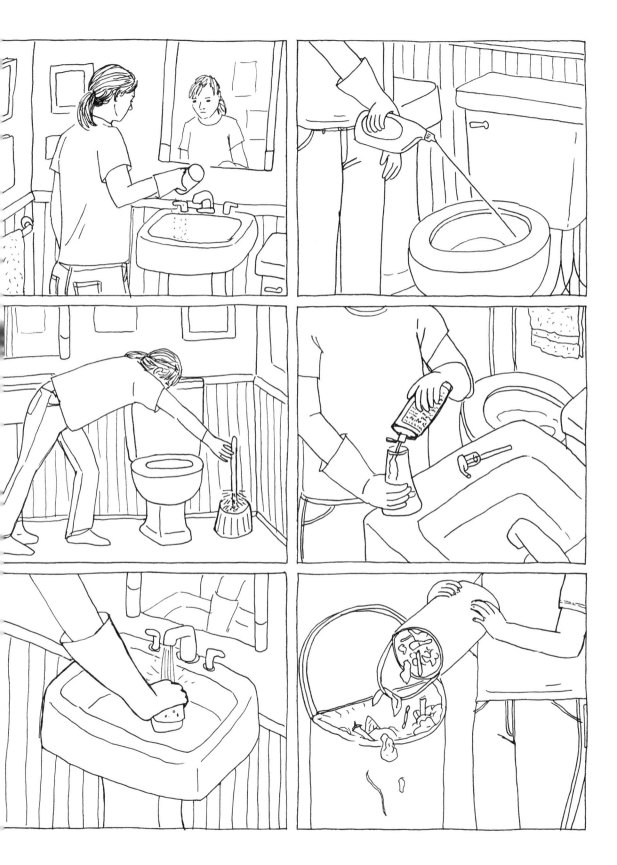

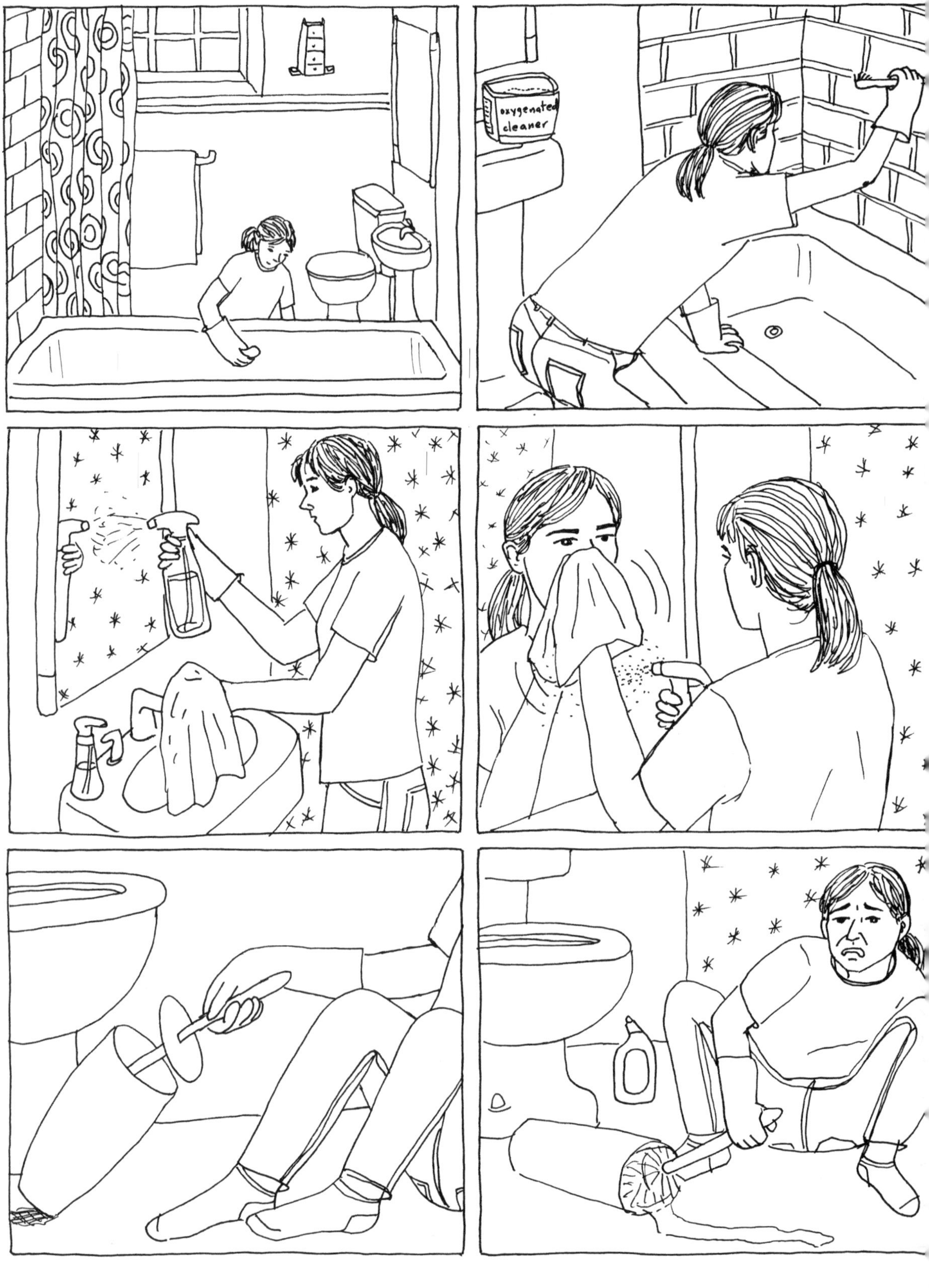
oxygenated cleaner

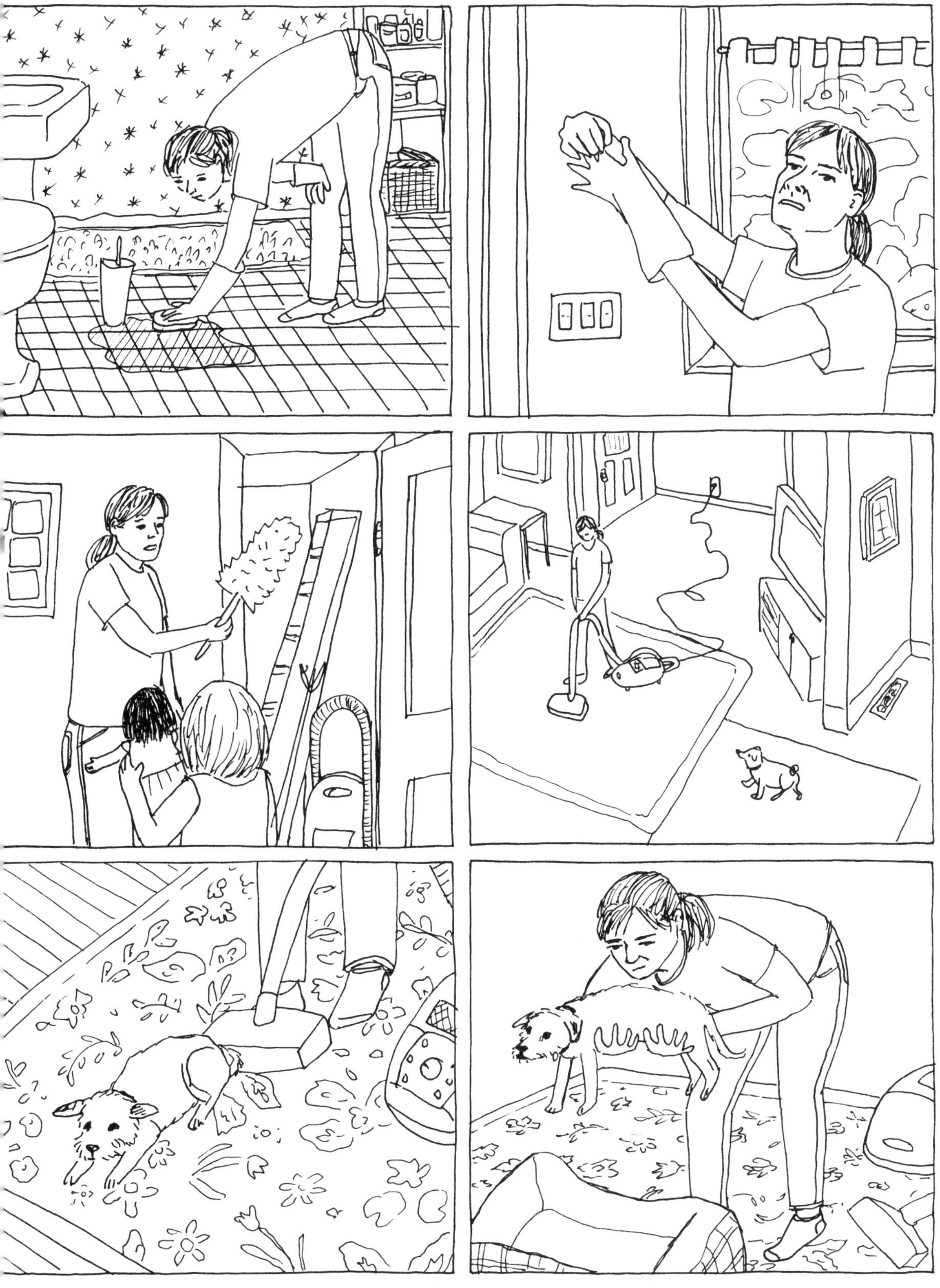

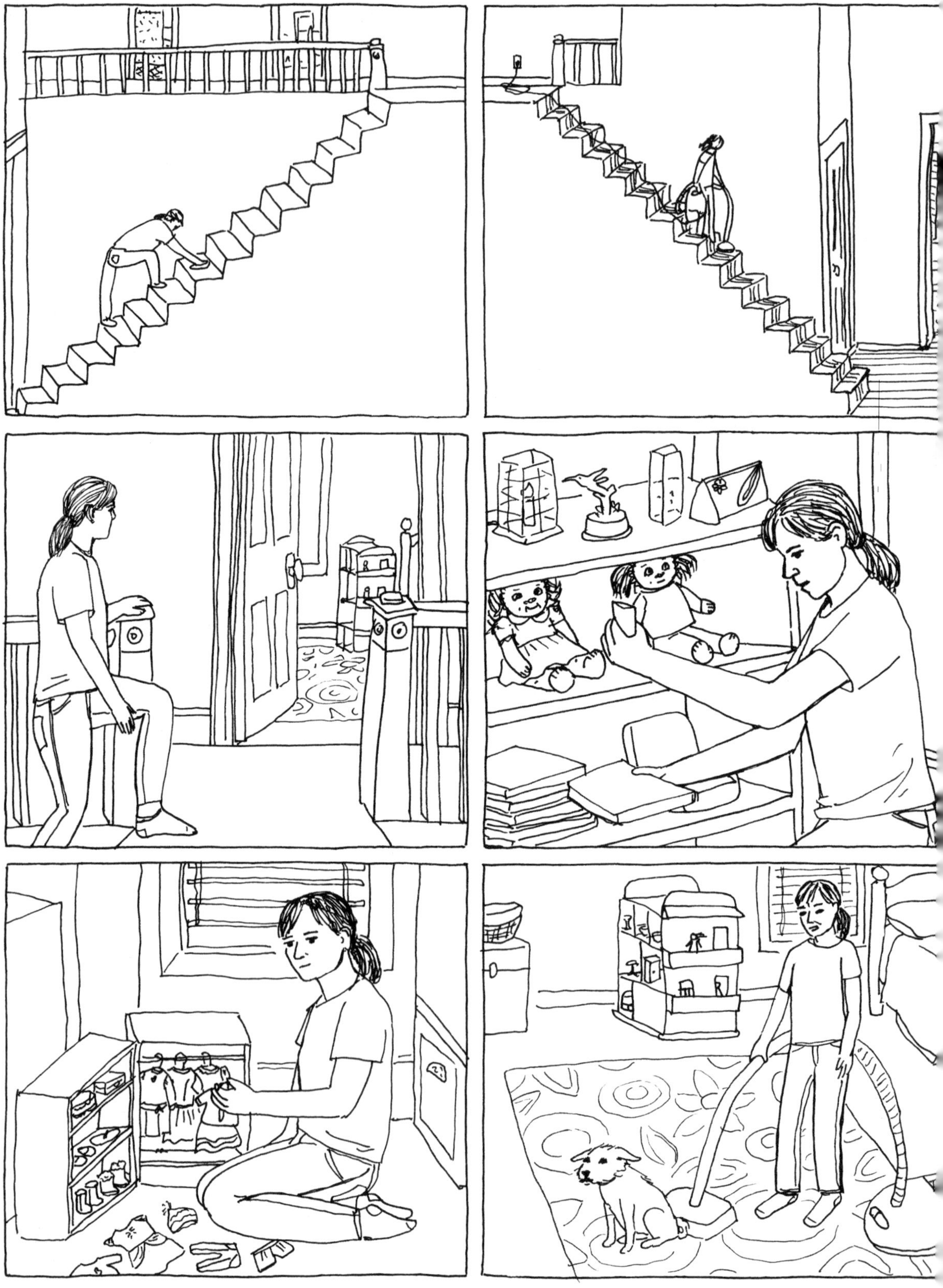

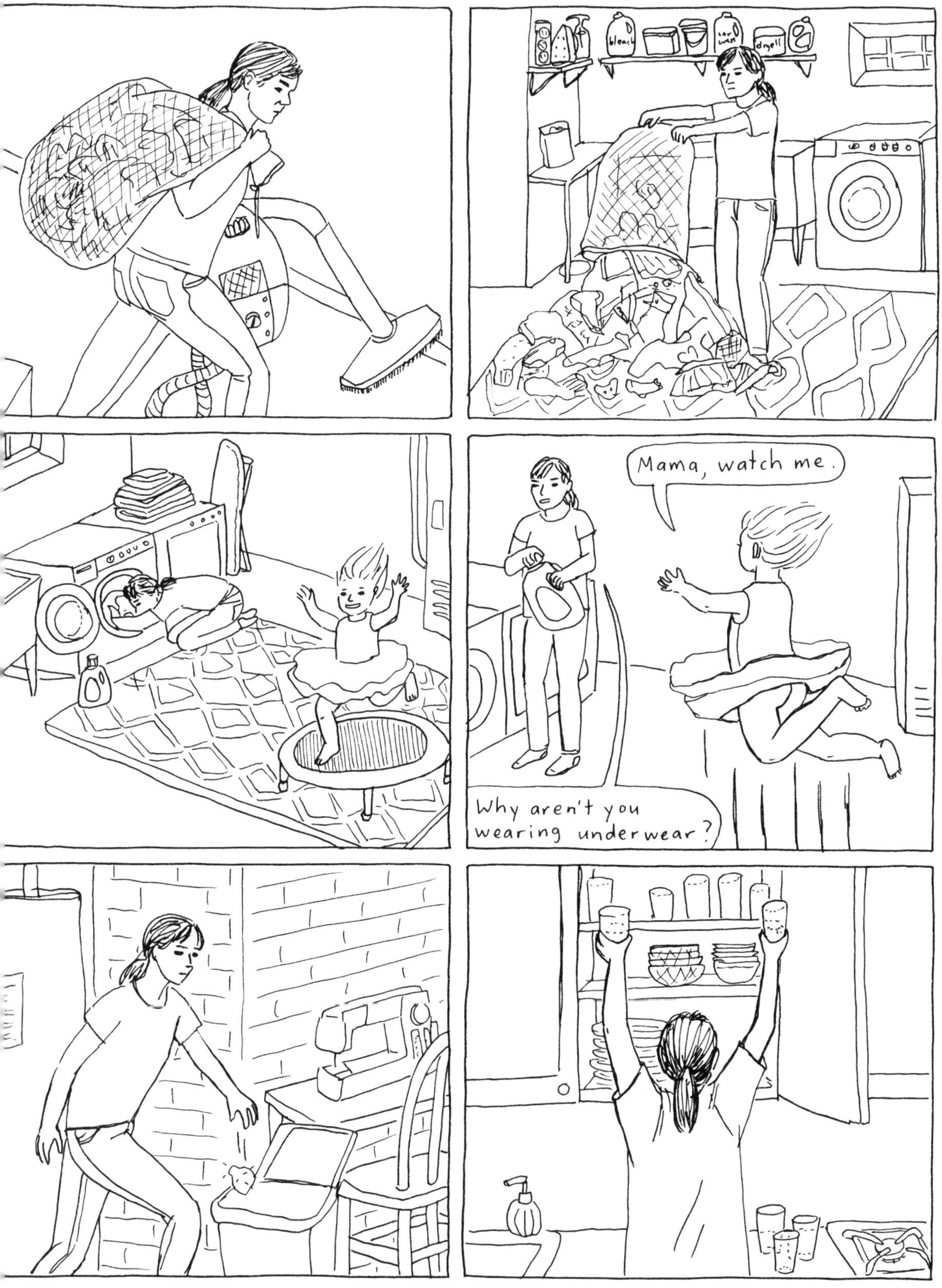
bleach
Mama, watch me.
Why aren't you wearing underwear?

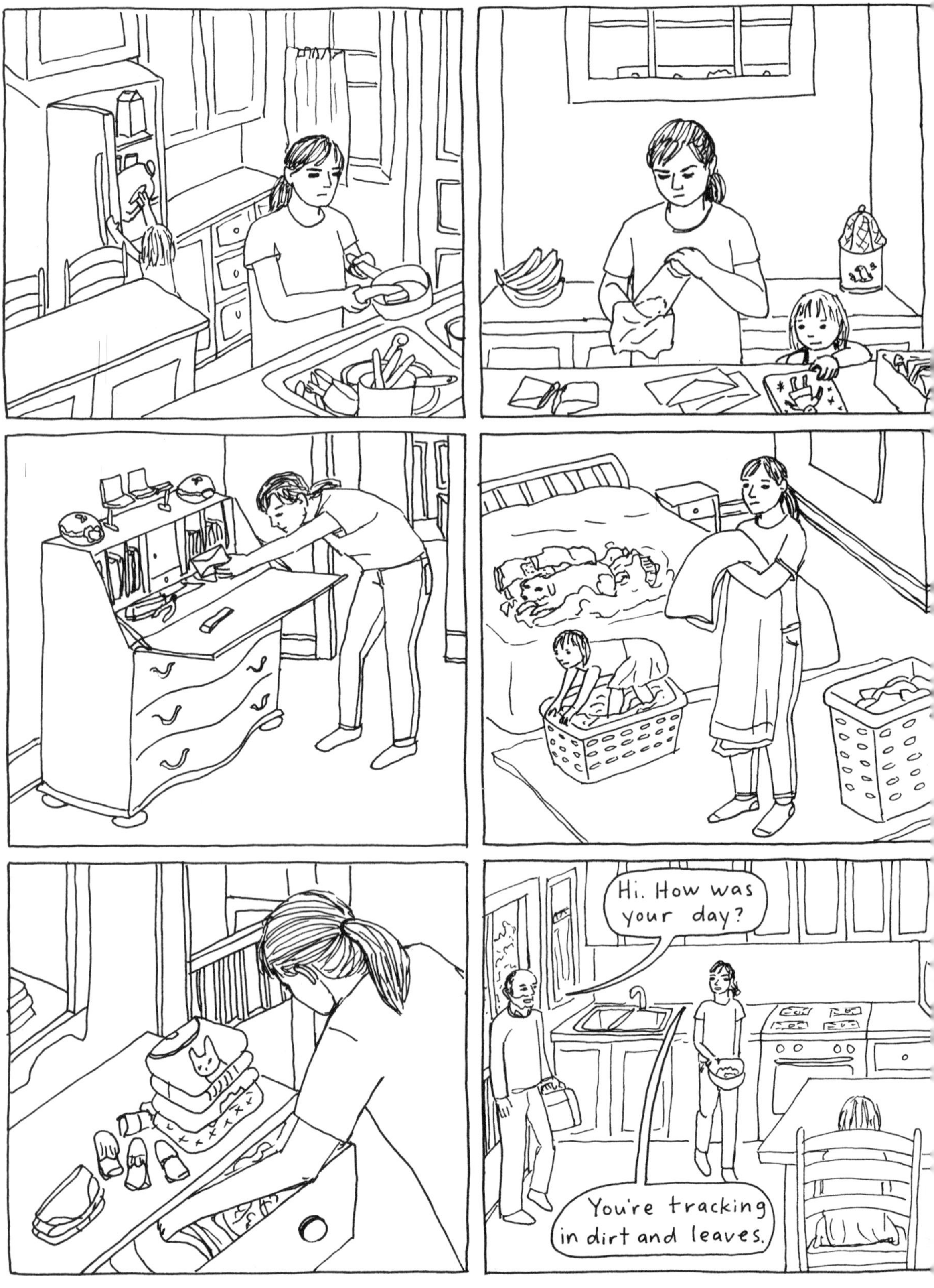
Hi. How was your day?
You're tracking in dirt and leaves.

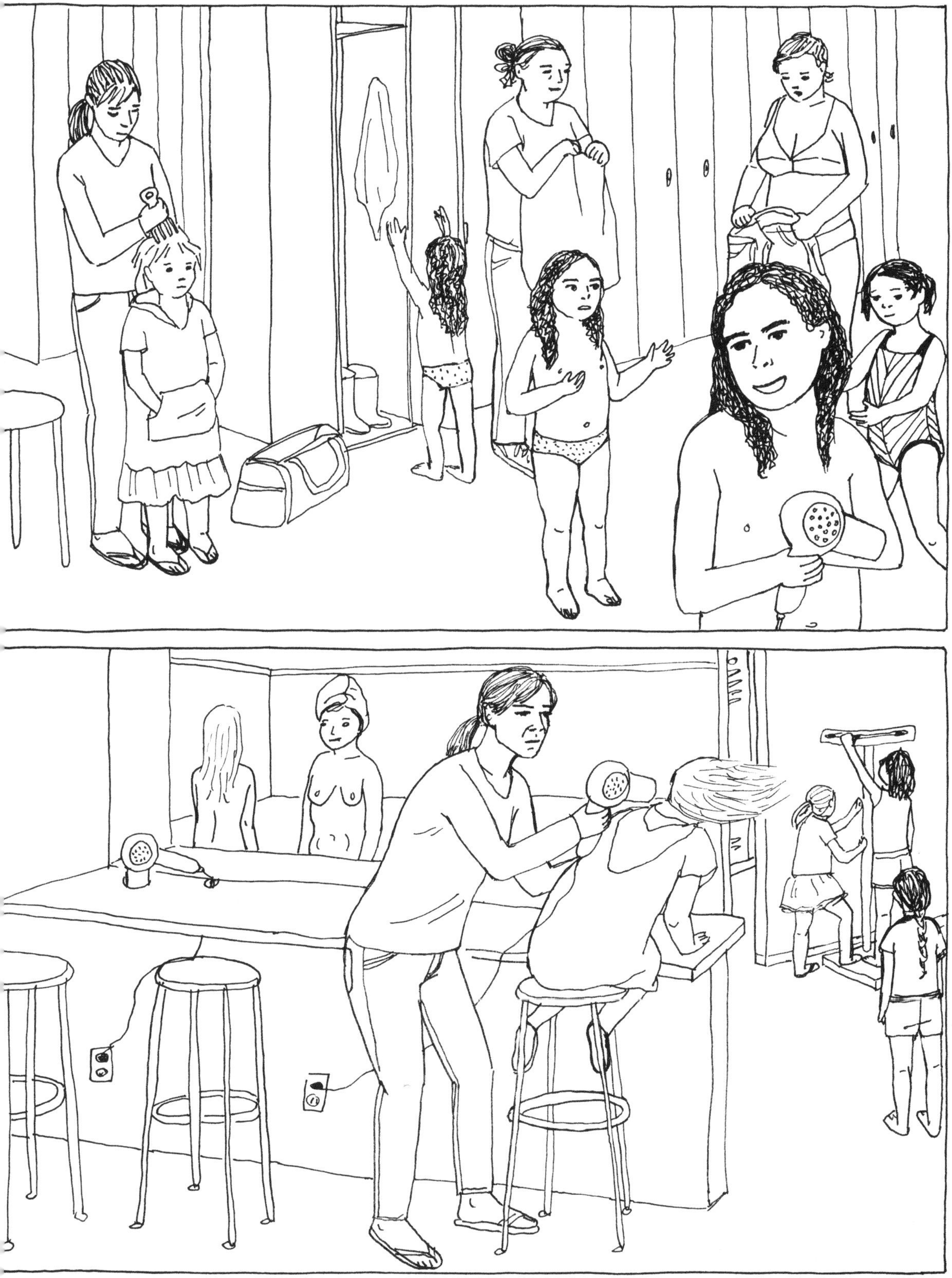

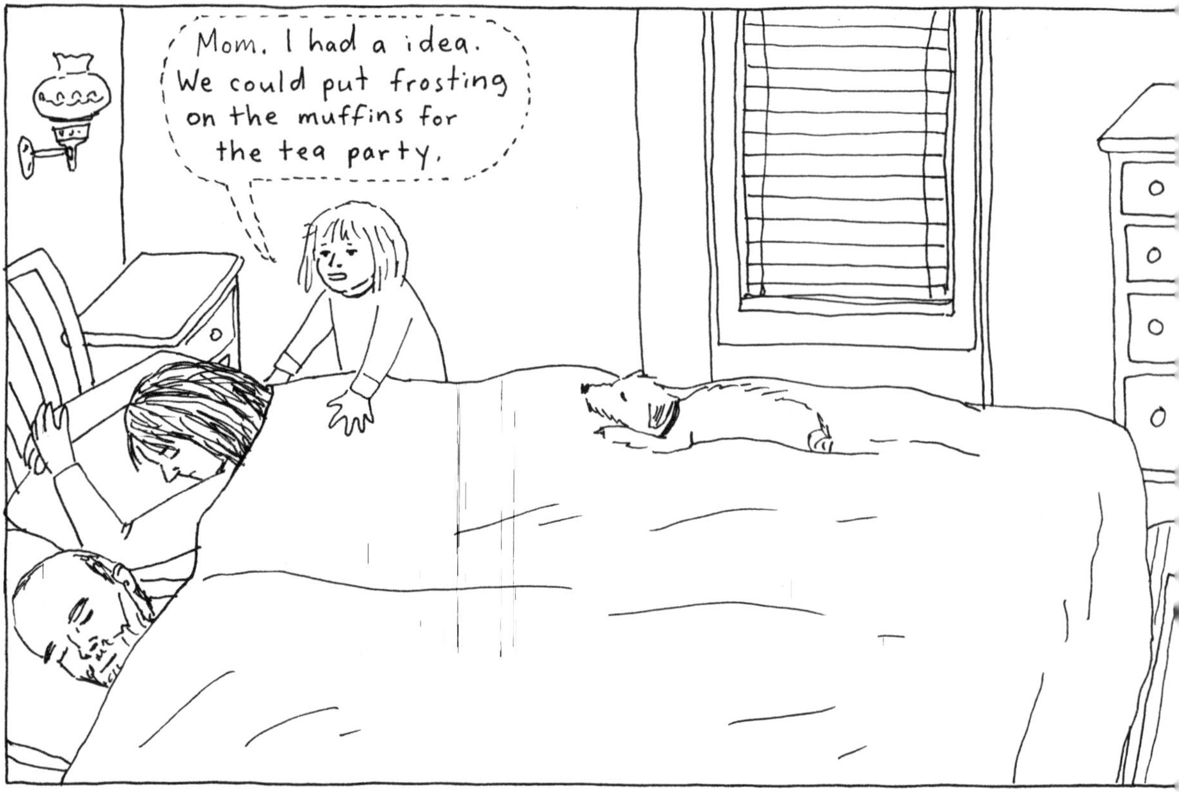
Mom. I had a idea. We could put frosting on the muffins for the tea party.

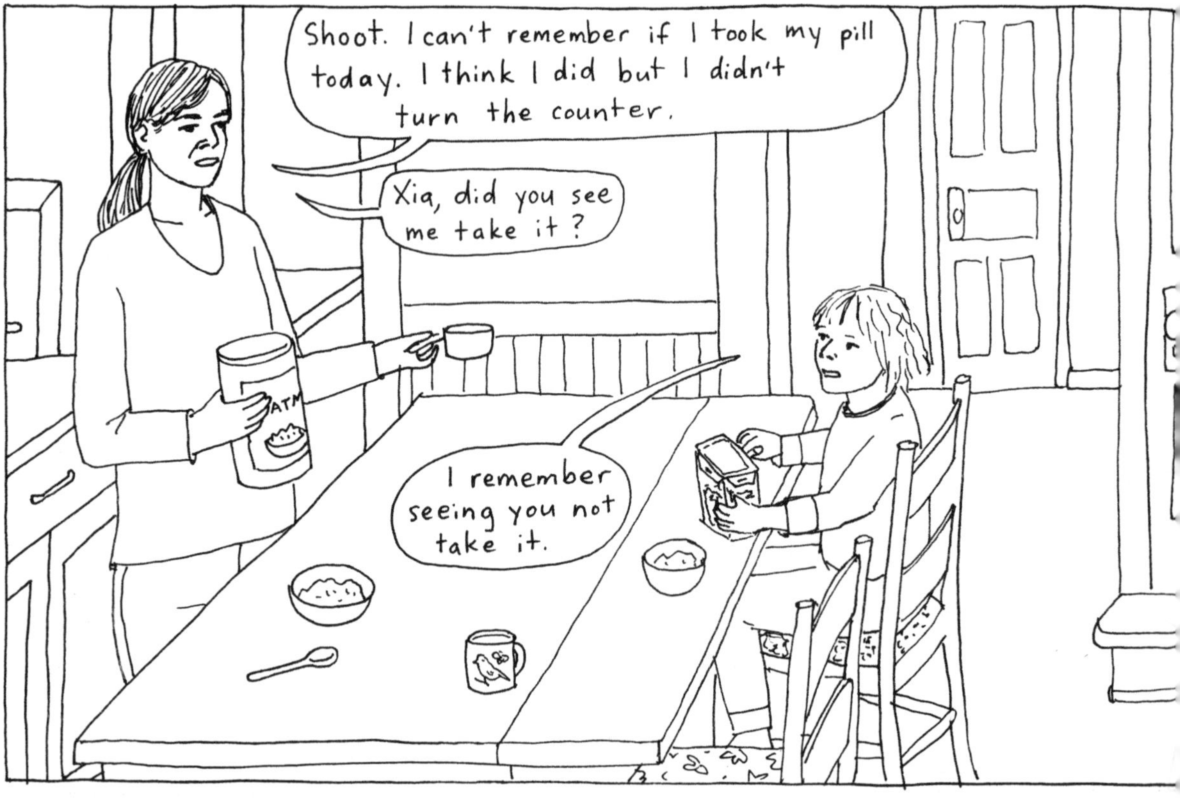
Shoot. I can't remember if I took my pill today. I think I did but I didn't turn the counter.
Xia, did you see me take it?
I remember seeing you not take it.

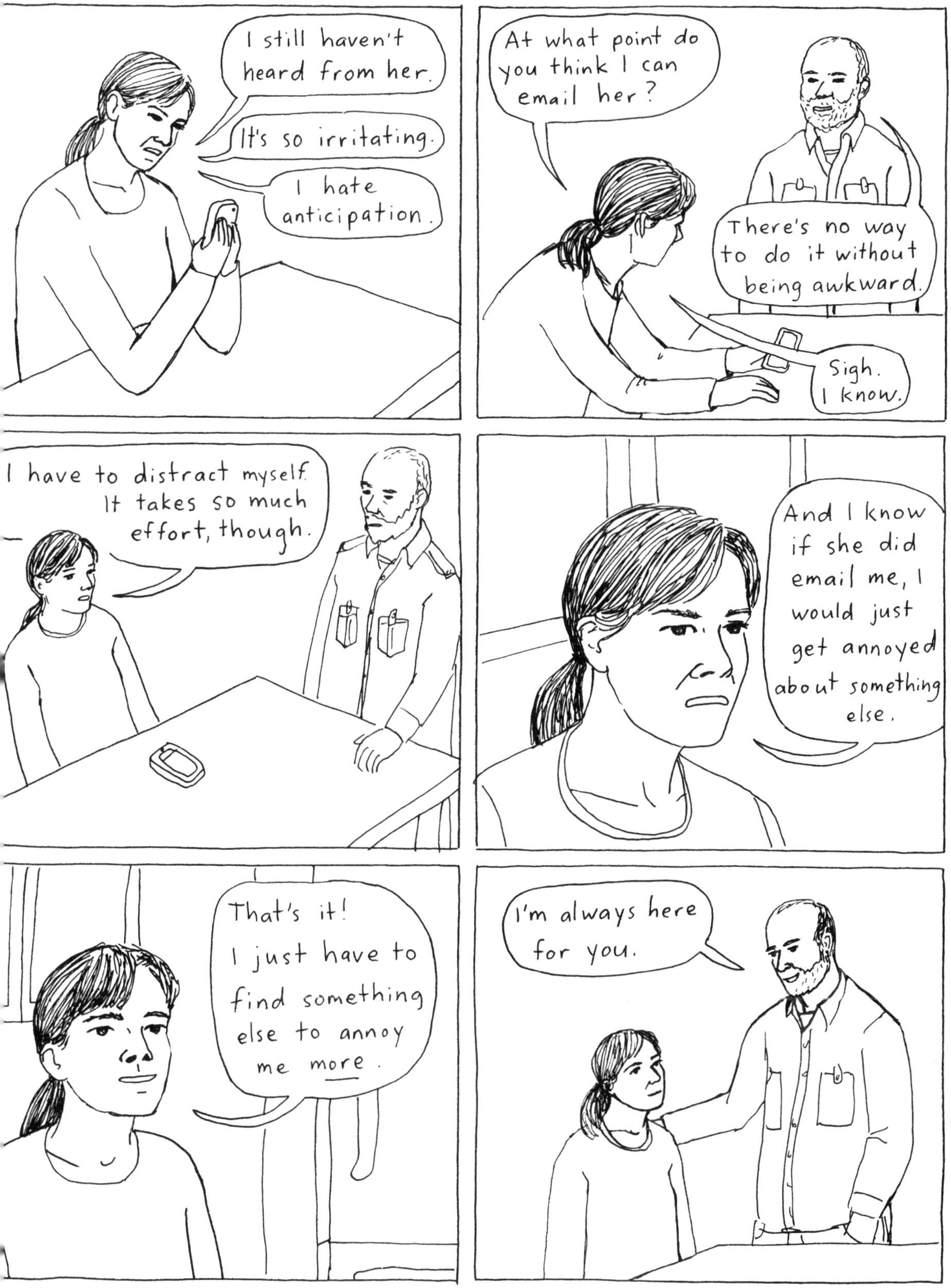
I still haven't heard from her.
It's so irritating.
I hate anticipation.
At what point do you think I can email her?
There's no way to do it without being awkward.
Sigh. I know.
I have to distract myself. It takes so much effort, though.
And I know if she did email me, I would just get annoyed about something else.
That's it! I just have to find something else to annoy me more.
I'm always here for you.

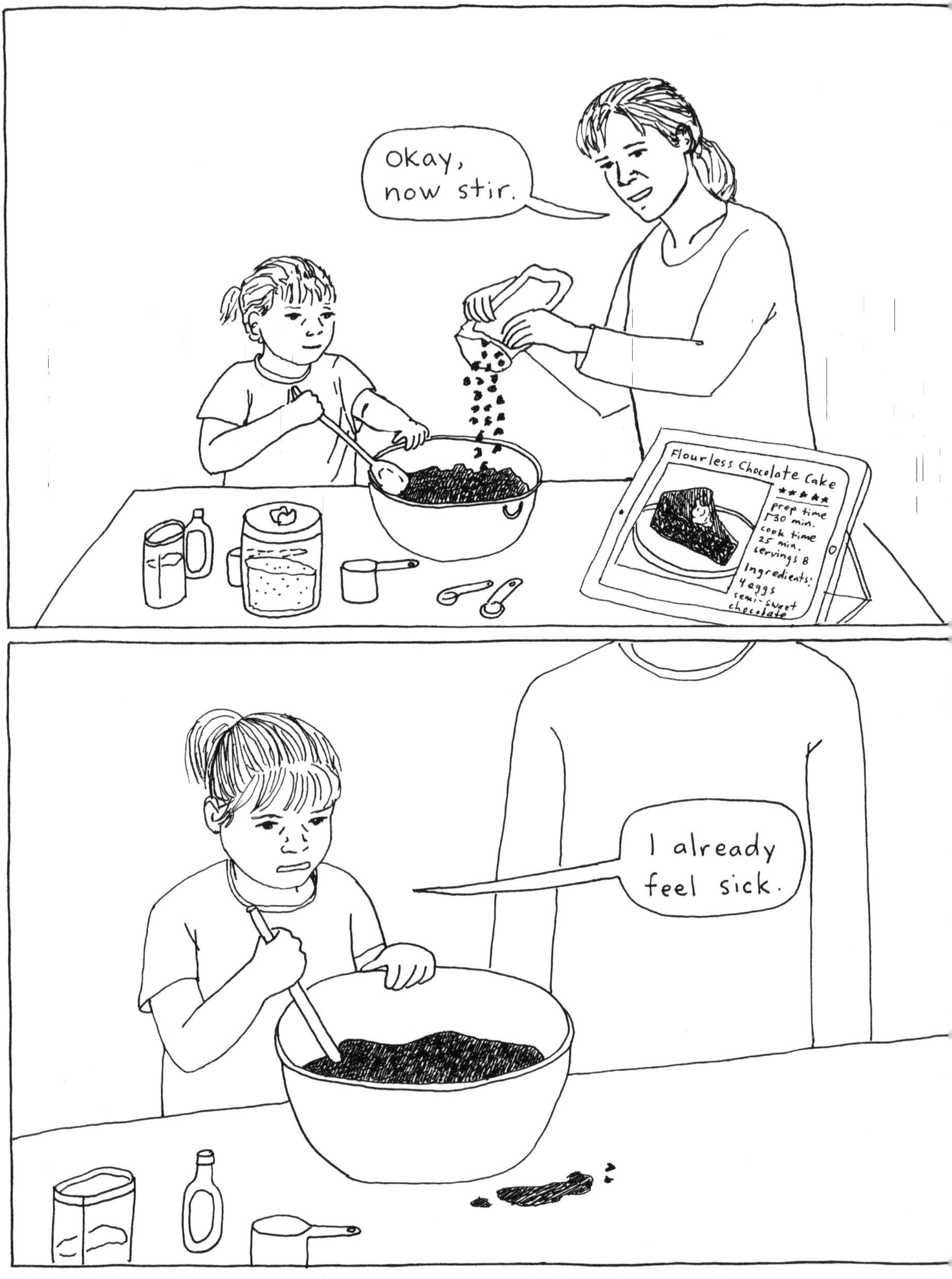
Okay, now stir.
Flourless Chocolate Cake
prep time 30 min.
cook time 25 min.
servings 8
Ingredients:
4 eggs
semi-sweet chocolate
I already feel sick.

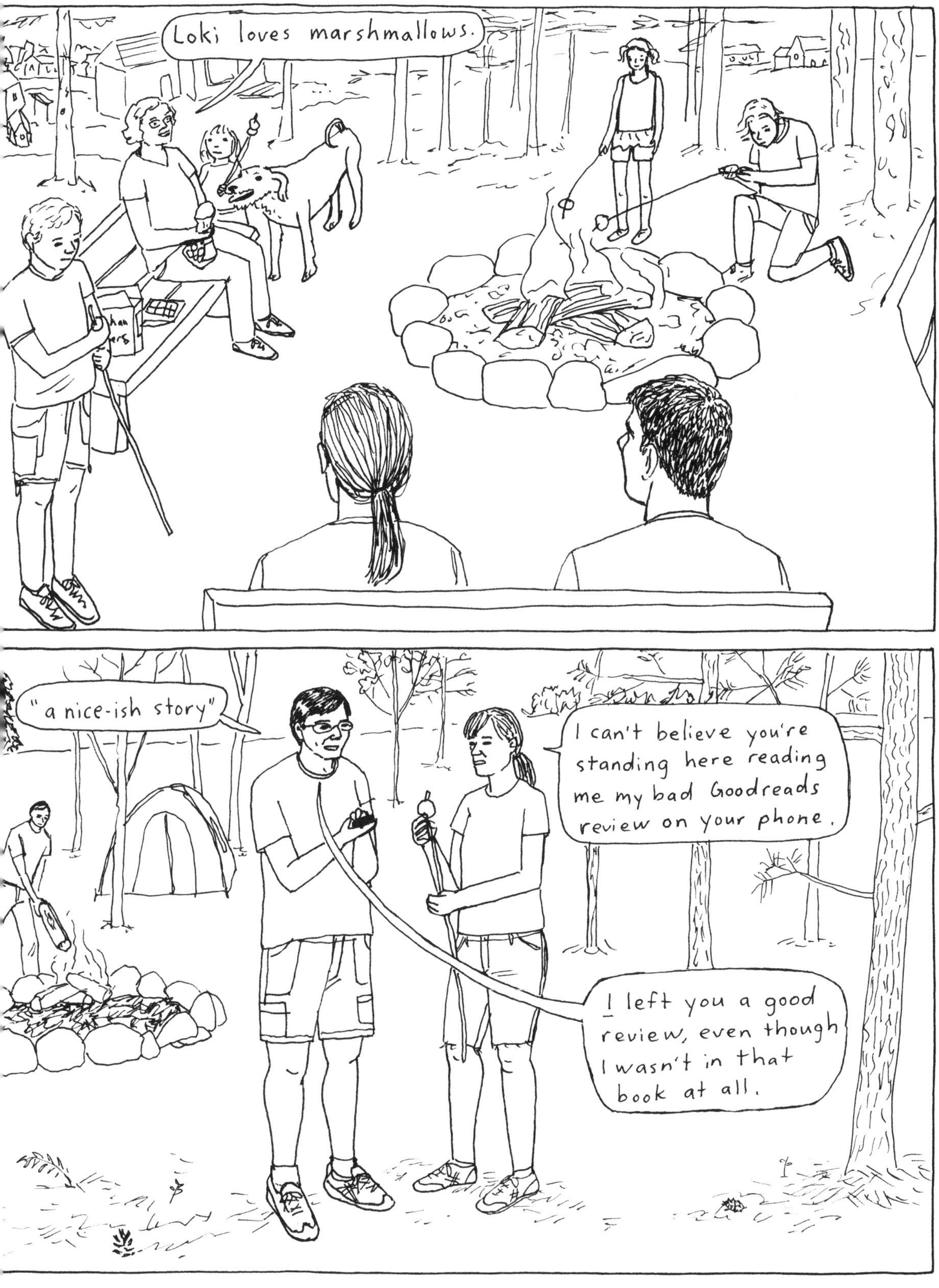
Loki loves marshmallows.
"a nice-ish story"
I can't believe you're standing here reading me my bad Goodreads review on your phone.
I left you a good review, even though I wasn't in that book at all.

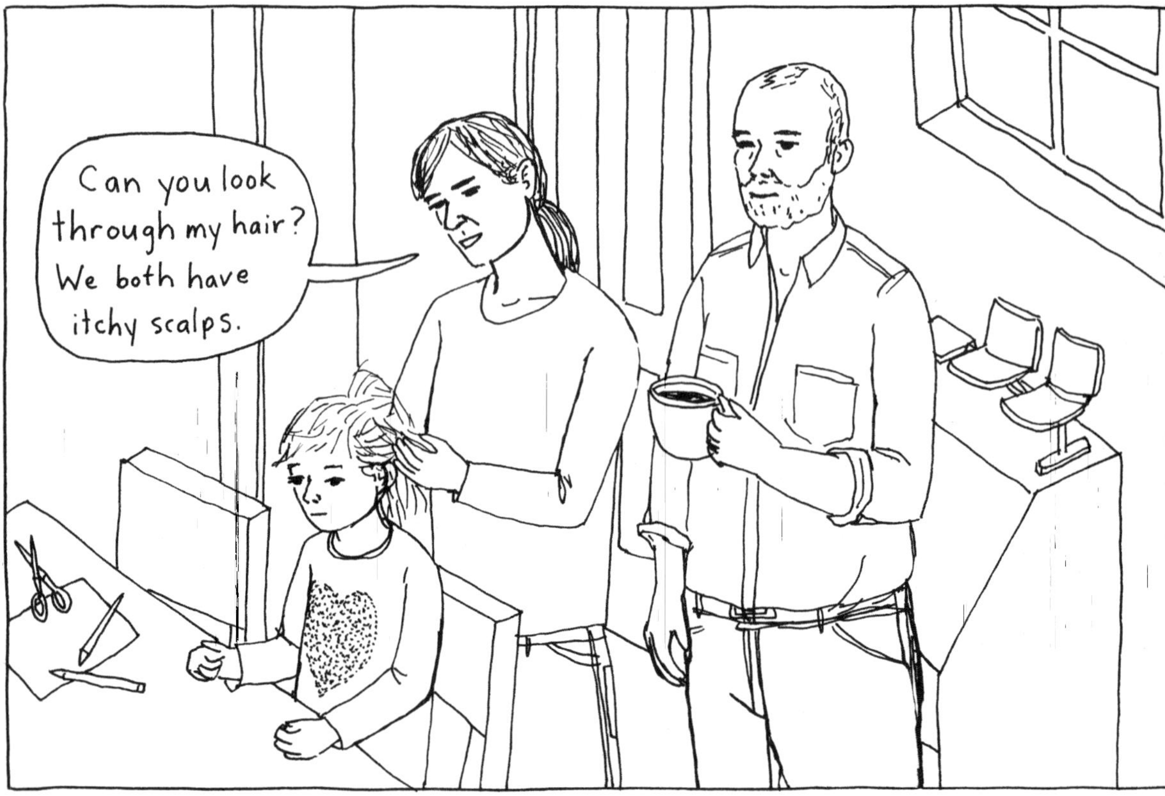
Can you look through my hair? We both have itchy scalps.

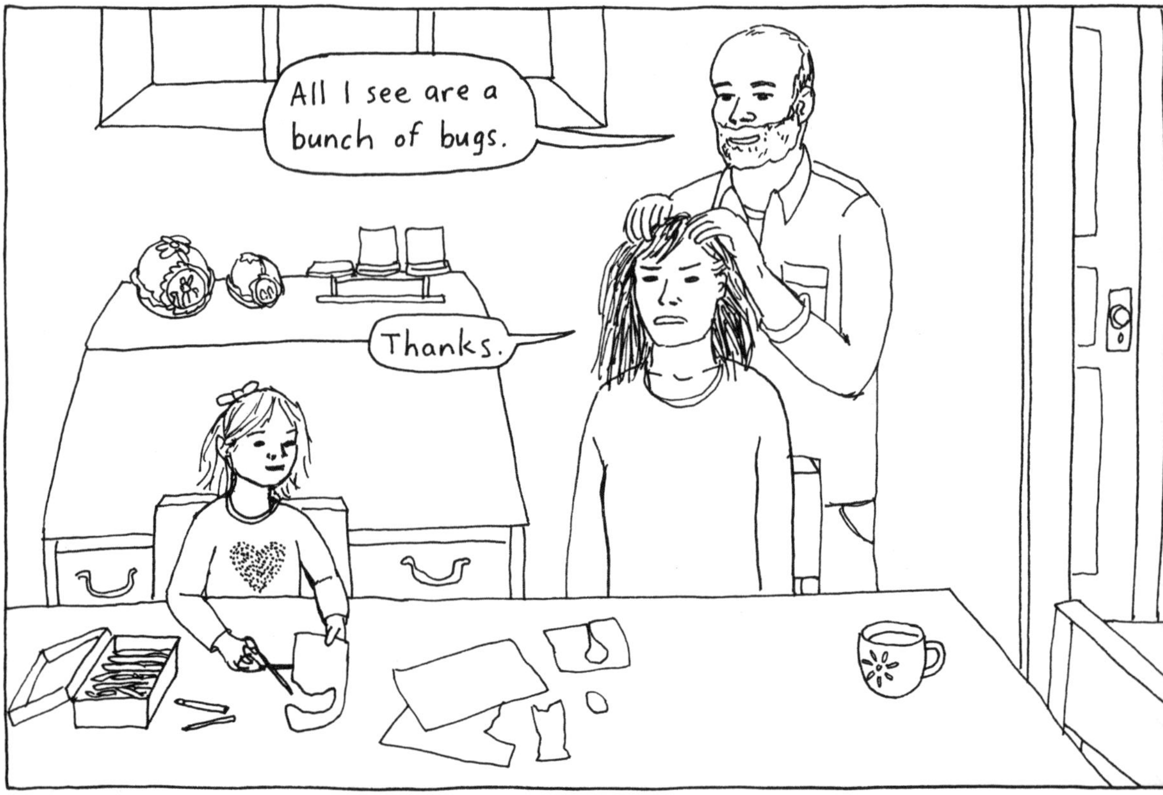
All I see are a bunch of bugs.
Thanks.

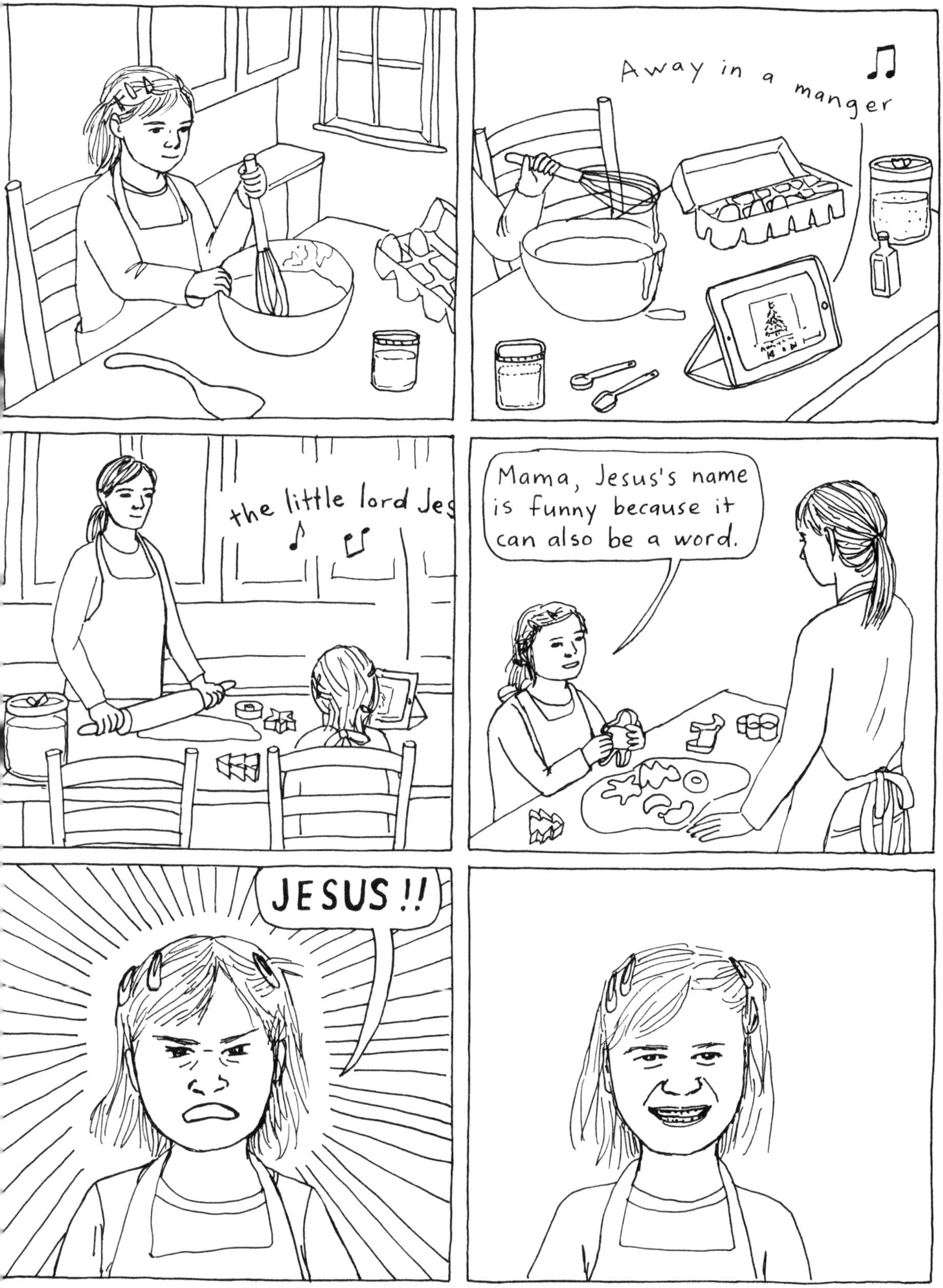
Away in a manger
the little lord Jes
Mama, Jesus's name is funny because it can also be a word.
JESUS!!

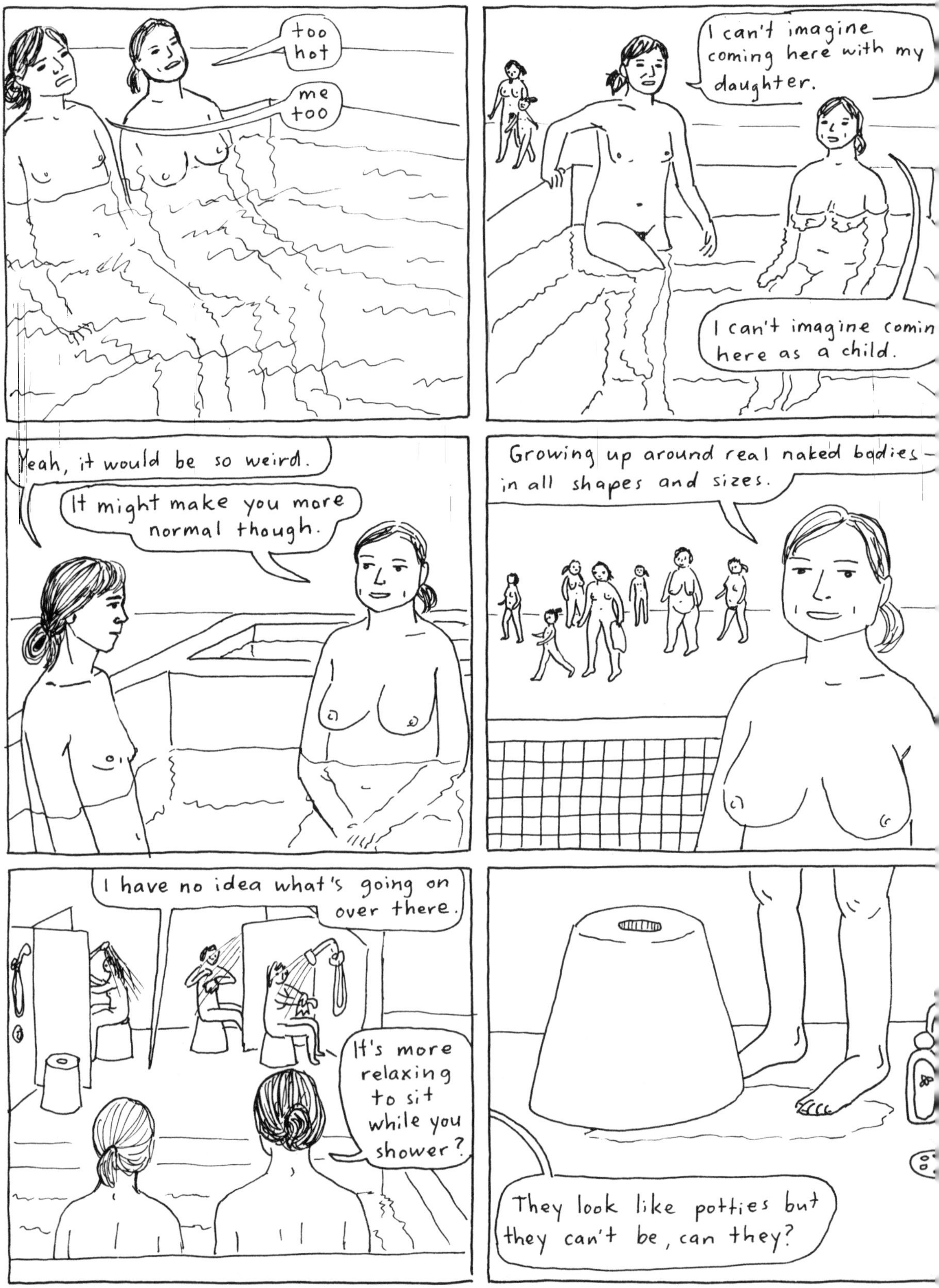
too hot
me too
I can't imagine coming here with my daughter.
I can't imagine comin here as a child.
Yeah, it would be so weird.
It might make you more normal though.
Growing up around real naked bodies — in all shapes and sizes.
I have no idea what's going on over there.
It's more relaxing to sit while you shower?
They look like potties but they can't be, can they?

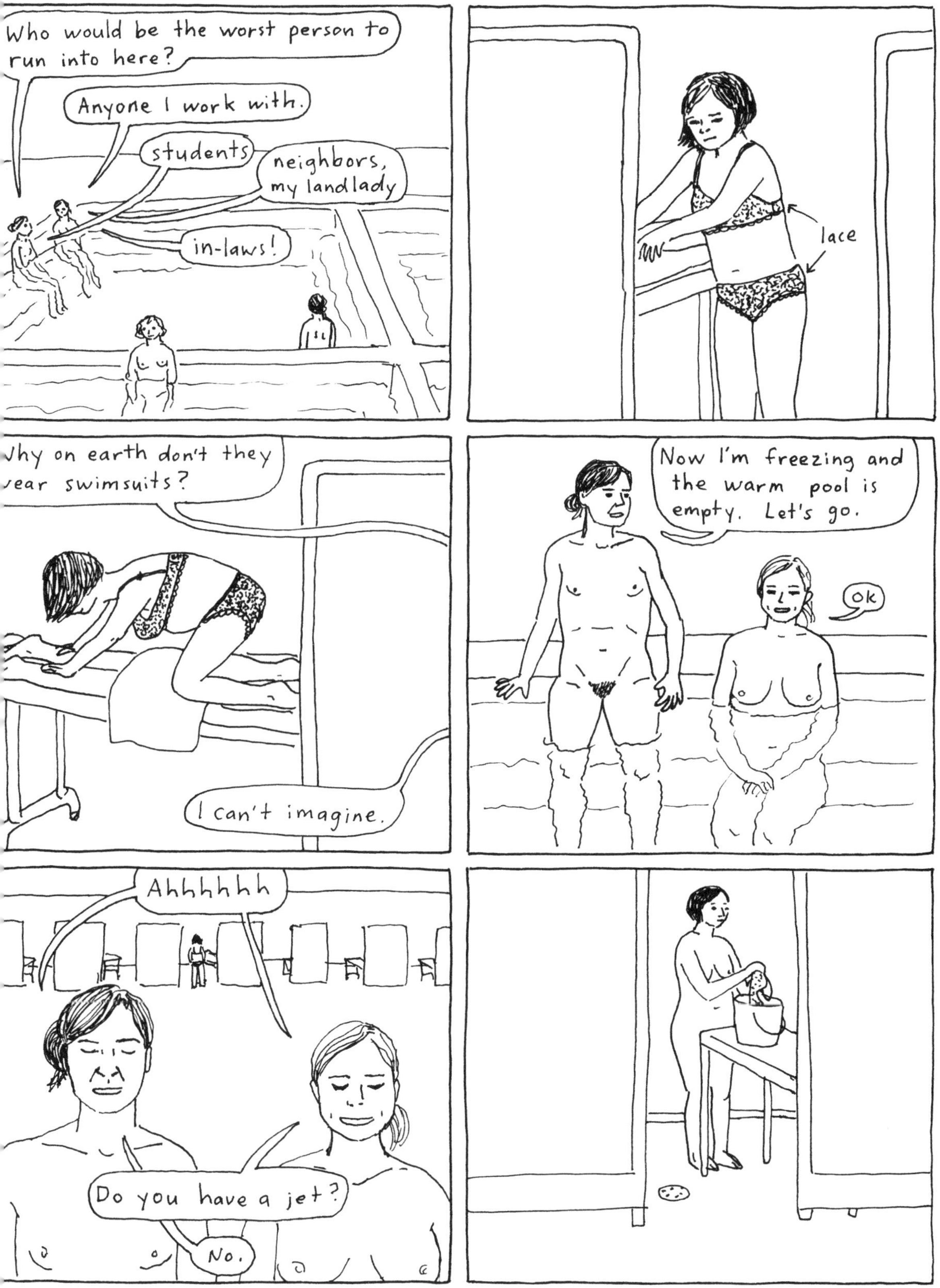
Who would be the worst person to run into here?
Anyone I work with.
students
neighbors, my landlady
in-laws!
lace
Why on earth don't they wear swimsuits?
I can't imagine.
Now I'm freezing and the warm pool is empty. Let's go.
ok
Ahhhhhh
Do you have a jet?
No.

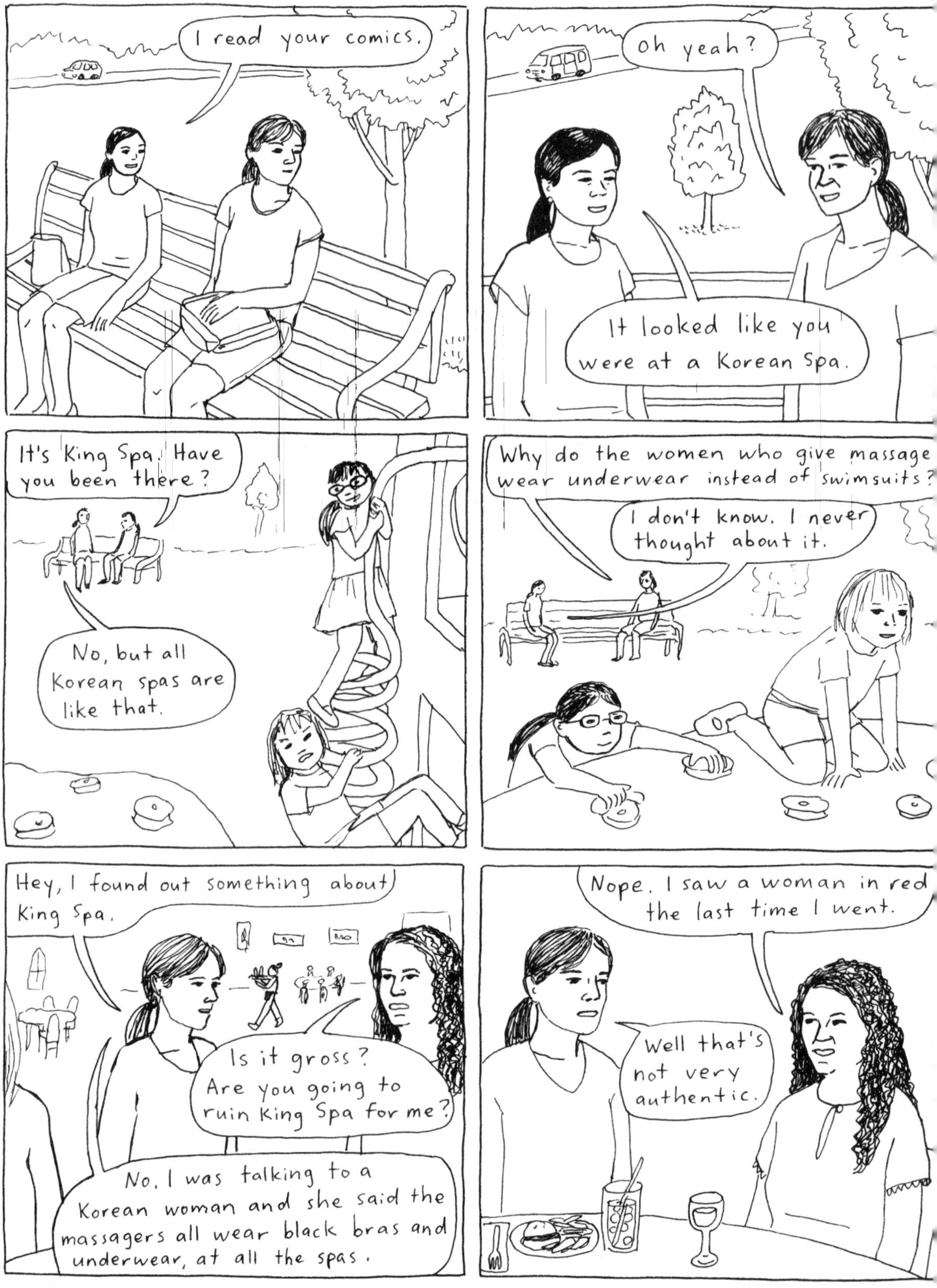
I read your comics.
Oh yeah?
It looked like you were at a Korean Spa.
It's King Spa. Have you been there?
No, but all Korean spas are like that.
Why do the women who give massage wear underwear instead of swimsuits?
I don't know. I never thought about it.
Hey, I found out something about King Spa.
Is it gross? Are you going to ruin King Spa for me?
No. I was talking to a Korean woman and she said the massagers all wear black bras and underwear, at all the spas.
Nope. I saw a woman in red the last time I went.
Well that's not very authentic.

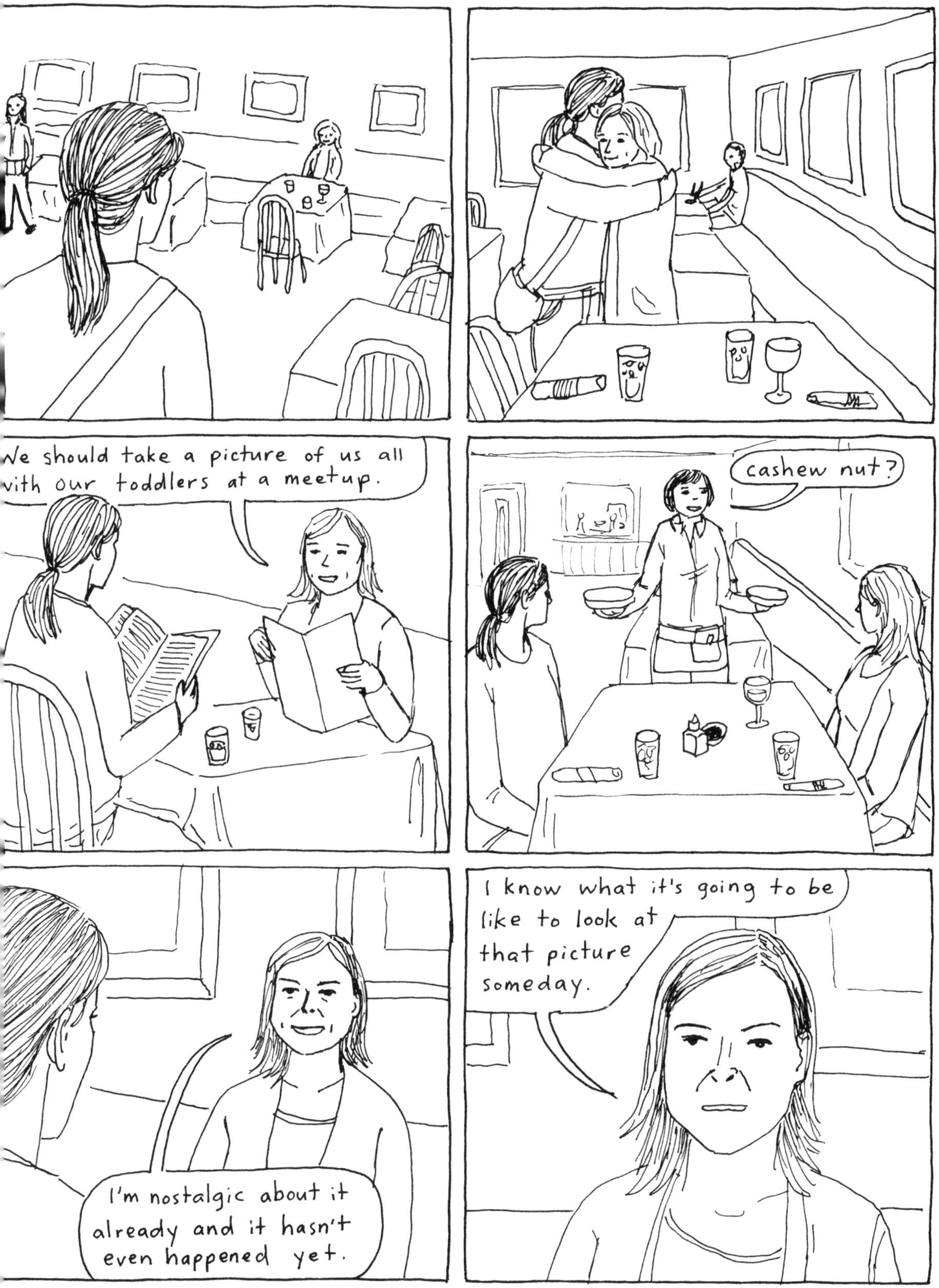
We should take a picture of us all with our toddlers at a meetup.
cashew nut?
I'm nostalgic about it already and it hasn't even happened yet.
I know what it's going to be like to look at that picture someday.

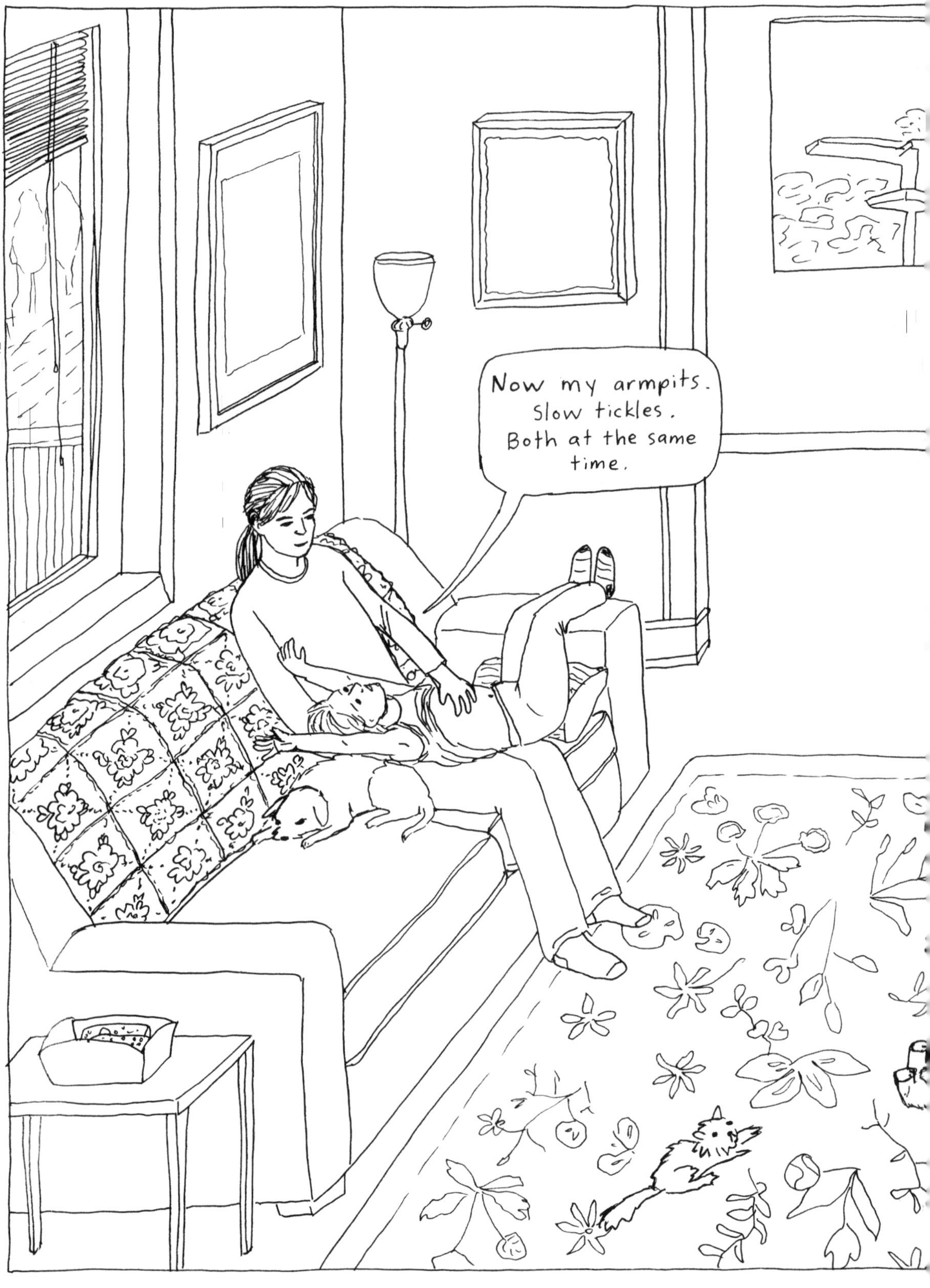
Now my armpits. Slow tickles. Both at the same time.

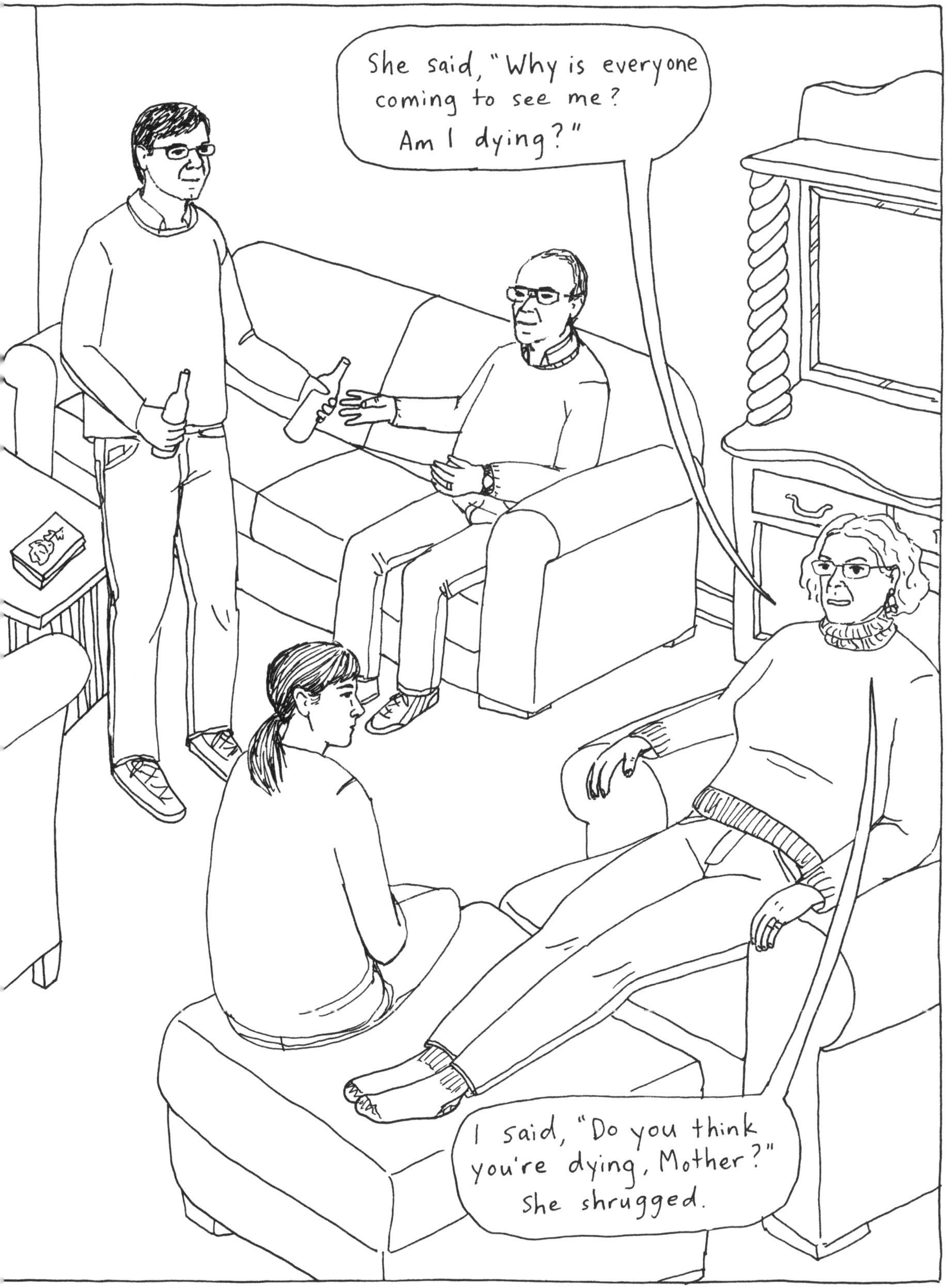
She said, "Why is everyone coming to see me? Am I dying?"
I said, "Do you think you're dying, Mother?" She shrugged.

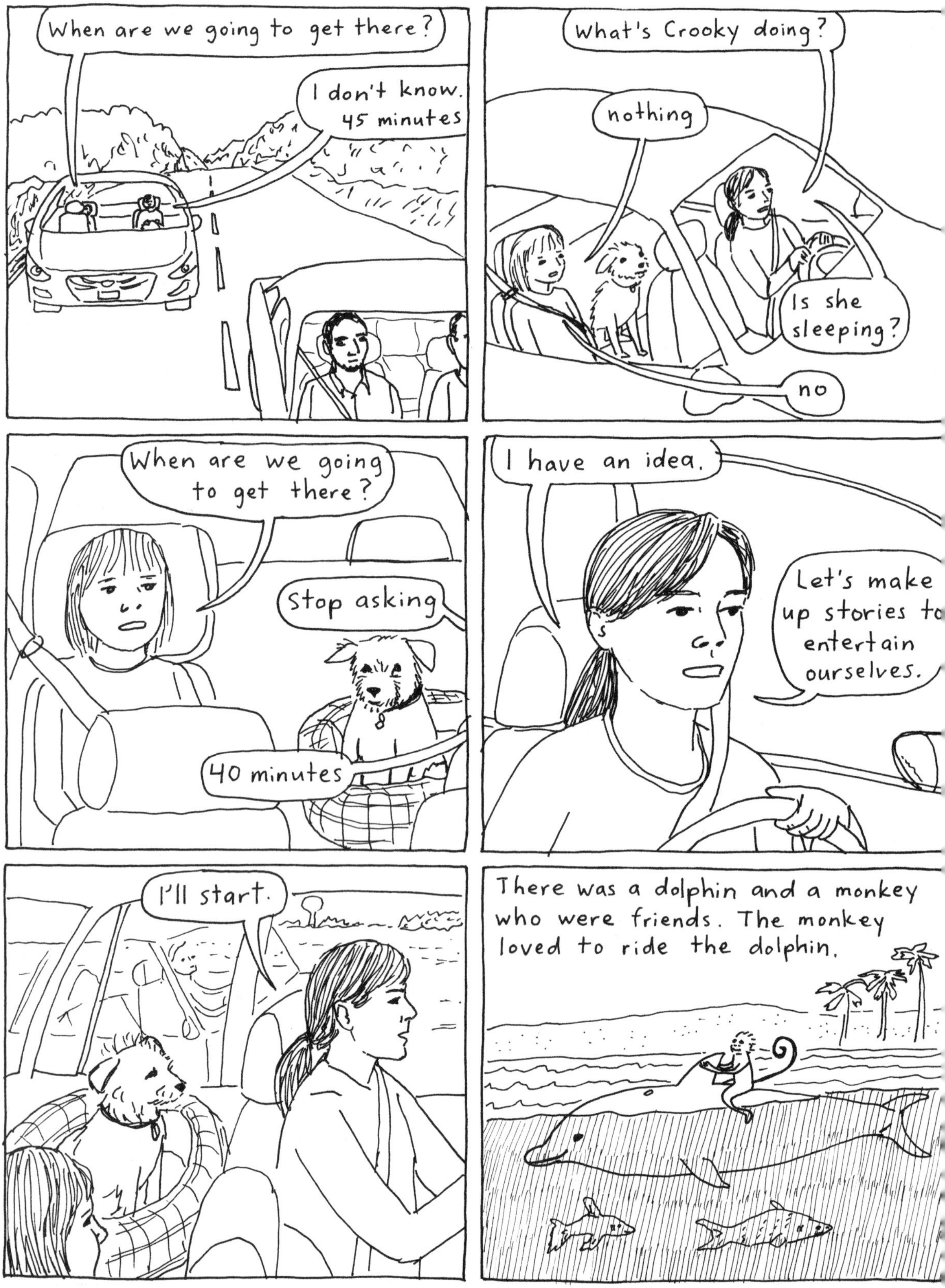
When are we going to get there?
I don't know. 45 minutes
What's Crooky doing?
nothing
Is she sleeping?
no
When are we going to get there?
Stop asking
40 minutes
I have an idea.
Let's make up stories to entertain ourselves.
I'll start.
There was a dolphin and a monkey who were friends. The monkey loved to ride the dolphin.

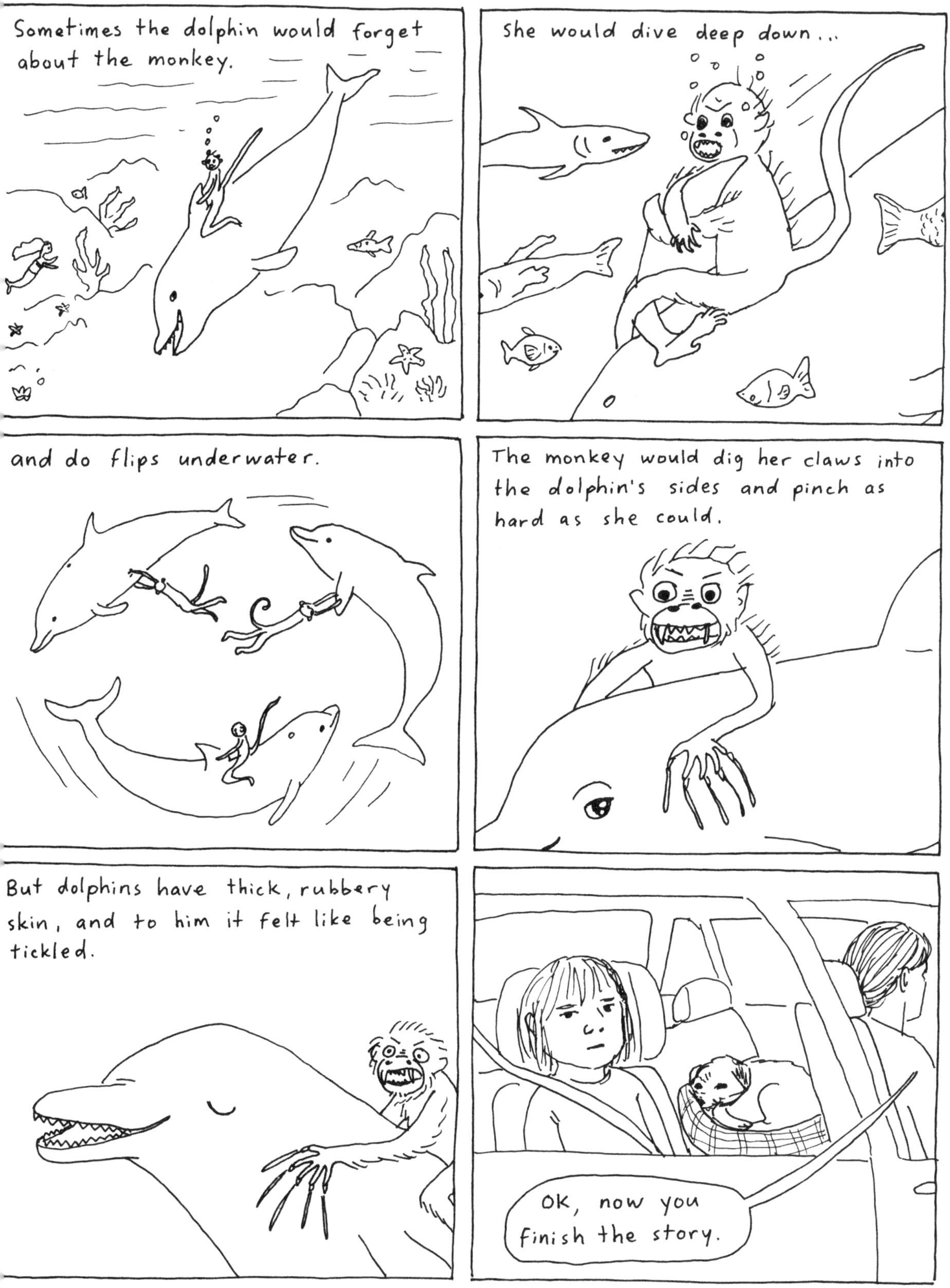
Sometimes the dolphin would forget about the monkey.
She would dive deep down...
and do flips underwater.
The monkey would dig her claws into the dolphin's sides and pinch as hard as she could.
But dolphins have thick, rubbery skin, and to him it felt like being tickled.
OK, now you finish the story.

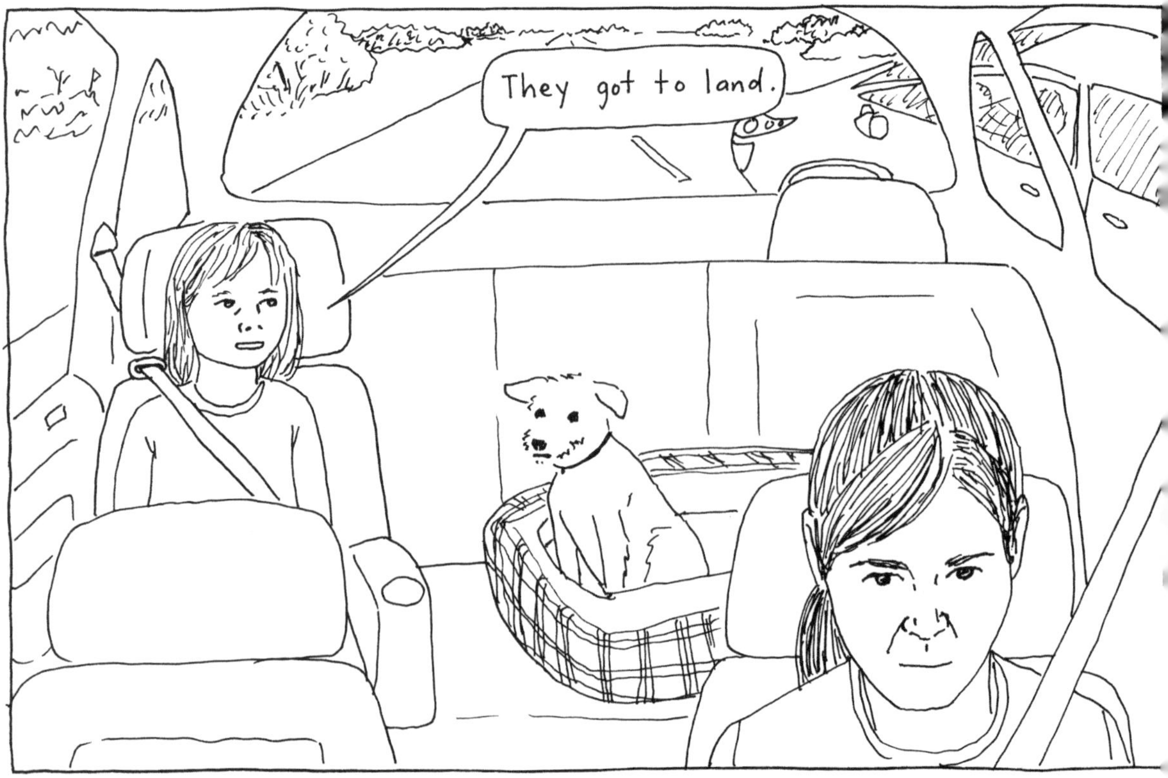
They got to land.

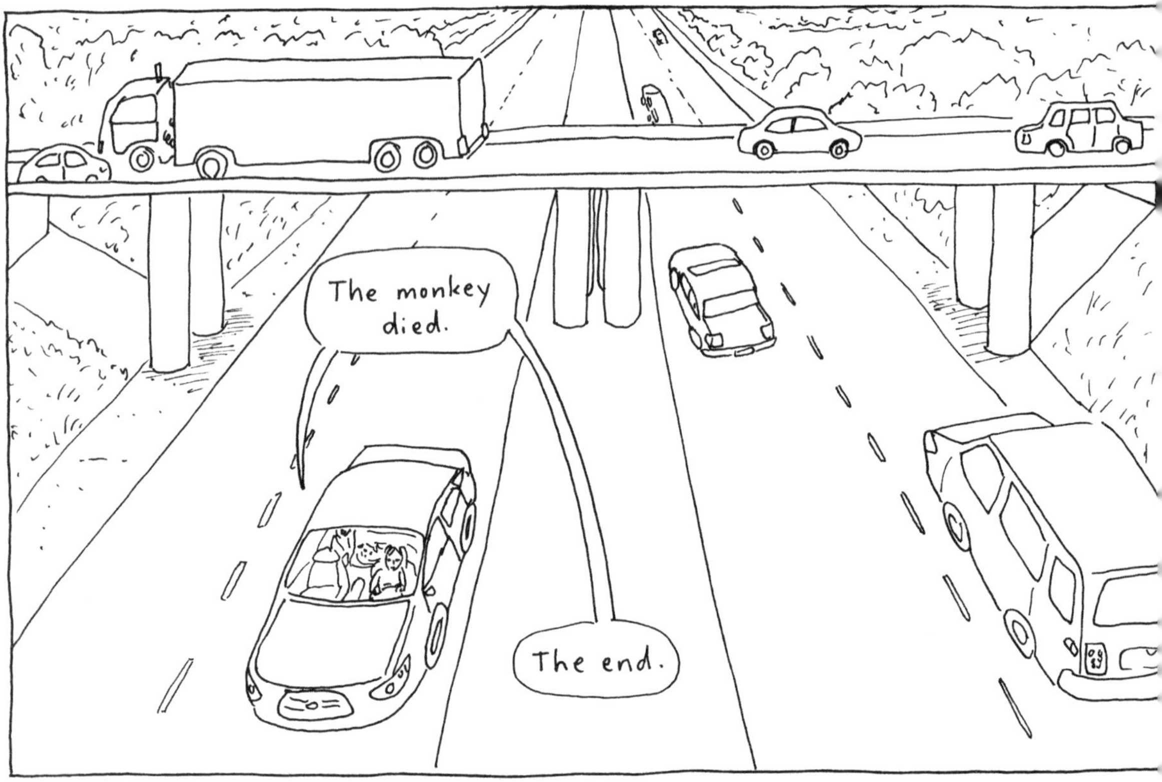
The monkey died.
The end.

Special thanks to the following people:

my family (especially Xia), Annie Koyama, Ed Kanerva, Helen Koyama, Roz Chast, John Porcellino, Meg Lemke at MUTHA Magazine, Rob Kirby, Bill Kartalopoulos, Tom Spurgeon, Neil Brideau at Radiator Comics, Rob Clough, Brian Cremins, Andy Oliver, Heidi MacDonald, Alex Hoffman, Amie Larkin, Sharon Fiffer, Justin Witte, Ben Crothers, CAKE, Chicago Zine Fest, DePaul University, The School of the Art Institute, Quimby's, Jarrett Dapier, Ruth Bell, and all librarians.

Thank you, Scott Roberts. I love you.

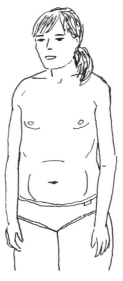

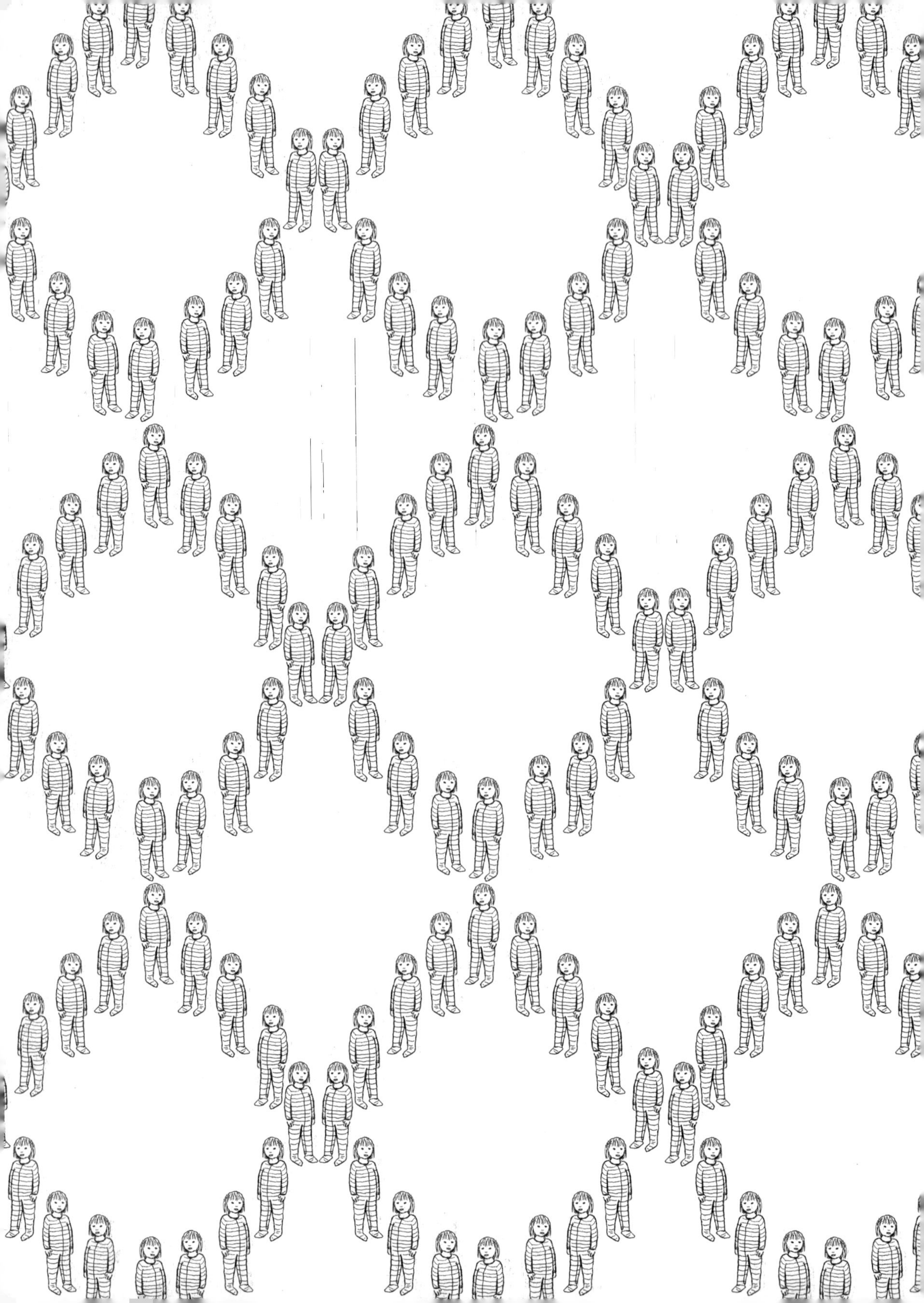